THE
EATINGWELL™
COOKBOOK

THE
EATING WELL™
COOKBOOK

Volume I
Favorite Recipes from
EATING WELL
The Magazine of Food & Health

Edited by
Rux Martin, Patricia Jamieson
and Elizabeth Hiser, M.S., R.D.

CAMDEN
•HOUSE•
PUBLISHING

Camden House Publishing, Inc.
A division of Telemedia Communications (USA) Inc.

Camden House Publishing, Inc.
Ferry Road
Charlotte, Vermont 05445

Library of Congress Cataloging-in-Publication Data

The Eating well cookbook: favorite recipes from Eating well,
the magazine of food and health /
edited by Rux Martin, Patricia Jamieson and Elizabeth Hiser.
p.   cm.
Includes index
ISBN 0-944475-19-1 (v. 1 : hardcover)
ISBN 0-944475-22-1 (v. 1 : softcover)
1. Cookery.   I. Martin, Rux.   II. Jamieson, Patricia.
III. Hiser, Elizabeth.   IV. Eating well.
TX714.E23   1991
641.5 – dc20   91-22875
CIP

Design by Eugenie S. Delaney
Cover photograph by Fred Bird

Trade distribution by
Firefly Books Ltd.
250 Sparks Avenue
Willowdale, Ontario
Canada M2H 2S4

Printed and bound in Canada by
D.W. Friesen & Sons, Altona, Manitoba

CONTENTS

To James M. Lawrence

INTRODUCTION

"The primary requisite for writing about food is a good appetite," the great journalist A.J. Leibling once said, and as *Eating Well, The Magazine of Food & Health,* recently neared the end of its first year of publication, a small feast for those who helped create it seemed the appropriate celebration. The ranks of guests would include many with excellent appetites, but as I surveyed the list, I realized it would be far from a homogeneous group: recipe testers with advanced French-cooking-school degrees; hard-to-please editors with finely honed critical sensibilities; a typesetter openly disdainful of low-fat food; a hawk-eyed nutritionist; several members of the staff with specific aversions to meat, chips and dips; and about 35 assorted others. To spread the pressures of serving this difficult group, everyone was invited to bring a dish of his or her choice from the pages of *Eating Well*.

Despite the diverse and intimidating guest list, I was reassured by the fact that some of the best cooks from several countries would be catering the event—in absentia—from the pages of the magazine.

With the aid of some well-thumbed issues, I sat down to plot the back-up dishes. To get things rolling, I decided on 'Ti Punch, a potent Caribbean cocktail of rum and lime. For appetizers, mushroom caps stuffed with wild rice; canapés spread with smoked trout; marinated vegetables; phyllo triangles filled with feta and spinach; and endive leaves with smoked salmon and goat cheese.

Without much more difficulty, the main course took shape: a group of savory and spicy fillings for flour and corn tortillas: shredded beef, fiery chicken and avocado with *chile chipotles,* and Shrimp With Lime and Crunchy Vegetables. Mixed greens and a Caribbean fruit salad would round out the meal, fol-lowed by a pineapple chiffon cake. If the recipes worked as well multiplied for several dozen as they had in the magazine's test kitchens, the food would be worthy of the event.

I couldn't help noticing the difference between this dinner and one that I had given more than a decade earlier. Grease-stained pages in one of my favorite cookbooks of the period chart the fat-laden progression of that meal: baked Camembert cheese; chili-cheese dip; crab-filled mushrooms; chicken and rice with avocados; and miniature cheesecakes and brownies. For good measure, we added a roast of bear shot by a neighboring hunter. The percentage in fat of the meal must have totalled an unseemly 60 percent, not counting the bear. Luckily, few people worried about that then, though, and I concentrated on impressing my guests.

Even to someone with no grasp of nutritional numbers, the contrast between those two menus was dramatically visible in the shopping cart the day before the party. It held little meat, no cream, no sour cream and very little cheese, save for some goat cheese and low-fat cottage cheese, but instead, shrimp, trout and salmon. At the produce section, the vegetables took up an entire cart of their own.

As the guests began to arrive, a meal of surprisingly well-balanced proportions appeared on the table: Shrimp & Snow Pea Hors d'Oeuvres with Currant-Mustard Dip; a dip of smoky-tasting eggplant puree; chicken and macaroni from the Greek island of Corfu; and whole-grain breads. Despite its plenitude, the meal was well under the widely recommended 30 percent calories from fat. Not that any of the guests were counting. At least not that night. Still, as our typesetter conceded the following day, "It was nice to know that all the dishes were good for you."

The potluck of recipes from readers, staff, writers and chefs on the following pages is offered to those who, like ourselves, want to eat well in the fullest sense. They bear testimony that healthful food need involve no compromise in taste. Despite contrary scientific evidence on the finer points of the relationship between diet and health, age-old nutritional truths still hold: rice, pasta, grains and beans should form the center of the meal, along with plenty of vegetables and fruits, while meat and desserts play supporting roles.

Accordingly, the recipes in this cookbook come from a variety of sources, many of them from cultures that have never abandoned these sound principles: Greece, Guadeloupe, Vietnam, Italy and China, to name a few. Still others rest squarely in the heart of the American tradition, sent to us by cooks who revised their eating habits and redid their recipes to make them more healthful. Others took shape when readers sent in their favorite recipes for revision in our test kitchen.

Regardless of their source, these recipes were first reviewed by nutritionist Elizabeth Hiser, R.D., who looked at the proportions of nutrients and suggested adjustments where appropriate. The most important consideration is how much fat the recipes contain. Often, it can be reduced without affecting taste. Small measures make a big difference: using a nonstick skillet, adding less oil (health-conscious cooks should remember that a single tablespoon contains about 14 grams fat), or replacing it with defatted chicken stock. Other dishes called for more ingenuity: making a low-fat mayonnaise without raw eggs, or a flaky, flavorful tortilla with a minimum of saturated fat. (For tips on revising conventional recipes, see "Rx for Recipes," page 238.)

The standard for whether a dish is sufficiently low in fat to be included is not a hard-and-fast rule: a chocolate cake cannot be judged by the same benchmark as a broccoli stir-fry. We are often asked why individual dishes do not always meet the 30-percent-calories-from-fat limit. Simply put, this recommendation applies to the overall diet and can include dishes that contain more than 30 percent fat, as well as those that contain far less. While our menus fall easily under the 30 percent limit, individual recipes must be looked at in the context of the total meal, but all are healthful alternatives to other recipes of their kind. (For more information on how to interpret the nutritional analyses, consult our Culinary Math box.)

The dishes have been tested, refined and streamlined where necessary in our test kitchen under the direction of Patricia Jamieson. In the last analysis, each recipe was selected for one reason only: because it won the unanimous approval of all who tasted it.

This first annual collection of *Eating Well* recipes would not have been possible had it not been for the support of writers, photographers and readers, who wrote to encourage and occasionally to correct us, and an assorted cast of publishing consultants, advertising staff, print suppliers, family and other visitors who stop into the test kitchens to offer opinions or to sample a slice of chocolate-potato cake or a steaming bowl of Beef Soup With Herbs.

Particular thanks go to Elizabeth Lowe, Melissa McClelland, Maria Kourebanas and Irving Smith, who tested recipes; Susan Walker, editorial assistant of Camden House Publishing, who secured permissions; proofreaders Sharon Smith and Faith Hanson; copyeditors Wendy Ruopp and Alice Lawrence, who oversaw the manuscript during all stages; art director Eugenie Delaney, who designed the book; and Camden House Editorial Director Sandra Taylor, who weeded out inconsistencies.

The lion's share of credit belongs to Barry Estabrook, editor of *Eating Well*, who distributes equal parts wisdom and good cheer, and especially to Publisher James M. Lawrence, who, a little more than a year ago, set out on what then seemed an impossible dream: to launch "the most authoritative food magazine in the world" from a small village in Vermont.

—Rux Martin

Culinary Math

The following numbers are given to help interpret the nutritional analysis included with each recipe.

	Per day for a 120-lb. person	Per day for a 170-lb. person
Calories	1,800	2,550
Protein	Min. 44 gm	Min. 62 gm
Fat*	Max. 60 gm	Max. 85 gm
Carbohydrate	Min. 248 gm	Min. 351 gm
Sodium**	Max. 6,000 mg	Max. 6,000 mg
Cholesterol	Max. 300 mg	Max. 300 mg

*An easy way to limit fat consumption to the recommended 30 percent of calories is to divide your ideal weight in half. This number is an estimate of the allowed fat in grams per day for a moderately active person. The above values are given as a reference only, since calories needed to maintain ideal body weight vary from person to person.
**Unlike fat, there is no general consensus for healthy people to reduce sodium below this moderate level.*

MENUS

Breakfast for a
Post-Egg-and-Bacon World

Cranberry-Grapefruit Cooler, p. 236

---

*Smoked Salmon & Potato Cakes
With Dill Cream, p. 31*
or
Vegetable Hash Baked in a Skillet, p. 32
or
Potato & Smoked Fish Frittata, p. 34

Toasted Cornmeal-Apple Muffin Wedges, p. 35

Maple-Walnut Yogurt Swirl, p. 37

*This menu contains from 738 to 771 calories
per serving with 22 to 23 percent of calories from fat,
depending on the entrée chosen.*

Potato & Smoked Fish Frittata

A Simple Spring Dinner

Fresh Pea Soup, p. 47

Broiled Lamb Chops, p. 175

Rhubarb Chutney Sauce, p. 180

New Potatoes & Peas, p. 111

Warm Dandelion Greens, p. 73

Young Salad Greens
with Garlic-Tip Dressing, p. 80

Lemon Meringue Kisses, p. 218

Ginger Sorbet, p. 231

This menu contains a total of 794 calories
per serving with 22 percent of calories from fat.

A Three-Pasta Party

Marinated Mushrooms & Peppers, p. 76

Pappardelle With Squab, p. 96

Spaghetti With Shrimp, p. 89

Orecchiette With Vegetable Sauce, p. 93

Salad of Mixed Greens, p. 80

Poached Dried Fruit, p. 229

This menu contains a total of 1,166 calories
per serving with 14 percent of calories from fat.

A Midsummer Barbecue

Bruschetta With Tomatoes & Capers, p. 23

Crusty Herbed Chicken, p. 120

Roasted Bell Peppers, p. 70

Italian Potato Salad, p. 109

Fruit Cup With Marsala Sauce, p. 225

Biscotti, p. 219, and Iced Coffee

Frascati, Dry Orvieto or Pale Ale

This menu contains a total of 986 calories
per serving with 24 percent of calories from fat.

A Chinese Barbecue

Steak & Vegetable Kebabs, p. 162

Grilled Salmon Steaks
With Black-Bean Sauce, p. 135
or
Grilled Swordfish
With Spicy Hot-&-Sour Sauce, p. 143

Chinese Rice Salad With Vegetables, p. 87

Rainbow Salad With Spicy Chili Dressing, p. 86

Fruit Compote With Almond Jelly, p. 226

This menu contains a total of 1,037 calories
per serving with 22 percent of calories from fat.

A Healthful Holiday Banquet

Pumpernickel Toasts With Smoked Salmon, p. 15

Chicken Soup With Mushrooms, p. 54

Lacquered Cornish Game Hens, p. 113

Wild Rice Pilaf, p. 102

Glazed Onions, p. 76

Sweet Potatoes Anna, p. 79

Spicy Pear Chutney, p. 181

Pumpkin Caramel Custard, p. 222

Almond Tuiles, p. 218

*This menu contains a total of 1,483 calories
per serving with 25 percent of calories from fat.*

BEGINNINGS

~

Pumpernickel Toasts With Smoked Salmon

An easy beginning for a holiday meal.

½ cup low-fat yogurt
2½ Tbsp. chopped scallions or chives
1 Tbsp. chopped fresh dill
⅛ tsp. salt

⅛ tsp. freshly ground black pepper
8 oz. pumpernickel bread, cut into 1½" rounds
6 oz. thinly sliced smoked salmon
dill sprigs for garnish

Combine yogurt, scallions or chives, dill, salt and pepper. *(Yogurt sauce can be made ahead and held in the refrigerator for up to 2 days.)* Preheat oven to 350 degrees F. Toast bread rounds on an ungreased baking sheet in the oven for 5 minutes, turning once.

To assemble toasts: Place about 1 tsp. yogurt sauce on a toast round. Slice a piece of salmon in half, lengthwise, and roll each half into a rose. Place the rose on top of the sauce and garnish with a dill sprig. Makes 24 appetizers; serves 6.

143 CALORIES PER SERVING: 10 G PROTEIN, 3 G FAT, 20 G CARBOHYDRATE; 487 MG SODIUM; 7 MG CHOLESTEROL.

Pumpernickel Toasts With Smoked Salmon

Belgian Endive With Smoked Salmon & Goat Cheese

Softened light cream cheese may be substituted
for goat cheese; in that case, reduce the yogurt to 4 Tbsp.

5 oz. goat cheese
5 Tbsp. nonfat yogurt
1 lb. Belgian endives (5-6 small), leaves
  separated, washed and dried

6 oz. thinly sliced smoked salmon, cut into
  thin strips
1 lemon
approximately 2 Tbsp. chopped fresh dill
freshly ground black pepper

Mix together goat cheese and yogurt until smooth and spreadable. *(The filling can be made up to 2 days ahead and held in the refrigerator.)* Spread about 1 tsp. filling onto each endive leaf. Top with salmon and arrange on a platter. *(The endive leaves can be stuffed up to 8 hours ahead and stored in the refrigerator.)* Just before serving, squeeze on a little lemon juice and sprinkle with dill and pepper.

Makes 60 to 70 stuffed endive leaves.

13 CALORIES EACH: 1 G PROTEIN, 1 G FAT, 0 G CARBOHYDRATE; 31 MG SODIUM; 3 MG CHOLESTEROL.

Smoked Fish Canapés

These pleasing canapés require little labor. Look for good-quality smoked haddock or trout. If it
seems very salty or tough, soak it in milk for 1 hour, drain and pat dry.

8 oz. smoked haddock or trout, skin removed
4 Tbsp. fresh lime juice (2 limes)
1 Tbsp. olive oil
freshly ground black pepper

20 ½"-thick slices baguette (stick of French
  bread) or small pieces good-quality bread
1 clove garlic (optional)
chopped fresh chervil, dill or parsley for garnish

Flake fish into small pieces. Mix lime juice and 1½ tsp. olive oil together and toss fish in the mixture. Grind in some pepper and toss again. *(The fish may be prepared up to this point and stored, covered, in the refrigerator overnight.)* Preheat oven to 350 degrees F. Toast bread for 10 minutes and rub with a cut clove of garlic (if using). Brush the toast lightly with remaining 1½ tsp. oil and top with the fish. Drizzle any marinade remaining in the bowl over the toasts. Sprinkle with fresh herbs.

Makes 20 canapés.

106 CALORIES EACH: 5 G PROTEIN, 1 G FAT, 18 G CARBOHYDRATE; 241 MG SODIUM; 3 MG CHOLESTEROL.

Belgian Endive With Smoked Salmon & Goat Cheese

Shrimp & Snow Pea Hors d'Oeuvres

These are pretty and easy to assemble, as well as tasty. Serve with Currant-Mustard Dip.

36 snow peas (about ¼ lb.)
36 medium-sized shrimp, unpeeled
(about 1 lb.)

Currant-Mustard Dip
(recipe follows)

String snow peas. Place pods in a pot of boiling, salted water and blanch them for 45 seconds, counting from when the water returns to a boil. Immediately remove from water with a slotted spoon and run under cold water. Drain. Place shrimp in the cooking water and boil for 2 to 3 minutes, or until pink.

Drain and run under cold water. Peel and devein. Place each shrimp on a blanched snow pea and secure with a toothpick, or wrap the pea pod around the shrimp. Repeat until all are done.

Makes 36 hors d'oeuvres.

15 CALORIES EACH: 3 G PROTEIN, 0 G FAT, 0 G CARBOHYDRATE; 19 MG SODIUM; 19 MG CHOLESTEROL.

Currant-Mustard Dip

This is one of those sauces people say they could eat a telephone book with. It has no fat to speak of, and it's fun to make people guess what's in it. Almost everyone says "mayonnaise," and no one believes it consists of only two ingredients.

½ cup red-currant jelly

4 Tbsp. Dijon mustard

Combine jelly and mustard in a small bowl and beat vigorously with a wire whisk. Small flecks of jelly will appear not to have dissolved, but in 5 minutes or so, they will melt and the sauce will be smooth. Alternatively, combine jelly and mustard in a blender until smooth.

Makes ¾ cup.

38 CALORIES PER TABLESPOON: 0 G PROTEIN, 0 G FAT, 9 G CARBOHYDRATE; 70 MG SODIUM; 0 MG CHOLESTEROL.

Phyllo Triangles With Spinach Filling

Phyllo (also spelled filo) pastries can be filled a day in advance.
They can be frozen and transferred directly from the freezer to the preheated oven.
(They will take an extra 5 to 10 minutes to cook.)

2 lbs. fresh spinach, stems removed
3 Tbsp. plus 1 tsp. olive oil
2 medium-sized onions, finely chopped
2 cloves garlic, minced
1 tsp. dried thyme
1 tsp. dried oregano
2 egg whites, beaten with a fork until frothy

3 oz. feta cheese, crumbled
⅓ cup low-fat cottage cheese
2 Tbsp. freshly grated Parmesan
½ tsp. salt
¼ tsp. freshly ground black pepper
½ lb. phyllo dough

Wash spinach but do not dry. Steam it in a covered stock pot, without additional water, for about 5 minutes, or just until it wilts. Drain, squeeze out the excess moisture and chop finely. Heat 1 tsp. oil in a nonstick skillet over medium-low heat and sauté onions, stirring often, until they begin to brown, about 3 to 5 minutes. Add garlic, spinach, thyme and oregano and cook, stirring, for 1 to 2 minutes. Remove from the heat. In a large bowl, combine egg whites, feta, cottage cheese, the spinach mixture, Parmesan, salt and pepper.

Place rack in the middle of the oven and preheat oven to 350 degrees F. Lay the phyllo dough across a cutting board, with the long side of the rectangle facing you, and cut it into five 2½-inch-wide strips. As you work, keep strips covered with a sheet of wax paper and a damp towel to prevent them from drying out. Place 1 strip vertically in front of you and brush it lightly with some of the remaining 3 Tbsp. oil. Place 1 tsp. of the filling on the right side of the base, about ½ inch from the end. Fold the left-hand corner of the pastry diagonally over the filling, forming a triangle so that the filling is enclosed. Fold the triangle over, down the same side of the strip, and then fold it diagonally again. Continue folding up the pastry as you would a flag, until you reach the end. Brush the outside lightly with oil and place it on a nonstick or lightly oiled baking sheet. Continue until all the filling and oil are used. Bake the pastries for 25 to 30 minutes. Serve hot.

Makes 72 pastries.

25 CALORIES EACH: 1 G PROTEIN, 1 G FAT, 3 G CARBOHYDRATE; 59 MG SODIUM; 1 MG CHOLESTEROL.

Crostini With Mushroom Topping

Sautéed mushrooms make a delicious topping for garlic toasts.

1 Tbsp. olive oil
¾ lb. mushrooms, stems trimmed, cleaned, minced
4 cloves garlic
3 Tbsp. dry white wine
1 tsp. sodium-reduced soy sauce (optional)

½ tsp. dried thyme
pinch crumbled dried rosemary
salt and freshly ground black pepper to taste
3 Tbsp. minced fresh parsley
48 ½"-thick slices baguette (stick of French bread)

Heat 1½ tsp. oil in a large, nonstick skillet over medium heat. Add mushrooms and cook for 2 minutes, stirring, until they begin to release their liquid. Mince 3 garlic cloves and add to the mushroom mixture. Cook, stirring, for 1 minute. Add white wine, soy sauce (if using), thyme, rosemary, salt and pepper. Cook, stirring, for 2 to 3 minutes. The mushrooms should be slightly moist. Stir in parsley and remove from the heat. Taste and adjust seasonings. *(The mixture may be made up to 2 days ahead and held*

in the refrigerator until ready to use.)
Preheat oven to 350 degrees F. Toast bread slices about 4 minutes on each side until they just begin to turn golden. Cut remaining garlic clove in half and rub each slice with the halves. Brush each slice lightly with remaining 1½ tsp. oil. Top the crostini with 1 tsp. mushroom mixture. Serve at room temperature or heat in a 300-degree F oven for 3 to 4 minutes before serving.
Makes 48 crostini.

5 CALORIES EACH: 0 G PROTEIN, 0 G FAT, 1 G CARBOHYDRATE; 1 MG SODIUM; 0 MG CHOLESTEROL.

Onion Confit Crostini

Sweet-onion jam contrasts nicely with the salty olive paste, available in specialty shops.

1 lb. sweet onions, coarsely chopped
1 tsp. olive oil
⅛ tsp. salt
⅛ tsp. freshly ground black pepper
2 Tbsp. dried currants
4 tsp. balsamic or red-wine vinegar

1½ tsp. drained capers
⅓ cup black-olive paste (olivada) or finely chopped pitted black olives
36 ½"-thick slices baguette (stick of French bread), toasted

Preheat oven to 375 degrees F. Place onions in a lightly oiled, shallow 2-qt. baking dish. Toss with oil, salt and pepper. Cover and bake for 45 minutes. Remove cover and bake for 10 minutes longer, or until tender and just starting to brown. Stir in currants, vinegar and capers. *(The onion confit can be made ahead*

and stored in the refrigerator for up to 4 days.)
Before serving, spread ½ tsp. olive paste or chopped olives over one side of each toast. Top with 2 tsp. of the onion confit.
Makes about 36 appetizers.

95 CALORIES EACH: 3 G PROTEIN, 1 G FAT, 18 G CARBOHYDRATE; 170 MG SODIUM; 0 MG CHOLESTEROL.

Smoky Eggplant Puree

This dip is best if made the day before. Tahini, a paste made of ground sesame seeds, is available in health-food stores and some supermarkets.

2½ lbs. eggplant (about 2½ medium-sized),
    pierced with a fork
2 tsp. olive oil plus extra for preparing
    baking sheet
3-4 Tbsp. fresh lemon juice
3 Tbsp. nonfat yogurt

1-2 cloves garlic, minced
2 Tbsp. tahini
½ tsp. ground cumin
salt and freshly ground black pepper to taste
2 Tbsp. minced fresh parsley

Preheat the broiler. Place eggplants on a lightly oiled baking sheet and broil 4 inches from the broiler. Turn every 5 minutes or so, until charred and soft, about 20 minutes. Cool.

Remove all the charred skin, carefully squeeze out the flesh and discard the liquid. With a food processor or blender, puree the eggplant until smooth, along with 2 tsp. oil, lemon juice, yogurt, garlic, tahini, cumin, salt and pepper. Taste and adjust seasonings, and transfer to a serving bowl. Cover and refrigerate, preferably overnight.

Shortly before serving, sprinkle on parsley. Serve with thickly sliced raw vegetables, crackers or pita bread.

Makes about 2 cups.

14 CALORIES PER TABLESPOON: 0 G PROTEIN, 1 G FAT, 1 G CARBOHYDRATE; 3 MG SODIUM; 0 MG CHOLESTEROL.

Serbian Vegetable Caviar

Mexican-cooking authority Diana Kennedy prefers to let this smoky-flavored spread sit overnight in the refrigerator before serving it on melba toast or crackers as an hors d'oeuvre.

1 eggplant (about 1 lb.)
2 green bell peppers, roasted *(page 242)*
1 red bell pepper, roasted *(page 242)*
2 cloves garlic, minced

2 Tbsp. vegetable oil
¼ tsp. freshly ground black pepper
¼ tsp. sea salt or to taste

Broil eggplant about 4 inches from the heat or cook over a charcoal fire for 20 to 25 minutes, turning often until the skin is charred and the flesh is cooked and soft. Remove from heat and make 3 vertical slashes from stalk to tip. Set the eggplant in a sloping position in a colander for about 15 minutes so that the brown, acrid juice can drain out. Remove the stalk and peel off the skin and discard. Reserve the flesh and seeds.

Chop or mash the eggplant and roasted peppers together and stir in the remaining ingredients. (If you use a food processor, which is not advisable, don't make a puree; there should be some texture to it.)

Makes 3 cups; serves 12 as appetizer.

30 CALORIES PER SERVING: 0 G PROTEIN, 2 G FAT, 2 G CARBOHYDRATE; 46 MG SODIUM; 0 MG CHOLESTEROL.

Bruschetta With Tomatoes & Capers

Bruschetta, or grilled bread, whose name comes from the Italian word
meaning "brushed," is a crisper, more flavorful alternative to American garlic bread.
Munch on this while you prepare the rest of the dinner. Note: If you like a strong garlic
taste, do not heat garlic in oil. Simply brush bread lightly with oil, then rub with a garlic clove.

3 large tomatoes
2 Tbsp. capers, chopped arugula or
    chopped fresh basil
1 tsp. plus 2 Tbsp. extra-virgin olive oil
1 tsp. red-wine vinegar

½ tsp. salt
½ tsp. coarsely ground black pepper
1 loaf Italian or French bread (about ½ lb.)
1 clove garlic, minced

Cut tomatoes in half and squeeze out the seeds. Dice the flesh and combine with capers or arugula or basil, 1 tsp. oil, vinegar, salt and pepper. *(The mixture can be made ahead and held in the refrigerator for up to 2 hours. Bring to room temperature before using.)*

Shortly before serving, cut bread into ¾-inch-thick slices. Grill on both sides over coals or under the broiler until lightly toasted. While the bread is grilling, place the remaining 2 Tbsp. oil and garlic in a small saucepan and warm over the coals, or if you are using the broiler, over low heat on top of the stove. Brush one side of bread with garlic oil and spoon tomato mixture over top. Serve immediately. Serves 6.

168 CALORIES PER SERVING: 4 G PROTEIN, 5 G FAT, 25 G CARBOHYDRATE; 374 MG SODIUM; 0 MG CHOLESTEROL.

Marinated Yogurt Cheese

This delicate, fresh cheese is a sensational appetizer.

yogurt cheese from 32 oz. low-fat yogurt
    (page 241)
3 Tbsp. olive oil, preferably extra-virgin
3 Tbsp. minced fresh parsley
1 Tbsp. minced fresh dill

2 cloves garlic, finely minced
½ tsp. dried thyme
½ tsp. dried rosemary
½ tsp. dried basil

Divide yogurt cheese into 4 rounds, shaping patties with your hands. Place in a wide, shallow bowl. Combine remaining ingredients and pour over cheese. Let stand at room temperature for ½ hour; cover and refrigerate overnight. Remove from refrigerator ½ hour before serving. Serve with crusty French bread or crackers.

Makes 4 small cheeses.

42 CALORIES PER OUNCE: 3 G PROTEIN, 2 G FAT, 3 G CARBOHYDRATE; 27 MG SODIUM; 4 MG CHOLESTEROL.

Mushroom Caps With Wild Rice

Wild rice makes a savory filling for mushroom caps.
Serve these any time of the year, adding fresh tarragon in spring and summer.

2 cups vegetable or defatted chicken stock
½ cup wild rice, rinsed
salt to taste
1 Tbsp. olive oil plus extra for preparing
   baking sheet
1 large shallot, chopped
2 large cloves garlic, minced
2¼ lbs. mushrooms (40-50 medium-sized),
   cleaned, caps whole, stems removed and
   chopped

1 tsp. butter
2 Tbsp. dry sherry
½ tsp. dried thyme
freshly ground black pepper to taste
¼ cup toasted almonds, finely chopped
2 Tbsp. chopped fresh parsley
1 tsp. chopped fresh tarragon or sage
   (optional)
2 egg whites, lightly beaten
6 Tbsp. fresh lemon juice (1 lemon)

Bring vegetable or chicken stock to a boil in a large saucepan. Add rice and a little salt if the stock does not already contain it. Return the water to a boil, reduce heat to low, cover and simmer for 40 to 45 minutes, until the rice is tender. Remove from the heat, drain off any remaining stock and set aside.

Heat 1 tsp. oil over low heat in a large, nonstick skillet and add shallots. Cook gently for 5 to 10 minutes, stirring often, until they begin to brown. Add garlic, mushroom stems and butter and sauté over medium heat until the mushrooms begin to release their liquid, about 1 to 2 minutes. Add sherry, thyme, salt and pepper and cook, stirring, for another 1 to 2 minutes. Stir in the wild rice, almonds, parsley and tarragon or sage (if using). Mix well. Adjust seasonings. Remove from heat and stir in egg whites. (*The filling can be made ahead to this point and stored, covered, in the refrigerator for up to 8 hours. The mushroom caps should be wrapped in paper towels, then in plastic, and refrigerated.*)

Preheat oven to 400 degrees F. Brush a baking sheet lightly with oil. Toss the mushroom caps in a bowl with lemon juice, remaining 2 tsp. oil and a little salt and pepper. Fill the caps with the wild-rice mixture. Place on the baking sheet, cover with foil and heat in the oven for 15 to 20 minutes, until they have cooked through but still hold their shape. Drain for a few seconds on paper towels if they are too moist and serve warm on doily-lined plates.

Makes 40 to 50 mushroom caps.

26 CALORIES EACH: 1 G PROTEIN, 1 G FAT, 3 G CARBOHYDRATE; 5 MG SODIUM; 1 MG CHOLESTEROL.

Chinese Dumpling Rolls

These dumplings are similar to egg rolls, but they are steamed, not fried. Serve them for lunch, for dinner or as hors d'oeuvres. (To make appetizer-sized dumplings, cut egg-roll wrappers in half.)

1 cup shredded bok choy or other Chinese cabbage
½ cup bean sprouts
½ cup sliced mushrooms (shiitakes add an Oriental flavor)
½ cup crumbled firm tofu
2 scallions, thinly sliced
1 tsp. peeled, minced gingerroot
2-3 tsp. vegetable oil
½ cup cooked brown rice

1 egg white, lightly beaten
1 Tbsp. soy sauce
½ tsp. mirin (Japanese sweet rice wine; sherry can be substituted)
¾ tsp. toasted sesame oil
1 pkg. egg-roll, spring-roll or wonton wrappers
additional soy sauce and hot mustard for dipping

Combine bok choy, bean sprouts, mushrooms, tofu, scallions and ginger. Heat 2 tsp. oil in a wok or skillet, and cook vegetables until cabbage softens. Combine with rice, egg white, soy sauce, mirin and sesame oil.

Place 1 egg-roll wrapper on the counter like a diamond. (Cover remaining wrappers with a damp cloth to prevent them from drying out.) Take 1 heaping Tbsp. of filling and squeeze out the excess liquid. Spread filling on the lower third of the wrapper. Starting at the point closest to you, bring the bottom half of the wrapper up to enclose the filling. Fold in the 2 sides and continue rolling up the dumpling. Brush

a little water over the inside of the tip and press edges together.

Line a steamer basket with parchment paper or lettuce or cabbage leaves to keep the dumplings from sticking. Set the filled dumplings in the basket over boiling water, cover and steam for 10 minutes, or until the wrappers are translucent. The dumplings can be served at this point, or crisped to a light brown by cooking them in a nonstick skillet in the remaining 1 tsp. oil for about 1 minute on each side.

Serve with soy sauce and hot mustard.

Makes 18 small or 12 large dumplings.

45 CALORIES PER LARGE DUMPLING: 3 G PROTEIN, 1 G FAT, 6 G CARBOHYDRATE; 113 MG SODIUM; 0 MG CHOLESTEROL.

Turban of Sole With Salmon-Yogurt Mousse

This fancy mousse encased in fillets of sole can be served warm or cold as an appetizer, a main course or as part of a buffet. Alternatively, the mousse can be baked without the sole in a lightly oiled 7-inch baking dish for 30 to 35 minutes in a pan of hot water and served with Yogurt-Dill Rémoulade. Fresh fish must be used; frozen will produce too watery a result.

¾ lb. salmon fillet, skinned
10 sole fillets (2½ lbs.)
4 egg whites
½ cup low-fat yogurt
2 Tbsp. minced fresh parsley plus extra for garnish

1 cup fresh bread crumbs
1 tsp. dried dill
1 tsp. salt
½ tsp. freshly ground black pepper
¼ tsp. cayenne pepper
¼ tsp. baking soda

Finely chop salmon and set aside. Lightly oil a 6-cup ring mold and line it with 8 sole fillets, radiating them out from the center of the pan so their sides touch and their tips hang over the rim of the pan. Set aside. Place the remaining 2 sole fillets in a food processor, puree, add egg whites and blend again. Add yogurt, parsley, crumbs, dill, salt, pepper, cayenne and baking soda and blend thoroughly. Place sole mixture in a large bowl and fold in salmon. Spoon the mixture into the mold and fold the ends of the sole over the mousse to enclose it completely.

Preheat the oven to 350 degrees F. Place the mold in a large, shallow pan filled with boiling water to come ⅔ up the sides of the mold. Bake for 30 to 35 minutes, or until the top is firm to the touch. Remove from oven. Carefully pour out any excess fish juice, then invert mold onto a serving plate. (Blot any excess fish juice with a paper towel.) Garnish with parsley and serve with Yogurt-Dill Rémoulade *(page 190)*.

Serves 8 to 10 as a main course or 14 to 16 as an appetizer.

256 CALORIES FOR EACH OF 8 SERVINGS: 35 G PROTEIN, 7 G FAT, 11 G CARBOHYDRATE; 502 MG SODIUM; 16 MG CHOLESTEROL.

Mussels on the Half Shell

A wonderful way to serve these shellfish.

MUSSELS
1 cup dry white wine
2 shallots or 1 onion, chopped
2 cloves garlic, crushed
few sprigs parsley
1 lb. mussels (about 1 qt.), scrubbed, beards
    removed
SALSA CRUDA
1 lb. ripe tomatoes, peeled, seeded and finely
    chopped

2 Tbsp. chopped fresh basil or ¼ tsp. dried
    plus 2 Tbsp. chopped fresh flat-leaved
    parsley
1-2 cloves garlic, minced
1 small hot chili pepper, minced
1 tsp. balsamic or red-wine vinegar
salt and freshly ground black pepper
    to taste
fresh basil for garnish (optional)

To make mussels: Combine wine, 1 cup water, shallots or onions, garlic and parsley in a large pot and bring to a boil. Add mussels, cover tightly and steam 5 minutes, shaking pan halfway through to redistribute the mussels. Drain, discarding any that have not opened.

To make salsa and assemble: Combine all in-gredients, taste and adjust seasonings. Remove mussels from their shells, keeping the shells. Add mussel meats to the salsa, stir gently, cover and chill in the refrigerator for ½ hour or up to 6 hours. Rinse the shells. To serve, spoon a mussel with a little salsa onto each half shell. Garnish with fresh basil.

Makes about 30 mussels.

11 CALORIES EACH: 1 G PROTEIN, 0 G FAT, 1 G CARBOHYDRATE; 23 MG SODIUM; 0 MG CHOLESTEROL.

BREADSTUFFS & BREAKFASTS

⁓

Corncakes With Maple-Yogurt Topping

Slightly crunchy, these pancakes are so light that you'll think they were made with yeast. Make the pancakes immediately, for this batter does not hold.

CORNCAKES
¾ cup stone-ground cornmeal
½ cup all-purpose white flour
½ cup whole-wheat flour
1 tsp. baking powder
2 Tbsp. sugar
½ tsp. salt

1¼ cups skim milk
¼ cup low-fat or nonfat yogurt
2 Tbsp. canola or corn oil
4 egg whites
TOPPING
8 oz. (1 cup) low-fat or nonfat yogurt
¼-½ cup maple syrup

To make corncakes: Combine dry ingredients in a large bowl. In a medium-sized bowl, mix together milk, yogurt and oil and stir into dry cornmeal mixture until blended. Beat egg whites to stiff peaks and fold gently into batter.

Fry pancakes over medium heat for 5 minutes on each side in a lightly oiled pan, until brown and puffed.

To make topping: Combine ingredients in a small bowl and spoon over pancakes.

Makes twelve 4-inch pancakes. Serves 6.

271 CALORIES PER SERVING: 10 G PROTEIN, 6 G FAT, 44 G CARBOHYDRATE; 333 MG SODIUM; 4 MG CHOLESTEROL.

Corncakes With Maple-Yogurt Topping

Ranch Granola

This healthful granola contains little oil or honey and has a lively orange-and-lemon flavor.

8 cups rolled oats
1 cup wheat bran
½ cup chopped almonds
2 Tbsp. cinnamon
1 tsp. ground cardamom
1 tsp. ground ginger
½ cup apple juice
⅓ cup fresh orange juice

⅓ cup fresh lemon juice
¼ cup canola oil
¼ cup honey
1½ Tbsp. grated orange zest (about 1 orange)
1 Tbsp. grated lemon zest (about 1 lemon)
1 Tbsp. vanilla extract
1 cup raisins or dates (optional)

Preheat oven to 300 degrees F. In a large bowl, combine oats, bran, almonds, cinnamon, cardamom and ginger. Set aside. In a small saucepan, over medium heat, heat juices, oil, honey and orange and lemon zests until warm. Stir in vanilla. Pour liquid ingredients into dry ingredients and mix thoroughly.

Spread mixture on two 11-by-16-inch baking sheets. Bake for 35 minutes, stirring every 5 minutes, or until golden brown. Let cool and stir in raisins or dates. *(The granola can be made ahead and stored in an airtight container for up to 3 months.)*
Makes about 10½ cups; serves 20.

204 CALORIES PER SERVING: 7 G PROTEIN, 7 G FAT, 31 G CARBOHYDRATE; 3 MG SODIUM; 0 MG CHOLESTEROL.

Oatmeal & Whole-Wheat Bread

This high-fiber quick bread takes only 1 hour to make.
Its contributor thinks it may be responsible for her long life.

2 cups rolled oats
2 cups whole-wheat flour
2 tsp. baking powder
3 large eggs, lightly beaten

1 cup packed brown sugar
2 tsp. baking soda
2 cups buttermilk

Preheat oven to 350 degrees F. In a large mixing bowl, mix together oats, flour and baking powder. In a medium-sized bowl, whisk together eggs and sugar. In a small bowl, stir baking soda into buttermilk. Add buttermilk mixture to the egg mixture. Pour liquid ingredients into the oatmeal mixture and

beat with a wooden spoon until evenly blended. Turn into a 9-by-5-inch lightly oiled loaf pan. Bake for 50 minutes, or until top is golden brown and a cake tester inserted in the center comes out clean.
Makes 1 loaf, 12 slices.

223 CALORIES PER SLICE: 8 G PROTEIN, 3 G FAT, 43 G CARBOHYDRATE; 258 MG SODIUM; 55 MG CHOLESTEROL.

Smoked Salmon & Potato Cakes With Dill Cream

*You can also make these in miniature form as hors d'oeuvres topped
with a dab of the dill cream and a small amount of red caviar (salmon roe).*

DILL CREAM
½ cup low-fat yogurt
2 Tbsp. chopped fresh dill or to taste
SALMON CAKES
3 large Idaho potatoes, peeled, cut in coarse
   chunks
1 tsp. olive oil plus 1½ tsp. for frying patties
3 scallions, trimmed and thinly sliced
2 large eggs plus 1 egg white

6 oz. smoked salmon, minced
½ cup chopped fresh dill
1 Tbsp. fresh lemon juice
1 Tbsp. low-fat yogurt
few drops Tabasco Sauce
¾ tsp. salt
freshly ground black pepper
1½ tsp. unsalted butter

To make dill cream: In a small bowl, stir together yogurt and 2 Tbsp. dill. Cover and refrigerate. *(The cream can be made ahead and stored, covered, in the refrigerator overnight.)*

To make salmon cakes: Cook potatoes in boiling, salted water until very tender, about 15 to 20 minutes. Drain potatoes thoroughly; return them to the saucepan. Place pan over low heat and stir for about 1 minute to dry potatoes out. Put the potatoes through a ricer or a food mill or transfer them to a bowl and mash. (Do not use a food processor.) You should have about 3 cups. Cover and chill thoroughly for at least 30 minutes or overnight.

Heat 1 tsp. oil in a nonstick skillet over medium heat. Sauté scallions, stirring, for 3 to 4 minutes. Set aside. Beat eggs and egg white together until smooth. Add them to the potatoes, along with the scallions, salmon, ½ cup dill, lemon juice, yogurt, Tabasco, salt and pepper. Chill the mixture, if not using im-

mediately. *(The recipe can be made ahead to this point and stored, covered, in the refrigerator overnight.)*

Just before serving, heat ½ tsp. butter and ½ tsp. of the remaining oil in a wide, nonstick skillet over medium-high heat. Gently form the potato mixture into 12 patties about 2 inches wide and ½ inch thick. Place 4 patties in the pan, lower the heat to medium and cook, shaking the pan occasionally to prevent sticking, until the patties are lightly golden, about 3 to 4 minutes. (Adjust the heat if necessary to maintain a steady, gentle sizzle in the pan as the patties cook. They should not cook too slowly.) Gently flip them and cook until the undersides are lightly golden, about 3 minutes. Repeat twice with remaining patties, using the rest of the butter and oil. The patties can be covered and kept warm in a 200-degree F oven. Serve hot with a dab of dill cream on the side.

Serves 6.

166 CALORIES PER SERVING: 11 G PROTEIN, 6 G FAT, 17 G CARBOHYDRATE; 544 MG SODIUM; 82 MG CHOLESTEROL.

Vegetable Hash Baked in a Skillet

The technique of using pureed vegetables to bind this hash,
replacing cream and eggs, is useful for all sorts of soups and stews too.

1 Tbsp. olive oil
1 large leek, well-washed, trimmed, and cut into ½"-thick slices (1½-2 cups)
1 medium-sized onion, chopped
2-3 cloves garlic, minced
1 fresh thyme sprig, leaves stripped, or pinch dried
1½ cups peeled, diced celery root
1-1½ cups diced carrots
1 cup peeled, diced potatoes
1 cup thickly sliced fresh mushrooms

½ cup thickly sliced shiitake mushrooms
1 medium-sized red bell pepper, seeded and diced
1 large egg
2 Tbsp. low-fat yogurt
3 Tbsp. chopped fresh parsley
1 tsp. salt
¼ tsp. freshly ground black pepper
1 Tbsp. low-fat milk
¼ cup grated Swiss cheese

Heat 1½ tsp. oil in a 10-inch ovenproof nonstick skillet over medium heat. Add leeks, onions, garlic and thyme. Cook, uncovered, stirring frequently, until leeks and onion are softened, about 6 to 8 minutes. Add celery root, carrots, potatoes and ⅓ cup water to the skillet. Cover and cook until the vegetables are almost tender and water is nearly absorbed, about 8 minutes. Remove and reserve 1 cup of the vegetables. Add mushrooms and red pepper to the skillet and sauté uncovered, stirring, for about 4 minutes.

In a food processor, process the reserved vegetables, egg and yogurt until smooth and transfer to a large mixing bowl. Add the vegetables from the skillet, parsley, salt and pepper and toss gently to combine.

Preheat oven to 450 degrees F. Heat remaining 1½ tsp. oil in a nonstick skillet over medium-high heat. (If the skillet is not ovenproof, use a flameproof shallow baking dish.) Add the vegetable mixture, spreading it evenly. Cook 3 to 5 minutes, shaking the pan occasionally to prevent sticking. Place the skillet in the oven and bake 5 minutes. Drizzle the top with milk. Bake until browned, 10 to 15 minutes.

Heat broiler. Sprinkle the hash with cheese. Broil until the cheese is nicely browned, for 1 to 2 minutes. Cool briefly and spoon out portions.

Serves 6.

123 CALORIES PER SERVING: 5 G PROTEIN, 5 G FAT, 17 G CARBOHYDRATE; 438 MG SODIUM; 40 MG CHOLESTEROL.

Potato & Smoked Fish Frittata

Whole eggs and egg whites replace the usual egg mixture in this pancake-style omelet.
It's especially important to cook it slowly and to avoid overcooking, since
protein-rich egg white coagulates at a lower temperature than yolks or whole eggs.
In plain English, it can turn to leather in seconds.

4 new potatoes, unpeeled, scrubbed (about
   12 oz. total)
2 tsp. olive oil
1 medium-sized onion, cut in slivers
3 scallions, trimmed and sliced
6 oz. smoked fish (sturgeon, trout or white-

fish), skin and bones removed, flaked
3 large eggs plus 3 egg whites
3 Tbsp. low-fat milk
¼ tsp. salt
¼ tsp. freshly ground black pepper

In a saucepan, cover potatoes with cold, salted water. Cover, bring to a boil and boil 15 to 20 minutes, or until just tender. Drain, cool in cold water, peel and slice. Heat 1 tsp. oil in a 10-inch nonstick oven-proof skillet over medium heat. Add onions and scallions and cook, stirring occasionally, until the onions begin to soften, about 5 to 6 minutes.

Add the potatoes to the skillet, spreading them gently to cover the bottom of the pan. Add remaining 1 tsp. oil. Toss briefly and sauté on medium heat for 3 to 5 minutes, or until they are lightly browned and crisp. Scatter the smoked fish over the potatoes.

Meanwhile, preheat the broiler and place the rack so that the top of the skillet will be about 1 inch from the heat.

In a mixing bowl, whisk together eggs, egg whites, milk, salt and pepper. Reduce the heat under the skillet to low. Carefully pour the egg mixture over the potatoes and fish, covering them evenly. Cover the pan and cook until the egg mixture has set around the edges but the center is still fairly liquid, usually 6 to 10 minutes. (Adjust the heat if necessary; the mixture should sizzle gently but steadily as the eggs cook.)

Place the skillet under the broiler and cook just until the surface is lightly golden, 1 to 2 minutes. Watch carefully to prevent overcooking, or the egg mixture will toughen. Cut the frittata into 6 wedges and serve hot or warm, passing the pepper mill at the table. Serves 6.

137 CALORIES PER SERVING: 12 G PROTEIN, 6 G FAT, 9 G CARBOHYDRATE; 185 MG SODIUM; 107 MG CHOLESTEROL.

Toasted Cornmeal-Apple Muffin Wedges

Food writer Richard Sax likes to make this breakfast bread with one tart apple,
such as 'Granny Smith,' and a sweeter one, such as 'McIntosh.' In summer, a cornmeal-berry
muffin is ideal. Chunks of pear work well too. Serve with Maple-Walnut Yogurt Swirl (page 37).
Note: *The cake is especially delicious made with Rhode Island Jonny Cake Meal,*
which is freshly ground from white flint corn. It is available from Gray's Grist Mill,
P.O. Box 422, Adamsville, RI 02801; (508) 636-6075.

1⅓ cups all-purpose white flour
⅔ cup cornmeal
⅓ cup light brown sugar
1 Tbsp. baking powder
1 tsp. baking soda
¼ tsp. salt
½ cup nonfat or low-fat yogurt
¼ cup low-fat milk

2 large eggs plus 1 egg white
2 Tbsp. vegetable oil
2 large apples, peeled, cored, and cut into chunks
½ cup currants or raisins
1¼ tsp. cinnamon
pinch nutmeg

Preheat oven to 375 degrees F. Lightly oil a 9-inch round cake pan; set aside. Place dry ingredients in a large mixing bowl and whisk to combine. In a small bowl, combine yogurt and milk. Whisk in eggs, egg white and oil and set aside.

Toss apples with currants or raisins, cinnamon and nutmeg. Add to the dry ingredients and toss to coat the fruit. Make a well in the center of the mixture and pour in the yogurt mixture all at once. With a rubber spatula, mix until moistened but still lumpy; do not overmix. Scrape the batter into the cake pan and spread gently, leaving the top lumpy.

Bake until the cake is golden brown and a toothpick inserted in the center comes out clean, 40 to 45 minutes. Cool in the pan on a rack. *(The cake can be stored, wrapped in plastic, at room temperature for up to 24 hours or in the freezer for up to 1 month.)*

Using a serrated knife, cut the cake into 6 large wedges. Split each wedge in half horizontally. Toast in a toaster oven or under a preheated broiler, cut side up. Serve hot.

Serves 6.

344 CALORIES PER SERVING: 9 G PROTEIN, 7 G FAT, 62 G CARBOHYDRATE; 451 MG SODIUM; 72 MG CHOLESTEROL.

Maple-Walnut Yogurt Swirl

Serve in small ramekins, alongside Toasted Cornmeal-Apple Muffin Wedges (page 35). It is also good when spread on top of them.

½ cup walnuts, toasted *(page 242)*, cooled and chopped

5 Tbsp. maple syrup, preferably chilled
2 cups nonfat yogurt, chilled

Stir nuts into maple syrup in a small bowl. Place yogurt in another small mixing bowl. Pour the nut-syrup mixture over the yogurt and swirl it in with a spoon, without combining thoroughly. Spoon the mixture gently into 6 small ramekins, cover and chill at least ½ hour or overnight.
Serves 6.

147 CALORIES PER SERVING: 7 G PROTEIN, 6 G FAT, 18 G CARBOHYDRATE; 58 MG SODIUM; 1 MG CHOLESTEROL.

Oat Scones

Whole-wheat pastry flour and yogurt, which retains water during baking, plus a small amount of browned butter, combine to give these scones the buttery flavor and crumbly texture of traditional versions, without all the fat.

2 Tbsp. butter
1¼ cups rolled oats
¾ cup all-purpose white flour
¾ cup whole-wheat pastry flour
¼ cup sugar
1 Tbsp. baking powder

½ tsp. baking soda
½ tsp. salt
½ cup raisins
1 egg, lightly beaten
½ cup low-fat yogurt
2 Tbsp. vegetable oil

Preheat oven to 425 degrees F. Melt butter in a small saucepan over low heat and cook until it begins to turn light brown, about 2 minutes. Do not burn. Skim foam and carefully pour the butter into a small bowl.

In a large bowl, mix oats, flours, sugar, baking powder, baking soda and salt. Stir in raisins and make a well in the center of the dry ingredients. Combine browned butter, egg, yogurt and oil and add to the dry ingredients, stirring just until moistened.

Turn out onto a lightly floured surface and gently knead several times to form a ball. Pat the ball into an 8-inch circle and cut into 8 wedges.

Place the wedges on a lightly oiled baking sheet and bake them for about 12 minutes, or until firm to the touch. Transfer to a rack and let cool slightly. Serve warm.

Serves 8.

254 CALORIES PER SERVING: 7 G PROTEIN, 8 G FAT, 40 G CARBOHYDRATE; 412 MG SODIUM; 35 MG CHOLESTEROL.

Toasted Cornmeal-Apple Muffin Wedges and Maple-Walnut Yogurt Swirl

The Best Corn Bread

One of the best things about this corn bread is that it takes only 15 minutes to prepare.

¾ cup plus 2 Tbsp. yellow cornmeal
2 Tbsp. all-purpose white flour
1 tsp. baking powder
1 tsp. sugar
½ tsp. salt

½ tsp. baking soda
1 cup buttermilk
1 large egg, lightly beaten
1 Tbsp. canola oil plus extra for preparing pan

Preheat oven to 475 degrees F. In a large bowl, stir together cornmeal, flour, baking powder, sugar, salt and baking soda. In a small bowl, whisk together buttermilk, egg and oil. Pour into flour mixture and stir until just combined.

Brush an 8-by-8-inch square cake pan with oil and heat in oven for 5 minutes. Pour the batter into the hot pan and bake for 8 to 10 minutes, or until the top springs back when touched lightly. Let cool on a rack and cut into 9 pieces. Serve warm or at room temperature.

Serves 9.

84 CALORIES PER SERVING: 3 G PROTEIN, 3 G FAT, 12 G CARBOHYDRATE; 237 MG SODIUM; 25 MG CHOLESTEROL.

Brioche Bread

Sesame seeds form a nice crust on this bread, which is particularly good toasted for breakfast.

approximately 5½ cups all-purpose white flour
1 cup yellow cornmeal
½ cup nonfat dry milk
½ cup oat bran
2 pkg. active dry yeast (2 Tbsp.)
1½ tsp. salt

1 tsp. sugar
¼ cup olive oil plus extra for preparing pan
¼ cup honey
1 large egg, lightly beaten plus 1 beaten white
1 Tbsp. sesame or poppy seeds

In a large bowl, stir together 2 cups flour, cornmeal, dry milk, oat bran, yeast, salt and sugar. In a small saucepan, over medium heat, heat 1¾ cups water, oil and honey for 8 minutes, or until very warm. Add the warm liquid and 1 egg to the flour mixture and blend with a mixer set at low speed or by hand until well combined. Gradually stir in remaining 3½ cups flour until the dough pulls away from the bowl.

Turn out onto a lightly floured board and knead for about 10 minutes, or until dough is smooth and elastic, adding additional flour as needed to prevent the dough from sticking. Place dough in a bowl, cover and let rise in a warm, draft-free place for about 1 hour and 15 minutes.

Punch the dough down, and divide it in half and shape each portion into a ball. Return the dough to the bowl, and let rest for 15 minutes, covered. Lightly oil two 8-by-4-inch loaf pans and sprinkle with cornmeal. Shape balls into oval loaves to fit pans, cover and let rise for about 1 hour.

Preheat oven to 350 degrees F. Uncover the dough and brush the tops of the loaves lightly with beaten egg white. Sprinkle with sesame or poppy seeds. Bake the loaves for 30 to 40 minutes, or until the tops are golden brown and the bottoms sound hollow when tapped. Remove from pan and let cool on a rack.

Makes 2 loaves, about 16 slices each.

129 CALORIES PER SLICE: 4 G PROTEIN, 2 G FAT, 23 G CARBOHYDRATE; 110 MG SODIUM; 7 MG CHOLESTEROL.

Hearty Grain Bread

This recipe, from Lucia's restaurant in Minneapolis, combines bulgur, oatmeal, wheat bran, sunflower seeds and whole-wheat flour for a hearty, crunchy texture. It will keep for several days and freezes beautifully.

2 pkg. active dry yeast (2 Tbsp.)
⅓ cup honey
2-2½ cups all-purpose white flour
1¾ cups whole-wheat flour
¾ cup rolled oats (not instant)
¾ cup raw bulgur

¾ cup wheat bran
¾ cup ground sunflower seeds (from ¾ cup whole)
1½ tsp. salt
vegetable oil for greasing bowl and baking sheet

In a large bowl, stir yeast and honey into 2½ cups lukewarm water. Let stand for 10 minutes, or until frothy. With a wooden spoon, stir in 1 cup white flour, ¾ cup whole-wheat flour, oats, bulgur and bran. Beat for 100 strokes. Cover with plastic and let rise for 1 hour in a warm, draft-free place.

Stir in sunflower seeds, salt, remaining 1 cup whole-wheat flour and enough of the remaining white flour to make a firm, soft dough. Turn out onto a lightly floured board and knead for about 10 minutes, or until dough is smooth and elastic, adding additional white flour as needed to prevent the dough from sticking. Place it in a lightly oiled bowl and turn to coat with oil. Cover with plastic and let rise for about 1½ hours, or until doubled in bulk.

Punch the dough down, cover and let rise again for 1 hour, or until doubled. *(Alternatively, refrigerate the dough, let it rise overnight, then allow it to return to room temperature.)* Divide dough in half and shape each portion into an oval loaf, about 8 inches long. Place loaves at least 3 inches apart on a lightly oiled baking sheet. Cover with a towel and let rise for about 45 minutes, or until almost doubled.

Preheat oven to 375 degrees F. Brush the tops of the loaves lightly with water. With a serrated knife, make 3 diagonal slashes about ¼ inch deep across the tops. Bake the loaves for 25 to 35 minutes, or until tops are golden brown and the bottoms sound hollow when tapped.

Makes 2 loaves, 12 slices each.

148 CALORIES PER SLICE: 5 G PROTEIN, 3 G FAT, 27 G CARBOHYDRATE; 134 MG SODIUM; 0 MG CHOLESTEROL.

Spinach & Red Pepper *Torta Rustica*

This double-crusted deep-dish tart is as exciting to look at as it is to eat, with its multicolored dark green, red and light green layers. The crust is a yeasted pizza dough with a rich flavor. It takes a while to make, so serve it for a dinner party on a weekend and dazzle your guests. Be sure to wring out as much moisture as possible from the cottage cheese so the torta filling will set properly.

PIZZA DOUGH
2 tsp. active dry yeast
1 tsp. sugar
1 cup semolina flour
1 Tbsp. olive oil
1 tsp. salt
1½ cups all-purpose white flour
FILLING
4 large red bell peppers, roasted *(page 242)*,
    or one 1-lb. jar good-quality peeled,
    roasted red peppers, or pimientos, drained
1½ lbs. fresh spinach, rinsed

1 Tbsp. olive oil
2 large onions, minced
4 cloves garlic, minced
1 tsp. dried thyme
2 eggs
½ cup freshly grated Parmesan
1½ tsp. salt
1 tsp. freshly ground black pepper
1 lb. cottage cheese (2 cups)
½ cup chopped fresh basil
2 Tbsp. chopped fresh parsley
1 egg beaten with 1 Tbsp. water for egg wash

To make the dough: Dissolve yeast and sugar in 1 cup lukewarm water in a large bowl. Let rest 10 minutes or until frothy. Stir in semolina flour, oil and salt. Stir in 1 cup unbleached flour and turn out on to a lightly floured board. Knead 10 to 15 minutes, adding additional unbleached flour as needed to prevent sticking, until dough is smooth and elastic, but still soft. Place in a lightly oiled bowl and turn once to coat with oil. Cover with a damp towel or loosely with plastic wrap, and let rise in a warm spot until doubled in bulk, for 1 to 1½ hours, then punch down. *(Dough can be made ahead to this point and held in the refrigerator for up to 2 days.)*

To make the filling: Cut peppers in half lengthwise, remove seeds and membranes, chop roughly and pat dry.

Steam spinach in a covered pan without adding additional water for about 5 minutes or until it wilts. Drain and squeeze out all excess moisture. Heat oil in a large skillet over medium heat and sauté onions and garlic until onions are tender, 3 to 5 minutes. Stir in spinach and thyme. Cook for a few minutes,

then remove from heat and let cool completely. Lightly beat 1 egg and stir into spinach mixture along with ¼ cup Parmesan, ¾ tsp. salt and ½ tsp. pepper. Set aside.

Place cottage cheese in a cheesecloth-lined sieve over a bowl. Gather cheesecloth into a ball and squeeze out moisture. (You should have about 1 cup cottage cheese solids.) Transfer to a bowl; lightly beat remaining egg and stir into cottage cheese, along with remaining Parmesan, basil, parsley, remaining ¾ tsp. salt and ½ tsp. pepper.

To assemble the tart: Preheat oven to 375 degrees F. On a lightly floured board, roll out ⅔ of the dough into a 14-inch-diameter circle. Transfer to a lightly oiled 10-inch springform pan. Firmly press the dough into place up the sides.

Place half the spinach mixture in the dough, followed by half the chopped peppers, the cottage cheese mixture, the remaining peppers and finally the remaining spinach mixture. Roll out the remaining third of the dough for the top crust. Using a cookie cutter or sharp knife, cut a large steam vent about 1 inch in diameter in the center of the crust. Place the dough over the filling, fold in edges of bottom crust, and pinch the crusts together. Brush the top crust with egg-water wash and bake for 50 to 60 minutes or until puffed and golden. Remove from oven and let cool 10 to 15 minutes. Carefully remove the ring of the pan and serve, or allow to cool still more and serve at room temperature.

Serves 8 to 10.

333 CALORIES FOR EACH OF 8 SERVINGS: 20 G PROTEIN, 11 G FAT, 40 G CARBOHYDRATE; 1,106 MG SODIUM; 93 MG CHOLESTEROL.

Rumanian Zucchini-Potato Latkes

"Latke" is the Yiddish word for pancake. Every latke lover seems to know how to make these potato pancakes and has strong opinions about them. They can be served for breakfast, brunch, lunch, dinner or cocktail parties. They can be eaten plain or fancy, with applesauce or even chicken soup.

2 lbs. zucchini squash, peeled and seeded
  (4 medium-sized)
1 lb. potatoes, peeled (2 large)
1 medium-sized onion
1 egg plus 2 egg whites
1 tsp. vegetable oil plus 1 Tbsp.
½ tsp. salt
½ tsp. freshly ground black pepper
½-¾ cup matzo meal

Grate zucchini, potatoes and onions by hand or in a food processor. Place the grated vegetables in a tea towel and wring firmly to remove excess moisture. (You may need to do this in batches.)

Place the grated vegetables in a large bowl. Stir in egg and egg whites, 1 tsp. vegetable oil, salt and pepper until well combined. Add ½ cup matzo meal and blend well. Add additional meal if needed to help the mixture hold together.

Lightly brush a large nonstick skillet with some of the remaining vegetable oil and heat over medium heat until a drop of water sizzles when dropped on the surface of the pan. Drop batter by ¼ cupfuls into the pan and flatten to form pancakes. Cook for 3 to 4 minutes per side, or until latkes are golden brown and the centers are cooked through. Repeat until all the batter has been used, brushing pan with oil as needed to prevent sticking. Keep pancakes warm in a 175-to-200-degree-F oven while the remaining ones are being prepared. Serve hot with yogurt or applesauce.

Serves 6 to 8.

151 CALORIES FOR EACH OF 6 SERVINGS: 6 G PROTEIN, 4 G FAT, 25 G CARBOHYDRATE; 213 MG SODIUM; 36 MG CHOLESTEROL.

Hortopitta (Pie of Assorted Greens)

*Before phyllo dough became available in frozen packets, the rural population
of the Greek island of Corfu used a different kind of pastry, known locally as* petouro,
*for their pies. In comparatively isolated communities, it is still the most popular pie crust.
It is not only simpler to prepare and easier to handle than phyllo, but lower in fat.*

DOUGH
1½ tsp. active dry yeast
½ tsp. sugar
2¾ cups all-purpose white flour, plus more
    for kneading
1 tsp. salt
1 egg
⅔ cup skim milk
2 Tbsp. olive oil
FILLING
1½ lbs. mixed greens (chard, dandelion,
    escarole, spinach), washed

1 Tbsp. olive oil
4 large scallions, with green tops, finely
    chopped
1 Tbsp. finely chopped fresh fennel leaves
1 Tbsp. finely chopped fresh dill
1 Tbsp. finely chopped fresh parsley
½ lb. feta cheese, finely crumbled (1½ cups)
⅓ cup skim milk
¼-½ tsp. salt
¼ tsp. freshly ground black pepper or to taste
2 eggs, beaten
2 Tbsp. uncooked rice

To make dough: Dissolve yeast and sugar in ¼ cup warm water and let stand for 10 minutes until foamy. Meanwhile, combine flour and salt in a large bowl. In a separate bowl, beat egg and stir in milk, oil and yeast mixture. Make a well in the center of the flour and pour in the liquid; mix with a wooden spoon, stirring until mixture comes together and forms a soft dough. Turn out onto a lightly floured surface and knead until smooth and elastic, about 5 minutes, adding flour as needed to prevent sticking. Shape the dough into a ball, place it in a lightly oiled bowl and turn dough to coat. Cover with a damp cloth and set in a warm place for about 45 minutes, or until doubled in size.

To make filling: Bring a large pot of water to a boil. Add greens, return to a boil and cook for 2 to 3 minutes. Drain, refresh in cold water, squeeze out moisture and chop greens finely. Place

them in a large bowl and set aside.

In a large, nonstick skillet, heat oil over medium heat and fry scallions, fennel, dill and parsley for 2 to 3 minutes, or until softened. Stir into the greens, along with feta, milk, salt and pepper. Mix well, taste and adjust seasonings. Mix in eggs and rice.

To assemble *Hortopitta*: Preheat oven to 350 degrees F. Punch down dough and divide into 2 balls, one slightly larger than the other. On a lightly floured surface, roll out the larger ball into a 12-by-16-inch rectangle. Place it in a lightly oiled 9-by-13-inch baking dish. Press the dough up the sides and spread the filling evenly throughout. Roll out the remaining dough, place it over the top of the dish and pinch the edges of the top and bottom crusts together. Bake 45 to 50 minutes or until crusts are crisp and golden. Cool on a rack for 10 minutes before serving.
Serves 8.

353 CALORIES PER SERVING: 15 G PROTEIN, 14 G FAT, 42 G CARBOHYDRATE; 827 MG SODIUM; 106 MG CHOLESTEROL.

Hortopitta *(Pie of Assorted Greens)*

Wheat-Flour Tortillas

*To reduce the fat in the tortillas, we added a little flour to
vgetable oil and froze the mixture so it would act like shortening.
Adapted from Rick Bayless's recipe, these tortillas are much better than store-bought.
Note: To steam-heat tortillas, wrap a stack of 12 tortillas in a clean, heavy
towel, place in a steamer over ½ inch of water, cover and bring to a boil over medium-high
heat. When steam is released, time 1 minute, then remove from the heat and let stand 15 to
20 minutes. Held in a very low oven, the tortillas will stay warm and moist for an hour or more.*

**2¾ cups all-purpose white flour, plus a little
extra for rolling out the tortillas**

3 Tbsp. vegetable oil
¾ tsp. salt

Combine ½ cup of the flour and the oil in a small bowl and place in the freezer for 1 hour. Place the remaining 2¼ cups flour in a large bowl and work in the oil-flour mixture quickly with your fingers, until pea-sized lumps remain. Dissolve salt in ¾ cup very warm tap water. Pour it over the dry ingredients and immediately work it in with a fork; the dough will be in large clumps rather than a homogeneous mass. If all the dry ingredients haven't been dampened, add a little more water, 1 tsp. at a time, until the dough clumps together. Scoop the dough onto your work surface and knead until smooth, about 3 minutes. It should be a medium-stiff consistency—definitely not firm but not quite as soft as most bread dough either. (The tortillas may also be mixed in the food processor. Pulse several times, then blend until the fat is thoroughly incorporated. Dissolve salt in ¾ cup warm water. With the machine running, pour the liquid through the feed tube in a steady stream. Let the machine run until the dough has collected into a ball. If it's too stiff, divide the dough into several pieces, sprinkle with 1 Tbsp. water and process until it forms a ball again.)

Divide the dough into 12 portions and roll each

into a ball. Set them on a plate, cover with plastic wrap and let rest at least 30 minutes to make the dough easier to roll.

Heat an ungreased griddle or heavy skillet over medium to medium-high heat. On a lightly floured surface, roll out a portion of the dough into an even 7-inch circle. To do this, flatten a ball of dough, flour it, then roll forward and back across it; rotate a sixth of a turn and roll forward and back again; continue rotating and rolling until you reach a 7-inch circle, lightly flouring the tortilla and work surface from time to time.

Lay the tortilla on the hot griddle (you should hear a faint sizzle and see an almost immediate bubbling across the surface). After 30 to 45 seconds, when there are browned splotches underneath, flip it over. Cook 30 to 45 seconds more, until the other side is browned; don't overbake the tortilla or it will become crisp. Remove and wrap in a heavy towel. Roll and griddle-bake the remaining tortillas in the same manner, stacking them one on top of the other wrapped in the towel.

Makes 12 tortillas.

134 CALORIES PER TORTILLA: 3 G PROTEIN, 4 G FAT, 22 G CARBOHYDRATE; 134 MG SODIUM; 0 MG CHOLESTEROL.

Pizza Provençal

A delicious pizza for onion lovers, with a pleasing blend of caramelized onions, tomatoes and peppers.

PIZZA DOUGH
1 pkg. active dry yeast (1 Tbsp.)
pinch sugar
approximately 3 cups all-purpose white flour
1 tsp. salt
FILLING
2 heads garlic, unpeeled, plus 2 minced cloves
6 cups thinly sliced red onions
½ cup medium-dry red wine
¼ cup balsamic vinegar
2 Tbsp. sugar
1½ tsp. dried thyme

1 tsp. dried marjoram
½ tsp. salt
cornmeal for sprinkling over pan
4 plum tomatoes, cut in eighths
1 red bell pepper, roasted and cut into thin strips *(page 242)*
1 yellow bell pepper, roasted and cut into thin strips *(page 242)*
4-5 fresh basil leaves, torn
1 tsp. dried rosemary
½ tsp. dried oregano

To make dough: Dissolve yeast and sugar in 1¼ cups lukewarm water in a small bowl. Let stand for 10 minutes, or until frothy. Combine 3 cups flour and 1 tsp. salt in a food processor fitted with the metal blade. With the motor running, gradually pour the yeast mixture through the feed tube and process until the dough forms a ball. Let the dough spin for 30 seconds to 1 minute, or until smooth and elastic. Alternatively, mix dough in a bowl and knead on a lightly floured surface for 10 minutes until no longer sticky.

Transfer dough to a lightly oiled bowl. Cover with a damp towel or plastic wrap and let rise in a warm, draft-free place for 30 to 60 minutes, or until doubled in bulk. Punch down and knead for 1 minute. *(The dough can be made ahead and held in the refrigerator overnight.)*

To make filling: Preheat oven to 450 degrees F. Separate 2 heads of garlic into cloves and place them in a small nonstick baking pan with ¼ cup water. Cover with foil and bake for 40 to 60 minutes, or until garlic is very soft. Let cool.

Meanwhile, in a large saucepan, combine remaining 2 cloves minced garlic, onions, wine, vinegar, sugar, 1 tsp. thyme, marjoram and salt. Cook, covered, stirring frequently, over low heat for 45 to 60 minutes, or until the liquid has evaporated and the onions are slightly caramelized. Cool. *(The filling can be made ahead to this point and held overnight in the refrigerator.)*

To assemble pizza: Preheat oven to 450 degrees F. Stretch or roll the dough into a 14-inch circle or a 9-by-14-inch rectangle, leaving it slightly thicker around the edges. Sprinkle cornmeal over a pizza stone or a heavy baking sheet and place the dough on the pan. Arrange tomatoes over the dough and distribute the onion mixture and peppers over the tomatoes. Squeeze the baked garlic cloves over top (discard skin) and sprinkle basil, rosemary, oregano and remaining ½ tsp. thyme over top. Place the baking stone or sheet on the bottom rack of the oven and bake for 10 to 15 minutes, or until the pizza crust is golden brown.

Serves 6.

333 CALORIES PER SERVING: 10 G PROTEIN, 1 G FAT, 69 G CARBOHYDRATE; 556 MG SODIUM; 0 MG CHOLESTEROL.

SOUPS

Fresh Pea Soup

*Soups like this play up the best qualities
of peas, yet mask any falling-off from perfection.*

2½ cups fresh or frozen peas
¼ tsp. salt or to taste
1½ tsp. chopped fresh tarragon or ½ tsp. dried
6 cups Potato-Vegetable Stock *(page 50)*
¾ cup buttermilk (optional)
¼ tsp. freshly ground black pepper
minced raw leek for garnish (optional)
pinch nutmeg

(Recipe continues on next page)

Fresh Pea Soup

In a saucepan, barely cover peas with lightly salted water, add tarragon and bring to a boil. Reduce heat and simmer 2 to 5 minutes until tender. Remove 1 cup of the peas; set aside. Continue cooking the remaining peas for 3 to 5 minutes, until very tender. Drain, reserving ¼ cup of the cooking water. Puree the peas in a food processor or blender with the reserved cooking water and return the mixture to the saucepan. Add stock and reserved peas. Stir in buttermilk (if using) and pepper. Heat through. *(The soup can be made ahead and stored in the refrigerator for up to 2 days.)* Garnish with a few curls of leek (if using) and a sprinkling of nutmeg.

Makes 8 cups.

137 CALORIES PER CUP: 6 G PROTEIN, 0 G FAT, 28 G CARBOHYDRATE; 231 MG SODIUM; 0 MG CHOLESTEROL.

Puree of Vegetable Soup

This green soup, thickened with potatoes and bursting with vegetables,
may be served cold. To create a swirled pattern, drop several teaspoons of yogurt
onto the soup and draw the tip of a knife through the surface.

1 tsp. olive oil
2 leeks, white part only, well-rinsed and sliced
1 medium-sized onion, chopped
5 cups defatted chicken stock
1 lb. potatoes (about 3 medium), peeled and cut into 1" chunks
1 clove garlic, coarsely chopped
bouquet garni: 1 bay leaf, few sprigs thyme and parsley, tied with string or in cheesecloth

1 head Boston lettuce, leaves separated and chopped
5 cups fresh sorrel or spinach, stems removed
1 bunch parsley, stems removed (3 cups)
salt and freshly ground black pepper to taste
6 Tbsp. low-fat yogurt
sprigs of fresh parsley, tarragon, chervil or basil for garnish

Heat oil over low heat in a heavy-bottomed soup pot and add leeks and onions. When they begin to sizzle, stir over low heat for 1 minute, then add 3 Tbsp. water. Stir, cover and cook over low heat for 8 minutes, stirring often. The vegetables should soften but not brown. Add chicken stock, potatoes, garlic and bouquet garni, and bring to a boil. Reduce heat, cover and simmer 30 minutes, or until potatoes are soft. Add lettuce and half the sorrel or spinach and simmer another 5 to 8 minutes, covered, or until greens are wilted and cooked through. Add parsley and remaining sorrel or spinach and remove from the heat. Discard bouquet garni. In a blender or food processor, puree the soup in batches until completely smooth. Return to soup pot and reheat over low heat. Taste and add salt and pepper. Spoon into bowls, top each serving with a scant Tbsp. yogurt and garnish with herbs.

Serves 6.

155 CALORIES PER SERVING: 11 G PROTEIN, 2 G FAT, 27 G CARBOHYDRATE; 81 MG SODIUM; 1 MG CHOLESTEROL.

Puree of Vegetable Soup

Potato-Vegetable Stock

This stock owes its depth to last summer's crop of potatoes and leeks, simmered into a thick broth.
If you don't have leeks, a fat head of garlic, unpeeled and coarsely chopped, makes a fine substitute.

5 medium-sized potatoes (2 lbs.), scrubbed,
   unpeeled, cut in 1" chunks
4 large leeks (2 lbs.), white part only, split,
   well-rinsed and cut in chunks
2 medium-sized carrots, scrubbed, unpeeled,
   cut in 1" chunks
½ tsp. freshly ground black pepper
½ tsp. salt
½ tsp. lemon thyme or ordinary thyme or
   pinch dried

Combine all ingredients in a heavy-bottomed stock pot, along with 8 cups water or more as needed to cover the vegetables. Bring to a boil, reduce heat, cover and simmer for 30 minutes. Pass broth through a food mill or a sieve, pressing on vegetables to extract as much juice as possible.

Makes about 10 cups.

97 CALORIES PER CUP: 2 G PROTEIN, 0 G FAT, 22 G CARBOHYDRATE; 125 MG SODIUM; 0 MG CHOLESTEROL.

Barley-Root Chowder

This hearty soup with down-to-earth flavors makes good
use of root vegetables. Vegetable stock may be used in place of beef.
The soup can be frozen in 2- or 4-cup containers for easy microwave resuscitation.

4 cups defatted beef stock
½ cup pearl barley
1 celery root, peeled and cut into ½" chunks
1 turnip, peeled and cut into ½" chunks
1 rutabaga, peeled and cut into ½" chunks
1 carrot, peeled and cut into ½" chunks
1 parsnip, peeled and cut into ½" chunks
1 cup chopped green cabbage
1 onion, peeled and cut into ½" chunks
2 tomatoes, chopped, or 1 16-oz. can
   tomatoes, with juice
1 bay leaf
1 tsp. salt
½ tsp. dried sage
½ tsp. dried thyme
pinch freshly ground black pepper

In a large stock pot, bring stock and 4 cups water to a boil. Add barley. Reduce heat, cover and simmer 20 minutes, or until barley is tender. Add the remaining ingredients and bring to a boil. Reduce heat to low, cover and simmer 30 minutes, or until all of the vegetables are tender. Discard bay leaf before serving.

Serves 12.

71 CALORIES PER SERVING: 4 G PROTEIN, 0 G FAT, 15 G CARBOHYDRATE; 298 MG SODIUM; 0 MG CHOLESTEROL.

Chicken in Miso Soup With Noodles

*Serve this soup for a light lunch, dinner or even for breakfast. Miso, a paste
made of salted, fermented soybeans, is found in Oriental markets or in health-food stores.*

1 3-lb. chicken, fat removed, cut into 6 pieces
5-6 slices gingerroot, about the size of a
quarter, smashed lightly
4 scallions, trimmed, smashed lightly, green
tops reserved

½ lb. ramen or dried buckwheat noodles (soba)
¼-⅓ cup medium-colored or light-colored
miso paste (*chu miso* or *Shinshu Ichi miso*)
2 Tbsp. toasted sesame seeds *(page 242)*

Cook chicken in 2 qts. boiling water for about 5
minutes. Remove and rinse under cold running water. Place 10 cups fresh water, chicken pieces, ginger and white stalks of scallions in a pot and bring
to a boil. Lower heat to medium so that the liquid
is at a simmer and cook about 1½ hours (skimming
the surface to remove any froth), or until the chicken
is no longer pink inside and is very tender.

Remove the chicken, cool, and using your hands
or a knife, shred or cut it into matchstick-sized pieces.
Discard ginger and scallions. *(The recipe may be prepared ahead to this point. Cover and refrigerate stock overnight.)* Skim fat from surface.

Place 3 qts. water in a large pot and bring to a boil.
Add noodles, scattering them over the surface, and
return to a boil. Cook for 3 to 5 minutes, or until
they are just tender, and drain. Rinse under cold running water and drain thoroughly. Portion the noodles into 6 serving bowls.

Reheat the chicken stock until hot. In a small bowl,
combine ¼ cup hot stock with ¼ cup miso. Stir the
miso-soup mixture back into the soup pot. Taste and
add more miso paste if desired. Sprinkle some of the
shredded chicken over the noodles and portion the
stock on top.

Sprinkle the top of each bowl with 1 Tbsp. reserved
chopped scallion tops and a sprinkling of toasted sesame seeds and serve immediately.

Serves 6.

338 CALORIES PER SERVING: 37 G PROTEIN, 7 G FAT, 32 G CARBOHYDRATE; 491 MG SODIUM; 82 MG CHOLESTEROL.

Chicken & Cellophane-Noodle Soup

This Vietnamese soup can be served as a light meal or as a soup course.

1 3-lb. chicken, fat removed
¼ cup peeled, chopped gingerroot
6 oz. cellophane noodles (bean threads)
¼ cup fish sauce

freshly ground black pepper
½ cup fresh cilantro leaves
2 scallions, trimmed and chopped

In a large pot, bring 6 cups water to a boil. Add chicken and ginger and reduce heat to low. Cover and simmer for 45 minutes, or until chicken juices run clear when thigh is pierced with a skewer. Remove chicken from broth and set aside to cool. Strain broth and place in the refrigerator to chill.

Soak noodles in warm water for 20 minutes. Drain. Using scissors, cut them into 3-inch lengths and set aside.

Discard the chicken skin, remove the meat from the bones and shred.

Skim fat from broth and place in a large pot. Bring to a boil, add noodles and fish sauce and simmer for about 3 minutes, or until noodles are tender. Remove noodles from broth and divide evenly among individual soup bowls. Place shredded chicken in each bowl, cover with broth and grind in black pepper. Garnish each bowl with cilantro and scallions.

Serves 4 as a main course or 6 as an appetizer.

395 CALORIES FOR EACH OF 4 SERVINGS: 45 G PROTEIN, 5 G FAT, 38 G CARBOHYDRATE; 150 MG SODIUM; 123 MG CHOLESTEROL.

Herkimer Chicken Soup

Joan Nathan's rich chicken soup is a traditional favorite prepared and served on Shabat. It is excellent with Matzo Balls With Ginger & Nutmeg (page 54).

1 4-5 lb. roasting or stewing chicken, cut up, skin and fat removed
4 parsnips
1 medium-sized onion, left whole
½ cup celery leaves
2 Tbsp. chopped fresh parsley

2 Tbsp. chopped fresh dill
1 Tbsp. salt
¼ tsp. freshly ground black pepper
1 cup defatted chicken stock
6 carrots, peeled and left whole

Bring 4 qts. water and all ingredients except carrots to a boil. Cover and simmer for 3 hours. Add carrots and simmer 1 hour more, or until everything falls apart. Strain, reserving chicken for another use, and skim fat. Serve with noodles or matzo balls.

Makes 12 to 15 cups; serves 6 to 8.

After the stock has been skimmed of fat, each 2-cup serving contains about 1,066 mg sodium, small amounts of protein and traces of fat, carbohydrate and cholesterol.

Matzo Balls With Ginger & Nutmeg

These light matzo balls match Herkimer Chicken Soup (page 53) particularly well.

1 cup matzo meal
6 Tbsp. defatted chicken stock
2 Tbsp. melted *pareve* margarine (made
    without milk or animal products)
2 Tbsp. chopped fresh parsley

2 tsp. plus 1 Tbsp. salt
1 tsp. peeled, minced gingerroot or ¼ tsp.
    ground ginger
¼ tsp. nutmeg, preferably freshly grated
2 eggs plus 2 egg whites

In a large bowl, combine matzo meal, chicken stock, margarine, parsley, 2 tsp. salt, ginger and nutmeg. Refrigerate for a few hours or overnight. Add eggs and egg whites, one at a time, whisking until well incorporated. Bring an 8-to-10-quart pot of water to a boil. Add remaining Tbsp. salt to water. Wet your hands with warm water and form the matzo mixture into balls the size of walnuts. Drop matzo balls into boiling water, cover and let simmer 30 minutes, or until they are fluffy and floating at the top. Remove with a slotted spoon to bowls of soup.

Makes about 20 matzo balls; serves 6.

151 CALORIES PER SERVING: 6 G PROTEIN, 6 G FAT, 19 G CARBOHYDRATE; 795 MG SODIUM; 71 MG CHOLESTEROL.

ɮ

Chicken Soup With Mushrooms

This light soup can be made in advance, with the spinach added just before serving.

6 dried shiitake mushrooms
2½ lbs. chicken parts
⅓ cup dry sherry
3 slices gingerroot, about the size of a
    quarter, smashed
6 fresh mushrooms, trimmed, cleaned and
    sliced

½ lb. fresh spinach, trimmed, rinsed, drained
    and shredded
1 tsp. salt or to taste
¼ tsp. freshly ground black pepper
3 Tbsp. minced scallions

Rinse shiitake mushrooms and drain. Soak them in hot water to cover for 15 to 20 minutes until soft and spongy. Drain, reserving ½ cup of the liquid. Place softened mushrooms, mushroom liquid, chicken parts, 8 cups water, sherry and ginger in a heavy-bottomed saucepan and heat until boiling. Reduce heat to low and simmer uncovered, about 1 hour, skimming the surface periodically.

Strain the liquid through a fine-meshed strainer, retaining the mushrooms. Discard the stems from the mushrooms and finely shred the caps. Place strained chicken broth, shredded mushrooms and sliced fresh mushrooms in a soup pot and heat until boiling. Reduce heat to low and simmer 5 minutes. *(The soup can be made ahead to this point and refrigerated for up to 2 days. Bring to a simmer before continuing.)*

Add spinach, salt and pepper and taste for seasoning. Portion into serving dishes and sprinkle with minced scallions. Serve immediately.

Serves 6.

38 CALORIES PER SERVING: 2 G PROTEIN, 0 G FAT, 6 G CARBOHYDRATE; 209 MG SODIUM; 0 MG CHOLESTEROL.

Mexican Soup

This thick main-dish soup, a cross between chili and soup, is good with corn bread.

1 tsp. canola oil
½ lb. lean ground beef
1 large onion, chopped
2 cloves garlic, minced
16 medium-sized tomatoes, chopped (8 cups)
1 Tbsp. chili powder
1 tsp. dried oregano
½ tsp. ground cumin

1 15-oz. can garbanzo beans, undrained
3 medium-sized carrots, sliced
1 4-oz. can minced green chili peppers
1 cup corn (1 ear)
salt and freshly ground black pepper
Tabasco Sauce, to taste (optional)
chopped fresh cilantro for garnish (optional)

In a large soup pot, heat oil over medium-high heat. Add meat, onions and garlic and sauté for about 3 minutes, or until meat is just brown and onions are tender. Drain fat. Add tomatoes, chili powder, oregano and cumin. Bring to a boil. Reduce heat to low, cover and simmer 45 minutes. Add garbanzo beans, carrots and chili peppers; cover and simmer another 45 minutes. Add corn and simmer, covered, another 15 minutes, or until corn is tender. Taste and add salt, pepper and Tabasco, if using. Garnish with cilantro, if using.

Serves 8.

188 CALORIES PER SERVING: 12 G PROTEIN, 4 G FAT, 27 G CARBOHYDRATE; 643 MG SODIUM; 20 MG CHOLESTEROL.

Portuguese Sausage Soup

Chock-full of vegetables, thick with kidney beans and gently seasoned with garlic and anise, this soup typifies the Portuguese way of cooking. It needs only about ½ hour to simmer.

½ lb. hot Italian sausage
½ lb. sweet Italian sausage
1 small zucchini squash, sliced
1 medium-sized onion, chopped
3 celery stalks, sliced
3 large potatoes, cut into ½" cubes

1 28-oz. can tomatoes, undrained
1 15-oz. can kidney beans, undrained
¼ cup sliced, pitted black olives
2 cloves garlic, minced
1 tsp. anise seed
½ tsp. freshly ground black pepper

Remove casings from sausages. Crumble meat into a large soup pot and sauté over medium heat for about 6 minutes, or until brown. Drain fat. Add remaining ingredients along with 5 cups water. Bring to a boil. Reduce heat to low, cover and simmer for 30 minutes, or until all vegetables are tender.

Serves 12.

163 CALORIES PER SERVING: 9 G PROTEIN, 7 G FAT, 17 G CARBOHYDRATE; 602 MG SODIUM; 22 MG CHOLESTEROL.

Provençal Fish Soup

*Although this heady soup isn't a bouillabaisse, it is decidedly Mediterranean,
with garlic, the saffron and the special perfume of an orange peel, which is added close
to the end of cooking. Food writer Martha Rose Shulman likes to serve it at dinner parties,
because everything up to the addition of the fish can be done in advance.*

1 Tbsp. olive oil
1 large onion, chopped
4 cloves garlic (or more to taste), minced
2 28-oz. cans tomatoes, with juice, seeded
   and chopped
2 Tbsp. tomato paste
½-1 tsp. dried basil or 1 Tbsp. fresh,
   minced
½-1 tsp. dried thyme
1 recipe Fish Fumet *(recipe follows)*
1 bay leaf
salt
¾ lb. new potatoes, scrubbed and diced
   (4 medium)
1 lb. zucchini squash, sliced (4 small)

1½ cups fresh corn, from 2-3 ears (optional)
freshly ground black pepper
pinch cayenne pepper or ¼ tsp. red-pepper
   flakes
½ lb. mussels or clams (enough for 4 per
   serving)
1 cup dry white wine
2 wide strips orange zest
generous pinch saffron threads
2-2½ lbs. fish fillets or steaks, such as any
   combination of cod, striped bass,
   monkfish, tilefish, snapper, redfish,
   bream, turbot or conger, cut into 2" cubes
3 Tbsp. chopped fresh parsley
lemon wedges

Heat oil in a large, heavy-bottomed soup pot or casserole and sauté onions with garlic until tender. Add tomatoes, tomato paste, dried basil (fresh basil goes in later) and thyme, and simmer 15 minutes. Add fumet, bay leaf and salt to taste. Bring to a simmer and cook, uncovered, for 30 minutes.

Add potatoes, cover (you cover the soup now because you want to cook the vegetables without letting any more of the liquid evaporate) and simmer 10 to 15 minutes, or until potatoes are cooked through but still have some texture. Add zucchini, corn and fresh basil (if using). Cover and simmer 15 minutes or until zucchini is tender. Add black pepper and cayenne or red-pepper flakes and adjust seasonings, adding salt, garlic or more herbs if you wish. At this point you may remove the soup from the heat and let it sit for up to 1 hour before serving, when you will bring it back to a simmer and cook the fish.

While the stew is simmering, prepare mussels or clams. Clean them well in several rinses of cold water. Bring wine and ½ cup water to a boil in a large, lidded pot and add mussels or clams. Steam 5 minutes or until the shells open, shaking the pan once to distribute evenly. Remove from the heat, drain, reserving liquid, and set aside. Discard any that have not opened.

Fifteen to 20 minutes before serving, bring the soup to a simmer and add orange zest and saffron. Add mussel liquid if the broth seems too thick or if there's not enough of it to cover the seafood. Taste and adjust seasonings. Add fish, cover, and simmer 5 to 10 minutes, until the flesh is opaque. Remove bay leaf.

Serve at once, garnishing each bowl with mussels or clams, parsley and a lemon wedge.

Serves 4 to 6.

274 CALORIES FOR EACH OF 4 SERVINGS: 37 G PROTEIN, 4 G FAT, 22 G CARBOHYDRATE; 280 MG SODIUM; 84 MG CHOLESTEROL.

Fish Fumet

1 lb. fish trimmings (heads and bones),
 rinsed
1 onion, quartered
1 carrot, sliced
1 celery stalk, sliced
1 leek, white part only, cleaned and sliced

2 garlic cloves, peeled
2 sprigs parsley
1 bay leaf
1 sprig thyme
1 cup dry white wine
salt

Combine fish trimmings, onions, carrots, celery, leeks, garlic, parsley, bay leaf, thyme and 1 qt. water in a medium soup pot or saucepan and bring to a simmer over medium heat. Skim off all the foam that rises. Reduce heat, and simmer 15 minutes. Add wine and simmer 15 minutes. Skim foam periodically.

Season with salt to taste. Remove from the heat and strain at once through a fine sieve or a strainer lined with cheesecloth. Don't cook any longer than this, or the fumet will be bitter. *(The fumet can be made 1 day ahead and refrigerated.)*

Makes about 4 cups.

Moroccan Ramadan Soup

The traditional version of this Moroccan soup contains lamb and sometimes chicken, as well as beans, herbs and vegetables. It makes a filling, delicious meal. An additional ½ cup chickpeas (garbanzos) can be substituted for the beans.

½ cup dried chickpeas, washed and picked over
½ cup dried white beans, such as Great Northern, washed and picked over
2 Tbsp. olive, safflower or sunflower oil
2 yellow onions, chopped
¾ cup chopped celery leaves and ribs
½ cup finely chopped fresh parsley
2 Tbsp. finely chopped fresh cilantro
1 tsp. turmeric
1 tsp. ground cinnamon
1 tsp. or more freshly ground black pepper
½ tsp. saffron threads or ¼ tsp. powdered saffron
¼ tsp. ground ginger
2 lbs. tomatoes, peeled, seeded and chopped or 2 28-oz. cans, well-drained and chopped
¾ cup lentils, picked over and rinsed
salt to taste
½ cup fine vermicelli, broken into small pieces
1 egg, beaten
juice of 1 lemon (5 Tbsp.)
lemon slices, cinnamon and cilantro for garnish

Soak beans overnight or use quick-soak method: cover beans with water three times their volume, bring to a boil and boil gently for 2 minutes. Remove from heat, cover and let stand 1 hour. Drain and set aside.

Heat oil over low heat in a heavy-bottomed soup pot and sauté onions over medium-low heat for 5 to 7 minutes, stirring, until tender and beginning to color. Add celery, parsley, cilantro, turmeric, cinnamon, 1 tsp. pepper, saffron and ginger, and sauté, stirring, for another 2 to 3 minutes. Add tomatoes, cover, and continue to cook, stirring occasionally, over medium-low heat for another 10 to 15 minutes. Add chickpeas and white beans to the pot, along with lentils and 2½ qts. water, and bring to a boil. Re-

duce heat and simmer, partially covered, for 1½ to 2 hours, or until the beans are thoroughly tender. Season to taste with salt and freshly ground pepper. Mash some of the beans against the side of the pot with a wooden spoon to thicken the broth slightly.

About 5 minutes before serving, remove ½ cup soup from the pot and set aside to cool. Stir vermicelli into the pot. Meanwhile, mix together egg and lemon. When the vermicelli is cooked, turn off the heat. Gradually add egg-lemon mixture to the cooled ½ cup soup and quickly stir into soup. Serve at once, garnished with lemon slices, a light sprinkling of cinnamon and chopped cilantro.

Serves 8.

185 CALORIES PER SERVING: 8 G PROTEIN, 5 G FAT, 29 G CARBOHYDRATE; 345 MG SODIUM; 27 MG CHOLESTEROL.

Beef Soup With Herbs

This aromatic, slightly spicy soup is one of the most typical of Georgia in the Soviet Union. The marigold petals are optional but give the dish an earthy dimension. They are available from health-food stores or can be dried from the garden. Unlike most soups, this one tastes best when served the same day it is made.

2 lbs. lean stewing beef, cut into ¾" cubes
1 lb. veal or beef bones
2 bay leaves
2 sprigs parsley
¼ tsp. whole peppercorns
2 oz. apricot leather (available at health-food stores)
1 Tbsp. lemon juice
¼ cup uncooked rice
3 large onions
1 Tbsp. olive oil

1¾ tsp. salt
2 cloves garlic, minced
½ tsp. (generous) each: ground coriander, dried basil, ground caraway seed and ground marigold petals (optional)
¼ tsp. cayenne pepper
¼ tsp. paprika
freshly ground black pepper
3 Tbsp. chopped fresh herbs (cilantro, parsley, dill)

Bring beef and bones to a boil in 2 qts. water and skim the foam from the surface. Add bay leaves, parsley and peppercorns, and simmer, covered, for 1½ hours. Strain broth, skim any fat and return to pot. Remove any peppercorns, bay leaves or parsley pieces clinging to the meat and set meat aside.

Put apricot leather in a bowl and pour ½ cup boiling water over it. Let stand for 15 minutes and stir until creamy. Add lemon juice. Add rice to the broth and simmer 10 minutes. Chop onions finely and cook in a nonstick skillet in olive oil until soft but not brown. Add onions to the soup along with salt. Cook 10 minutes more until rice is done.

Return meat to the pot. Stir in garlic, coriander, basil, caraway seed, optional marigold petals, cayenne, paprika, freshly ground pepper and apricot puree. Cook for 10 minutes more. Stir in fresh cilantro, parsley and dill and let stand for 5 minutes before serving.

Serves 6 as a main course.

523 CALORIES PER SERVING: 55 G PROTEIN, 21 G FAT, 27 G CARBOHYDRATE; 1,049 MG SODIUM; 152 MG CHOLESTEROL.

Beef Soup With Herbs

Dr. Hammerschmidt's Blood-Thinning *Mapo Doufu*

*This pungent Chinese soup-stew is not for the fainthearted, for it
will sting the throat and clear the sinuses. Don't be put off by the seemingly
long directions: the soup can be made easily in less than a half hour. As with all
Chinese cooking, the ingredients should be cut up and ready-to-hand before the wok is heated.*

¼ cup dried tree ear mushrooms
½ lb. lean ground pork or beef
3 Tbsp. peeled, finely chopped gingerroot
  (3" piece)
1 cup chopped scallions (about 5)
5 Tbsp. reduced-sodium soy sauce
2 tsp. sesame oil
1 Tbsp. Chinese rice wine or cooking sherry
2 tsp. plus 1 Tbsp. cornstarch
8 or more cloves garlic, coarsely chopped

2 Tbsp. peanut oil
1½ tsp. red-pepper flakes
1 Tbsp. hot-pepper paste or chili paste
6 fresh water chestnuts, skinned and finely
  chopped, or canned (optional)
1 cup diced firm tofu
1 tsp. sugar
1 tsp. Szechuan peppercorns (or more to
  taste), roasted in a dry pan and crushed

Put tree ears in a small bowl and pour 1 cup boiling water over them. Let them soak for about 15 minutes, until they become soft and gelatinous.

Mix thoroughly pork or beef, 1 Tbsp. chopped ginger, ¼ cup chopped scallions, 2 Tbsp. soy sauce, 1 tsp. sesame oil and rice wine or sherry. Combine 2 tsp. cornstarch and ¼ cup cold water in a small bowl.

Combine garlic and remaining 2 Tbsp. ginger and mince together until they are a thick paste. Set aside.

Drain tree ears, rinse and pick them over to remove any impurities, and mince.

Heat wok or pan over a moderately high heat for about 15 seconds, then add peanut oil until small bubbles begin to form. Quickly add garlic and ginger paste and vigorously stir-fry over a medium heat for about 30 seconds, stirring. Continue stirring, and add red-pepper flakes, hot-pepper or chili paste, water chestnuts and tree ears. Stir-fry for 30 seconds more.

Add meat mixture and keep stirring it as it cooks, breaking up any large chunks of meat, until it has lost its pinkish color—about 1 minute. Add tofu and remaining ¾ cup scallions and stir-fry for about 45 seconds. Add sugar and stir-fry for another 30 seconds.

Pour in remaining 3 Tbsp. soy sauce and ½ to 2 cups water (depending on what consistency is desired), bring to boil, and cook for 2 more minutes. Stir in cornstarch mixture and cook, stirring, for 30 seconds, or until thickened. Add Szechuan peppercorns and stir thoroughly.

If the dish seems watery, you can stir in remaining 1 Tbsp. cornstarch mixed with 2 Tbsp. cold water, and cook, stirring, until the sauce becomes clear and slightly thickened.

Stir in remaining 1 tsp. sesame oil; taste for seasoning.

Serves 4.

375 CALORIES PER SERVING: 24 G PROTEIN, 22 G FAT, 24 G CARBOHYDRATE; 699 MG SODIUM; 36 MG CHOLESTEROL.

Marbled Melon Soup

A refreshing, slightly sweet soup with a subtle hint of mint.

1 large cantaloupe, halved, seeded, peeled
   and coarsely chopped
2 Tbsp. fresh lemon juice
¼ tsp. ground coriander
¼ cup honey

1 medium-sized honeydew melon, halved,
   seeded, peeled and coarsely chopped
¼ cup fresh lime juice
2 tsp. chopped fresh mint plus additional
   sprigs for garnish

In a blender or food processor, puree cantaloupe, lemon juice and coriander until smooth. Stir in 2 Tbsp. honey and pour into a bowl. Set aside. Thoroughly rinse processor or blender. Place honeydew in the food processor or blender with lime juice and chopped mint. Puree until smooth. Stir in the remaining 2 Tbsp. honey and pour into another bowl. Cover both bowls and refrigerate until chilled for at least one hour, or overnight. At serving time, spoon about ½ cup of each puree into each soup bowl, allowing colors to mix in the middle. To create a swirl pattern draw the tip of a knife through the surface. Garnish with mint sprigs.

Serves 6.

111 CALORIES PER SERVING: 1 G PROTEIN, 0 G FAT, 28 G CARBOHYDRATE; 18 MG SODIUM; 0 MG CHOLESTEROL.

VEGETABLES & SALADS

Blanched Winter Vegetables With Thyme

This delicate dish has humble origins—turnips, rutabagas and the often-discarded stems of broccoli. Though it may sound unlikely, it has just the cheery element that's needed in a drab month like January or February. The dish can also be served with a squeeze of lemon juice as a warm vegetable salad, or it can be tossed with pasta.

(Recipe continues on next page)

Blanched Winter Vegetables With Thyme

3 small turnips
1 small rutabaga
2-3 broccoli stalks, peeled
2 medium-sized carrots, peeled

2 tsp. butter
1 Tbsp. finely chopped fresh parsley
½ tsp. fresh thyme leaves or 2 pinches dried
salt and freshly ground black pepper

Peel turnips and rutabaga. If you notice an area just below the skin that seems tougher in texture and a slightly different color from the rest of the vegetable, remove it as you peel. Slice turnips and rutabagas into rounds about ¼ inch thick; then slice the rounds into strips about the same thickness.

Slice broccoli stalks ¼ inch thick on the diagonal, then slice them again into narrow strips. Repeat with the carrots. Taste the vegetables to determine if any seem tougher than the others. Often the rutabagas will need to be cooked a little longer than the rest.

In a large pot of boiling, salted water, cook the vegetables, starting with those that are toughest. Boil for about 30 seconds, add the remaining vegetables and cook until just tender, about 1 minute or so. Remove the vegetables with a slotted spoon and put them in a wide, nonstick skillet set over medium heat. Add butter, parsley and thyme and cook gently to melt the butter and evaporate any water, leaving a little sauce. Don't let the vegetables fry. Season with salt and pepper.

Serves 4.

58 CALORIES PER SERVING: 2 G PROTEIN, 2 G FAT, 9 G CARBOHYDRATE; 72 MG SODIUM; 6 MG CHOLESTEROL.

❧

Broccoli With Roasted Peppers, Olives & Feta Cheese

Many people frequently make a meal of a single vegetable dish garnished with tasty tidbits and some bread or rice. Bottled roasted red peppers may be used as a convenient shortcut.

1 large bunch broccoli
2 tsp. olive oil
1 clove garlic, thinly sliced
5 Kalamata olives, pits removed, chopped
3 Tbsp. diced roasted red or yellow bell
  peppers *(page 242)*

1 Tbsp. finely chopped fresh parsley
2 tsp. finely chopped fresh marjoram or
  ½ tsp. dried
1 oz. feta cheese, crumbled
salt and freshly ground black pepper
lemon wedges (optional)

Cut broccoli into medium-large florets. Set aside stalks for another purpose or peel them, cut them in rounds and include a few of them. Steam the broccoli until it has cooked as much as you like, about 3 to 5 minutes for tender-crisp.

Warm oil and garlic in a large, nonstick skillet over medium heat. Remove the garlic when it has browned

(after 2 to 3 minutes) and add the steamed broccoli, olives, peppers, parsley and marjoram. Sauté over medium-high heat until everything is warmed. Scatter cheese over the top, season lightly with salt and add pepper to taste. If you like, include wedges of lemon and serve this dish as a warm salad.

Serves 4 as a side dish.

74 CALORIES PER SERVING: 4 G PROTEIN, 5 G FAT, 6 G CARBOHYDRATE; 129 MG SODIUM; 6 MG CHOLESTEROL.

Broccoli With Roasted Peppers, Olives & Feta Cheese

Winter Greens & Potatoes

The flavor of greens is softened by the potatoes and brightened with tomatoes,
chili pepper and garlic. The vegetables come together to make a hash, creating a
good one-dish supper. Beet greens, turnip tops, broccoli rabe, dandelion greens, spinach
and chard can also be good cooked in this fashion, although the cooking time will be shorter.

1 lb. mixed greens (mustard, collards, kale,
   escarole)
2 medium-sized potatoes, unpeeled, scrubbed,
   quartered and thinly sliced
1 Tbsp. olive oil

1-2 small dried chili peppers, seeds removed,
   torn into pieces, or ¼ tsp. red-pepper flakes
2 medium-sized fresh tomatoes, chopped, or
   1 16-oz. can, drained and chopped
2 cloves garlic, minced
salt and freshly ground black pepper

Remove any leaves from greens that are yellow or wilted and remove any tough, fibrous stems. Chop the leaves, rinse them well and set aside. Cook potatoes in boiling, salted water until tender, for 5 to 7 minutes. Remove with a slotted spoon. Add greens to the hot potato water and boil for 2 to 3 minutes, until they are tender. Drain.

Warm oil over medium heat in a wide, nonstick skillet and add chilies or red-pepper flakes. When the oil is hot, add the potatoes, stir to coat them well and cook for 1 minute or so. Add greens, tomatoes and garlic. Continue cooking for another 5 minutes or so, breaking up the potatoes with a wooden spoon. Taste for salt and add freshly ground black pepper.
   Serves 4.

112 CALORIES PER SERVING: 3 G PROTEIN, 4 G FAT, 18 G CARBOHYDRATE; 26 MG SODIUM; 0 MG CHOLESTEROL.

Slow-Baked Tomatoes

The secret of these sweet, savory tomatoes is to bake them for a very
long time at low heat. By the end of the baking time, they are almost caramelized.

4-6 large, ripe, fresh tomatoes, cut in half
   horizontally
4-6 tsp. olive oil

salt and freshly ground black pepper
2-3 cloves garlic, minced
3 Tbsp. chopped fresh basil or parsley

Preheat the oven to 325 degrees F. Place tomatoes on a baking sheet, cut sides up. Drizzle on oil and sprinkle with salt and pepper to taste.

Bake for 2 to 3 hours, until tomatoes collapse and begin to caramelize. Spread on garlic about halfway through the baking, or at the end, and sprinkle with herbs just before serving. Serve hot or at room temperature.
   Serves 4 to 6.

59 CALORIES FOR EACH OF 4 SERVINGS: 1 G PROTEIN, 4 G FAT, 6 G CARBOHYDRATE; 11 MG SODIUM; 0 MG CHOLESTEROL.

Escarole With Garlic & Chili

*Like most greens, escarole tastes good stewed in a little oil with
garlic and red chili pepper, with vinegar added at the end to sharpen the tastes.*

1 large head escarole
2 tsp. olive oil
2 cloves garlic, sliced
1 small dried red chili pepper, broken into
　　pieces, or a few pinches red-pepper flakes

salt
about 1 tsp. balsamic or red-wine vinegar
freshly ground black pepper

Separate escarole leaves at the base, discarding any that are tough or bruised. Cut them into large pieces and rinse them well. In a nonstick skillet, warm oil and garlic over low heat. When the garlic is golden brown, remove it. Add chili pepper or red-pepper flakes and the escarole, with the water still clinging to its leaves. Salt lightly and cook, uncovered, over medium-high heat for 5 to 7 minutes. (A pair of tongs is useful for turning the leaves while they are cooking.) When the leaves are wilted and tender, taste for salt and add a few dashes of vinegar and plenty of black pepper. Toss once more to combine.

Serves 2 generously.

58 CALORIES PER SERVING: 1 G PROTEIN, 5 G FAT, 4 G CARBOHYDRATE; 29 MG SODIUM; 0 MG CHOLESTEROL.

Greens With Garlic & Walnuts

*Food-and-health writer Jean Carper says this dish has been proclaimed by her
guests as "the best greens ever." It contains bountiful amounts of disease-fighting nutrients.*

1 lb. mixed greens, such as mustard, kale
　　and collards, tough stems removed, washed
½ lb. spinach, trimmed and washed
1 Tbsp. olive oil

4 large cloves garlic, minced
salt and freshly ground black pepper to taste
2 Tbsp. chopped walnuts

Place greens and spinach in a large stock pot and cook, covered, over high heat for 2 minutes. (The water on the leaves will be enough to cook them.) Stir and continue cooking for 2 to 3 more minutes, or just until wilted. (Alternatively, to cook in a microwave oven, place half the washed greens with the water still clinging to their leaves in a large microwave-proof casserole dish. Cover with a lid and microwave on high for 1 minute. Stir and microwave, covered, for 30 to 60 seconds longer. Repeat, using remaining greens and spinach.)

Drain greens and spinach. Chop them coarsely and press them gently to remove more liquid. Heat oil in a skillet, add garlic and sauté over medium heat for 2 to 3 minutes. Add all the greens and sauté until heated through. Season with salt and pepper, sprinkle on walnuts and stir again.

Serves 6.

63 CALORIES PER SERVING: 4 G PROTEIN, 4 G FAT, 5 G CARBOHYDRATE; 90 MG SODIUM; 0 MG CHOLESTEROL.

Red Cabbage Braised in Red Wine

The cabbage emerges coated with reduced wine, vinegar and pan juices. It is best served
with something uncomplicated, like a plump piece of baked winter squash. Juniper berries,
a bitter seasoning that gives gin its taste, can be found in the spice section of many supermarkets.

1 head red cabbage (about 1½ lbs.)
2 tsp. olive oil
2 large celery stalks, cut into ¼" dice
1 large carrot, peeled and cut into ¼" dice
1 medium-sized red or yellow onion, finely
   chopped
2 cloves garlic, minced
2 Tbsp. finely chopped fresh parsley

10 juniper berries (optional)
1 bay leaf
pinch dried thyme
salt and freshly ground black pepper
1 large tart apple, grated
1 cup dry red wine
red-wine vinegar, about 1 Tbsp.

Cut cabbage into quarters, remove cores and slice cabbage into narrow shreds. Cook in a large pot of boiling, salted water for 2 minutes, then drain in a colander.

Warm oil in a wide, nonstick skillet and add celery, carrots, onions, garlic, parsley, juniper berries (if using), bay leaf and thyme. Season with salt and plenty of pepper and cook over medium heat for 3 to 4 minutes, stirring frequently. Add the cabbage and apple and stir to combine.

Pour in wine and ½ cup water, cover the skillet and cook over medium heat for about 20 minutes. Turn the vegetables over. Continue cooking, uncovered, until the liquids are reduced and the cabbage is tender, about 20 to 25 minutes. Taste for salt, add enough red-wine vinegar to give a lively edge, and remove bay leaf.

Serves 6.

77 CALORIES PER SERVING: 3 G PROTEIN, 2 G FAT, 15 G CARBOHYDRATE; 54 MG SODIUM; 0 MG CHOLESTEROL.

Roasted Bell Peppers

Fat bell peppers taste like summer itself when grilled this way. They need no seasoning at all.

1 large red bell pepper
1 large yellow bell pepper

1 large green bell pepper

Wash peppers and pat dry. Cut each in quarters lengthwise. Remove seeds and pithy membrane. Grill for 5 minutes, placing them at the outer edge of the barbecue, then turn them over and grill for 5 more minutes or until barely browned and tender-crisp. Slice each piece into three strips. Serve hot or at room temperature.

Serves 6.

9 CALORIES PER SERVING: 0 G PROTEIN, 0 G FAT, 2 G CARBOHYDRATE; 1 MG SODIUM; 0 MG CHOLESTEROL.

Red Cabbage Braised in Red Wine

Warm Dandelion Greens

*Dandelion greens are at their best from first emergence through mid-spring,
when the maturing leaves begin to turn tough. (If large, store-bought dandelion
greens are used, blanch them for 1 to 2 minutes in boiling water before sautéing.)*

2 oz. lean back bacon or Canadian bacon
   (3 3"-by-¼" slices), diced
2 tsp. olive oil
1 clove garlic, minced

12 cups young dandelion greens, rinsed well
   and briefly shaken dry
2 Tbsp. balsamic or rice-wine vinegar
6 dandelion flowers and 12 small, whole
   leaves for garnish (optional)

Fry bacon in a large cast-iron skillet or Dutch oven over medium heat for 2 to 3 minutes, until edges curl. Remove from the skillet and drain on paper towels. Pour off excess fat from the skillet and add oil. Add garlic and sauté 1 to 2 minutes, stirring occasionally, until light brown. Add rinsed greens (which are still damp), stir to coat them with the oil, cover pan and steam about 3 minutes, or until just limp. Add vinegar and bacon, toss lightly and serve at once on small plates or in bowls, garnished with flowers and small leaves (if using).

Serves 6.

50 CALORIES PER SERVING: 3 G PROTEIN, 3 G FAT, 4 G CARBOHYDRATE; 181 MG SODIUM; 6 MG CHOLESTEROL.

✌

Parsnips With Brown Butter & Bread Crumbs

*The natural sweetness of parsnips goes well with brown butter, while the crisp
bread crumbs contrast with the soft vegetables. Parsnips have cores, but most of the time
it is not necessary to cut them away, unless the parsnip is old, with a fibrous, woody center.*

1 lb. parsnips, peeled
1 Tbsp. unsalted butter
juice of ½ lemon
salt

2 Tbsp. fresh bread crumbs, toasted
   (page 242)
1 Tbsp. finely chopped fresh parsley or a
   mixture of fresh tarragon, parsley and chives

Cut parsnips into even lengths. Halve or quarter the large ends so that all the pieces are about the same size. Set them in a steamer basket over boiling water, cover and cook for 3 to 5 minutes, or until they are tender but still just a little firm. Melt butter in a nonstick skillet and cook until it begins to turn nutty brown. Skim off the foam that collects on the surface. Add cooked parsnips, toss to coat with butter and sauté over medium-high heat for 3 or 4 minutes, stirring occasionally, until the parsnips begin to brown here and there. Squeeze in lemon juice, lightly salt the parsnips and add the bread crumbs and herbs. Toss several times and serve.

Serves 4.

120 CALORIES PER SERVING: 2 G PROTEIN, 4 G FAT, 22 G CARBOHYDRATE; 34 MG SODIUM; 8 MG CHOLESTEROL.

Warm Dandelion Greens

Cauliflower With Paprika & Garlic Sauce

The important point in working with paprika, as with other ground peppers,
is to have the oil warm but not hot when you add it; otherwise, the paprika will
burn and its flavor will be spoiled. Potatoes are also delicious when cooked in this way.

1 medium-sized cauliflower, about 1¼ lbs.
1 Tbsp. olive oil
3 medium-sized cloves garlic, peeled and left
  whole

2 Tbsp. chopped fresh parsley
salt
1 Tbsp. sweet paprika
2 Tbsp. red-wine or sherry vinegar

Cut cauliflower into bite-sized pieces. Steam them over boiling water until they are fairly tender but not completely cooked, about 4 to 5 minutes. Turn off the heat, cover and set aside.

While the cauliflower is steaming, heat oil in a small, nonstick skillet over medium-low heat. Add garlic and cook, turning often, for several minutes, until light brown. Turn off the heat and leave the oil in the skillet. Put the garlic cloves in a mortar and pound them with half the parsley and several pinches of salt, forming a coarse paste. Place the cauliflower on a serving platter, reserving the cooking water.

Return the skillet to low heat and stir in paprika, vinegar, ¼ cup cauliflower-cooking water and the garlic-parsley paste. Pour the sauce over the cauliflower and garnish with remaining parsley.

Serves 4.

56 CALORIES PER SERVING: 2 G PROTEIN, 4 G FAT, 6 G CARBOHYDRATE; 14 MG SODIUM; 0 MG CHOLESTEROL.

Green Beans Indian-Style

These beans are a nice accompaniment to roast lamb. Cauliflower may also be cooked this way.

1½ tsp. vegetable oil
1 tsp. mustard seeds
1 lb. fresh green beans, trimmed, cut
  diagonally into 1" pieces
2 medium-sized carrots, peeled and sliced

1 small onion, chopped
1 tsp. salt or to taste
1 tsp. ground coriander
⅛ tsp. ground ginger
2 Tbsp. fresh lemon juice

In a large, nonstick skillet, heat oil over medium-high heat. Add mustard seeds and sauté for 30 seconds, or until they start to pop. Stir in beans, carrots and onions and cook, stirring constantly, for 5 minutes. Stir in salt, coriander and ginger. Reduce heat to low, cover and cook, stirring often, for 8 to 10 minutes, or until the beans are tender-crisp. Stir in lemon juice and serve.

Serves 4.

72 CALORIES PER SERVING: 2 G PROTEIN, 2 G FAT, 13 G CARBOHYDRATE; 16 MG SODIUM; 0 MG CHOLESTEROL.

Cauliflower With Paprika & Garlic Sauce

Marinated Mushrooms & Peppers

If the mushrooms are marinated for 2 hours or less,
they will be whiter and firmer than after a longer marination.
The taste will change slightly if you choose to sliver the garlic instead of mincing it.

2 green bell peppers, seeded and sliced
2 red bell peppers, seeded and sliced
4 cloves garlic, minced
1 Tbsp. olive oil
approximately 4 Tbsp. fresh lemon juice

1 lb. fresh mushrooms, trimmed, cleaned and
  thinly sliced
salt and freshly ground black pepper to taste
16 brine-cured black olives, pitted (optional)

Preheat oven to 375 degrees F. Toss peppers, garlic and oil in a shallow baking pan. Bake for 20 to 25 minutes, or until peppers are tender. Let cool.

In a large bowl, combine lemon juice, mushrooms and peppers. Season with salt and pepper, cover and marinate for at least 30 minutes or for up to 6 hours. (If you plan to marinate the mushrooms for more than 2 hours, refrigerate them. Let them come to room temperature before serving.) You may wish to add more lemon juice to suit your taste. Serve on plates accompanied by sturdy bread and, if you like, a couple of black olives.

Serves 8.

42 CALORIES PER SERVING: 2 G PROTEIN, 2 G FAT, 6 G CARBOHYDRATE; 3 MG SODIUM; 0 MG CHOLESTEROL.

Glazed Onions

No holiday table would be complete without traditional offerings like
glazed onions. This dish is given a new twist with the addition of Madeira
and honey, creating a caramel-like coating. These onions are also delectable served cold.

2 lbs. small white onions, unpeeled
1 tsp. unsalted butter
1 tsp. vegetable oil

1 cup Madeira
1½ Tbsp. honey
¾ tsp. salt

Boil onions for 5 minutes in a large pot of water, drain and plunge into cold water. Drain again and peel. In a nonstick skillet, heat butter and oil over medium heat until hot. Add onions and pan-fry about 5 minutes, turning often, until lightly golden. Combine Madeira, honey and salt and add to onions. Reduce heat to moderately low, cover and simmer 12 to 15 minutes until crisp-tender. Uncover and cook over medium heat, spooning liquid over onions until the liquid has been reduced to a glaze and the onions are golden brown, about 15 minutes. *(The onions can be made ahead and held in the refrigerator for up to 2 days. To reheat: Place them in a nonstick skillet, cover and cook over low heat for 20 to 25 minutes.)*

Serves 6.

80 CALORIES PER SERVING: 2 G PROTEIN, 2 G FAT, 15 G CARBOHYDRATE; 271 MG SODIUM; 2 MG CHOLESTEROL.

Artichokes in Egg-Lemon Sauce

In its native Greece, this stew is often eaten for lunch or supper.

2 lemons
15 baby or 8 large artichokes
2 Tbsp. olive oil
1 lb. scallions, chopped (about 3 cups)
4 shallots, minced
1 clove garlic, minced
1 Tbsp. chopped fresh fennel leaves
pinch dried oregano
pinch chopped fresh parsley
pinch chopped fresh mint
3 carrots, coarsely chopped
1 tsp. salt
freshly ground black pepper
2 large potatoes, cut into bite-sized chunks
1 egg
⅓ cup fresh lemon juice

Squeeze 1 lemon into a bowl of cold water. Cut the stalks from artichokes and discard. Using a sharp paring knife held at an angle, trim off all the leaves from the artichokes, working your way around them to the heart. Discard leaves. Cut off soft purple petals and discard. Trim any remaining green parts from the hearts. Cut remaining lemon in half and rub artichokes with cut side. If you are using mature artichokes, scoop out fuzzy chokes with a melon baller or spoon. Rub again with lemon half. Cut hearts from mature artichokes into quarters. Place artichoke hearts in the lemon water to prevent discoloration.

In a Dutch oven, heat 1 Tbsp. oil and fry scallions, shallots, garlic, fennel, oregano, parsley and mint over medium heat for about 5 minutes, or until softened, stirring often. Add 3 cups water, drained artichokes, carrots, salt and pepper, and bring to a boil. Reduce heat to medium and simmer, covered, for 5 minutes. Add potatoes. Cook, covered, for about 15 to 20 minutes longer, or until vegetables are tender. With a slotted spoon, remove vegetables to a bowl and keep warm; reserve the cooking liquid.

In a small bowl, whisk egg with lemon juice and gradually whisk in ⅓ cup of the cooking liquid. Pour into remaining liquid in the Dutch oven and cook, stirring, for 2 to 3 minutes, or until steaming. Do not boil or it will curdle. Return vegetables to the Dutch oven. Taste and adjust seasonings with salt and pepper and stir in remaining Tbsp. oil. Serve immediately.

Serves 8.

156 CALORIES PER SERVING: 6 G PROTEIN, 4 G FAT, 28 G CARBOHYDRATE; 368 MG SODIUM; 27 MG CHOLESTEROL.

Sweet Potatoes Anna

Pommes Anna is a classic French dish in which slices of potato are layered with butter in a pan, baked until crisp and unmolded onto a serving platter. In Nina Simonds's variation, sweet potatoes, flavored with a touch of ginger and brown sugar, are baked in a similar manner.

1 Tbsp. vegetable oil
1 Tbsp. melted butter
3 medium-sized sweet potatoes (about
   1½ lbs. total)

1 tsp. peeled, minced gingerroot
1½ Tbsp. light brown sugar
¾ tsp. salt

Combine oil and butter in a small bowl. Line a 9-inch glass pie plate with aluminum foil and lightly brush with a little oil-butter mixture. Peel sweet potatoes and slice them thinly with a food processor fitted with a slicer blade or by hand.

Place the potato slices in a bowl and toss with ginger, brown sugar, salt and a scant Tbsp. of oil-butter mixture. Arrange the slices in slightly overlapping concentric circles around the bottom of the pie plate, adding another row around the sides. Brush the top lightly with oil-butter mixture. Layer the remaining slices and drizzle remaining oil mixture over the top.

(The dish can be made ahead to this point, covered with plastic wrap and refrigerated for up to 2 days.)

Preheat oven to 400 degrees F and place oven rack on the bottom rung of the oven. Cover potatoes with aluminum foil, weight with a flat, heavy lid or a cake pan or pie pan and bake on the bottom rack of the oven for 30 minutes. Remove the foil and bake for another 30 to 35 minutes, or until the potatoes are brown and crisp on top. Remove from the oven and invert onto a serving platter.

Serves 6.

109 CALORIES PER SERVING: 1 G PROTEIN, 4 G FAT, 17 G CARBOHYDRATE; 293 MG SODIUM; 5 MG CHOLESTEROL.

Sesame Asparagus

These asparagus are tender, with an Oriental flavor of sesame and soy.

1½ tsp. sesame oil
1 lb. thin asparagus, trimmed and cut
   diagonally into 1" pieces

1½ tsp. soy sauce
1 tsp. sugar

In a large, nonstick skillet, heat oil over medium heat. Add asparagus and stir-fry for 1½ to 2 minutes, or until asparagus begins to soften. Add soy sauce and stir-fry for 1 minute. Add sugar and stir-fry another 30 seconds. Remove from heat and serve.

Serves 4.

59 CALORIES PER SERVING: 4 G PROTEIN, 2 G FAT, 8 G CARBOHYDRATE; 136 MG SODIUM; 0 MG CHOLESTEROL.

Sweet Potatoes Anna

Salad of Mixed Greens

This salad may be served in the Italian fashion
as a pleasant interlude between the main course and the dessert.

1 head romaine lettuce
1 head radicchio
1 bunch arugula or watercress
1 small Belgian endive
¼ cup loosely packed Italian parsley leaves
2 Tbsp. red-wine vinegar or fresh lemon juice

½ tsp. Dijon mustard
1 small clove garlic, minced
2 Tbsp. extra-virgin olive oil
2 Tbsp. defatted chicken stock
salt and freshly ground black pepper to taste

Trim and carefully wash romaine, radicchio, arugula or watercress, endive and parsley, and dry them thoroughly. Tear the leaves into bite-sized pieces and place them in a large salad bowl. *(If you do not plan to serve the salad immediately, place the leaves in a bowl lined with paper towels, cover with plastic and refrigerate.)*

Combine vinegar or lemon juice, mustard and garlic in a jar or cruet. Shake vigorously until well blended. Add oil and chicken stock and shake again. Season with salt and pepper. *(The dressing can be made up to 2 days ahead and refrigerated.)* Just before serving, pour the dressing over the salad and toss lightly. Serves 8.

50 CALORIES PER SERVING: 2 G PROTEIN, 4 G FAT, 4 G CARBOHYDRATE; 24 MG SODIUM; 0 MG CHOLESTEROL.

Garlic-Tip Dressing

A mixture of minced garlic and chopped chives can be substituted for the green garlic tips.

¼ cup nonfat yogurt
1½ Tbsp. fresh lemon juice
2-3 tsp. honey
1 Tbsp. vegetable oil

1 Tbsp. chopped green garlic tips or 1 small
    clove garlic, chopped, plus 1 Tbsp.
    chopped chives
¼-½ tsp. salt
¼ tsp. freshly ground black pepper

In a small bowl, combine yogurt, lemon juice and 2 tsp. honey. Whisk in oil, stir in garlic tips or garlic and chives and ¼ tsp. salt and pepper. Taste and adjust seasonings, adding more honey or salt as

needed. *(The dressing can be made ahead and stored in the refrigerator for up to 2 days.)*
Makes ⅓ cup.

39 CALORIES PER TABLESPOON: 1 G PROTEIN, 3 G FAT, 4 G CARBOHYDRATE; 109 MG SODIUM; 0 MG CHOLESTEROL.

"Zero-Fat" Herb Dressing

A quick, easy salad dressing that contains no fat.

¾ cup tomato or V-8 juice (6-oz. can)
¼ cup red-wine or sherry vinegar
1 Tbsp. minced fresh Italian parsley
1 Tbsp. chopped chives or scallions
1 clove garlic, crushed

½ tsp. salt
pinch dried savory or oregano
pinch sugar
pinch cayenne pepper
freshly ground black pepper

Combine all dressing ingredients in a jar and shake to mix thoroughly. *(The dressing can be stored in the refrigerator for up to 1 week.)* Remove the garlic clove before serving.

Serves 8, with about 2 Tbsp. each.

6 CALORIES PER SERVING: 0 G PROTEIN, 0 G FAT, 2 G CARBOHYDRATE; 250 MG SODIUM; 0 MG CHOLESTEROL.

Japanese Spinach Salad With Sesame Seeds

This makes a lovely side dish to fish.

1½ lbs. fresh young spinach, cleaned and
    trimmed
¼ cup rice vinegar

2 Tbsp. mirin (rice wine)
1 Tbsp. reduced-sodium soy sauce
1 Tbsp. sesame seeds, toasted *(page 242)*

Have a large bowl of ice water ready to chill the spinach. Place a steamer basket over a large pot of boiling water. Steam spinach, covered, in 3 batches for 2 to 2½ minutes, or just until wilted, tossing several times so that it cooks evenly. Immediately plunge spinach into the ice water to stop the cooking process. Remove it, squeeze out the excess liquid and set aside on paper towels.

In a small bowl, mix rice vinegar, mirin and soy sauce. Combine the spinach and dressing in a serving bowl, toss gently and garnish with the sesame seeds. Serve within 2 hours.

Serves 4.

57 CALORIES PER SERVING: 6 G PROTEIN, 2 G FAT, 7 G CARBOHYDRATE; 307 MG SODIUM; 0 MG CHOLESTEROL.

Spinach With Strawberries & Honey Dressing

It's hard to say enough good things about spinach, since it, more than any other green, leafy vegetable except broccoli and kale, is full of identified compounds that protect cells in numerous ways. Strawberries also contain disease-fighting antioxidants.

6 oz. fresh spinach, cleaned, trimmed and
   thoroughly dried (8-10 cups)
2 Tbsp. balsamic vinegar
2 Tbsp. rice vinegar
1 Tbsp. plus 1 tsp. honey

2 tsp. Dijon mustard
salt and freshly ground black pepper to taste
1 cup thickly sliced fresh strawberries
1 Tbsp. sesame seeds, toasted *(page 242)*
1 small red onion, thinly sliced (optional)

Tear spinach into bite-sized pieces and place in a salad bowl. In a separate bowl, whisk together vinegars, honey, mustard, salt and pepper. Add to the spinach and toss lightly. Add strawberries, sesame seeds and onion, if using. Toss lightly.

Serves 4 to 5.

50 CALORIES FOR EACH OF 4 SERVINGS: 2 G PROTEIN, 1 G FAT, 11 G CARBOHYDRATE; 69 MG SODIUM; 0 MG CHOLESTEROL.

Red Slaw

*This slaw is a traditional accompaniment to barbecued pork at
Bill Neal's Crook's Corner restaurant in Carrboro, North Carolina.*

1 16-oz. can Italian tomatoes, with juice
1 3-oz. jar pimientos, drained
2 lbs. cabbage (1 small), finely chopped
1 small green bell pepper, chopped
½ cup apple-cider vinegar

¼ cup sugar
¾ tsp. salt
½ Tbsp. hot-pepper sauce or to taste
⅛ tsp. freshly ground black pepper
pinch celery seed

Puree tomatoes with pimientos. Pour mixture over cabbage and add remaining ingredients. Stir well, refrigerate for 2 hours and toss again before serving.

Serves 8 to 12.

70 CALORIES FOR EACH OF 8 SERVINGS: 2 G PROTEIN, 1 G FAT, 18 G CARBOHYDRATE; 308 MG SODIUM; 0 MG CHOLESTEROL.

Marinated Vegetables Vinaigrette

The vegetables will keep for hours in the refrigerator and can even be made
a day ahead of time, though the green vegetables will lose some of their bright color.

VEGETABLES

1 lb. new potatoes, scrubbed, steamed or boiled until tender-crisp, cut into bite-sized chunks

½ head cauliflower, broken into florets and steamed 5 minutes

1 pint cherry tomatoes (or combination of red and yellow), halved if tomatoes are large

2 red bell peppers (or 1 green or yellow and 1 red), halved, seeds removed, cut into bite-sized chunks

1 seedless cucumber, scored with a fork and sliced about ¼" thick

¾ lb. medium-sized mushrooms, stems removed, caps quartered

2 red onions, sliced in thick rings

2 Tbsp. sliced imported black olives

1 cup cooked giant white beans, such as cannellini (optional)

MARINADE

3 Tbsp. sherry vinegar, champagne vinegar or wine vinegar

1½ Tbsp. lemon juice (½ large lemon)

1½ tsp. Dijon mustard

½ clove garlic, minced, or more to taste

3 Tbsp. nonfat yogurt

2 Tbsp. olive oil

¼ cup chopped fresh herbs: basil, tarragon, thyme, chervil, parsley, dill, chives (singly or in combination)

¼ tsp. dried tarragon

salt and freshly ground black pepper to taste

leaf lettuce for platter (optional)

radish roses (optional)

fresh herb sprigs (optional)

Toss vegetables together in a large bowl.

To make marinade: Mix together vinegar, lemon juice, mustard and garlic and combine well. Whisk in yogurt and oil. Stir in 2 Tbsp. fresh herbs, dried tarragon, salt and pepper to taste. Pour the vinaigrette into the vegetables and toss well. Cover and refrigerate for at least 1 hour or up to 8 hours. (The herbs will lose their bright color.)

Shortly before serving, remove the vegetables from the refrigerator and add remaining 2 Tbsp. fresh herbs. Toss and adjust seasonings.

Line a platter with lettuce leaves (if using). Arrange the vegetables on the platter. Decorate with radish roses, more olives and sprigs of fresh herbs (if using). Serve with small plates, forks and plenty of napkins.

Serves 30 as an hors d'oeuvre, 20 as a salad.

43 CALORIES PER HORS D'OEUVRE: 1 G PROTEIN, 1 G FAT, 7 G CARBOHYDRATE; 14 MG SODIUM; 0 MG CHOLESTEROL.

Dr. Duke's Anticancer Slaw

*Dr. James Duke, a USDA expert on medicinal plants, is convinced
that this delicious slaw may help ward off colon cancer if eaten regularly.*

2 cups cauliflower florets
1 small, firm green cabbage, shredded
1 large carrot, shredded
½ green bell pepper, chopped
4 radishes, trimmed and thinly sliced
4 scallions, trimmed and thinly sliced
½ cup white-wine vinegar

2 Tbsp. reduced-sodium soy sauce
1 Tbsp. dark sesame oil
2 tsp. peeled, grated gingerroot
2 cloves garlic, minced
¼-½ tsp. red-pepper flakes
1 Tbsp. sesame seeds, toasted *(page 242)*

Steam cauliflower until tender-crisp, about 5 minutes. Place vegetables in a large bowl. Place vinegar, soy sauce, sesame oil, ginger, garlic and red-pepper flakes in a blender and process until smooth. Stir in sesame seeds. Pour the dressing over the vegetables and toss well. *(The slaw can be made up to 24 hours ahead and refrigerated.)*
Serves 8.

27 CALORIES PER SERVING: 1 G PROTEIN, 1 G FAT, 5 G CARBOHYDRATE; 79 MG SODIUM; 0 MG CHOLESTEROL.

Fennel & Lemon Green Bean Salad

*The Italians often enjoy fennel the way North Americans eat celery:
raw in salads. This salad is aromatic and crisp with a fresh lemon dressing.*

¼ lb. fresh green beans, trimmed and cut
　　into 1½" pieces
4 bulbs fresh fennel
¼ lb. mushrooms, cleaned, trimmed and
　　quartered

1 2"-by-½" strip lemon zest, cut julienne
2 Tbsp. balsamic vinegar
1 Tbsp. fresh lemon juice
1 Tbsp. olive oil
salt and freshly ground black pepper to taste

Steam beans for 3 to 5 minutes, or until tender-crisp. Cool them under cold water. Place them in a salad bowl. Trim fennel leaves, reserving 2 Tbsp. minced leaves. Set aside. Slice the stalks. Quarter bulb lengthwise, remove core and thinly slice. Add to salad bowl along with mushrooms and lemon zest.

In a small bowl, whisk vinegar, 2 Tbsp. water, lemon juice and oil until well blended. Pour the dressing over the salad and add the reserved fennel leaves. Toss lightly. Season with salt and pepper. Cover and refrigerate for 30 minutes to 1 hour.
Serves 6.

45 CALORIES PER SERVING: 1 G PROTEIN, 2 G FAT, 6 G CARBOHYDRATE; 35 MG SODIUM; 0 MG CHOLESTEROL.

Rainbow Salad With Spicy Chili Dressing

This salad, which can be made with leftover corn, will delight even strict corn lovers. Note: You can substitute canned water chestnuts for fresh. Blanch them in boiling water for 10 seconds to remove any metallic taste.

1 Tbsp. sesame oil
1 Tbsp. canola or corn oil
4 slices gingerroot, about the size of a
   quarter, smashed lightly
4 scallions, trimmed and smashed lightly,
   plus ¾ cup minced green tops for garnish
2½ Tbsp. reduced-sodium soy sauce
1½ Tbsp. rice wine or sake

1½ Tbsp. sugar
1½ Tbsp. Chinese black vinegar or ¾ tsp.
   Worcestershire sauce
½ tsp. hot chili paste or to taste
5 cups cooked corn (5 large ears)
1½ cups fresh water chestnuts, peeled
1 cup diced red bell pepper
3 cups shredded iceberg lettuce

Place a heavy-bottomed saucepan with a tight-fitting lid over high heat. Add oils and heat until smoking. Remove from heat. Add ginger and 4 scallions. Press down on the ginger and scallions with the back of a wooden spoon. Cover and let cool slightly, about 2 minutes. Strain into a small bowl, pressing down on solids to extract as much oil as possible. Discard solids. Whisk soy sauce, rice wine or sake, sugar, black vinegar or Worcestershire sauce and chili paste into the oil, stirring until sugar has dissolved. Taste and adjust seasonings. *(The dressing may be prepared ahead and stored in the refrigerator for up to 2 days.)*

Place corn in a large bowl. Boil water chestnuts for 5 minutes. Drain, cool under cold water and chop coarsely. Add them to the corn along with red pepper and ½ cup minced scallion greens. Add chili-oil dressing and toss lightly to coat. Arrange lettuce in a deep serving bowl, making a well in the center. Mound the corn mixture in the center of the lettuce and sprinkle the remaining ¼ cup minced scallion greens over the top. Serve at room temperature or chill for up to 2 hours.

Serves 6.

156 CALORIES PER SERVING: 3 G PROTEIN, 4 G FAT, 28 G CARBOHYDRATE; 245 MG SODIUM; 0 MG CHOLESTEROL.

Chinese Rice Salad With Vegetables

Chopped fresh dill or tarragon may also be added to this dressing.

1½ cups long-grain white rice
¼ cup soy sauce
¼ cup minced fresh parsley
2½ Tbsp. Chinese black vinegar or 1½ tsp.
  Worcestershire sauce
1 Tbsp. sugar
1 tsp. vegetable or sesame oil

½ tsp. salt
½ lb. asparagus, trimmed and cut into
  1" lengths
1 cup cherry tomatoes, halved
¾ cup diced red onion
1 yellow bell pepper, seeded and diced

Place rice in a colander and rinse under cold running water until the water runs clear. Place it in a saucepan with a tight-fitting lid. Add 3 cups water and bring to a boil. Reduce heat to low, cover and simmer for 20 minutes, or until water has been absorbed. Uncover and fluff with a fork. Transfer to a sieve or fine colander and rinse under cold water.

In a small bowl, whisk together soy sauce, parsley, black vinegar or Worcestershire sauce, sugar, oil and salt. Steam asparagus for 3 to 4 minutes. Cool under cold water, drain and place in a large bowl along with rice, cherry tomatoes, onions and peppers. Add the soy-sauce mixture and toss well. *(The salad can be stored in the refrigerator for up to 8 hours. Bring to room temperature before serving.)*

Serves 6.

218 CALORIES PER SERVING: 6 G PROTEIN, 1 G FAT, 46 G CARBOHYDRATE; 884 MG SODIUM; 0 MG CHOLESTEROL.

Orange & Olive Salad With Cumin

A refreshing salad for winter, when navel oranges are in season.

8 navel oranges, peeled and white pith
  removed, sliced
¾ cup good-quality black olives, cut in half
  and pitted
1 red onion, sliced very thinly

juice of 1 medium-sized lemon
½-1 tsp. ground cumin (to taste)
salt and freshly ground black pepper
1 Tbsp. olive oil

Toss together oranges, olives and onion. Mix together lemon juice, cumin, salt and pepper, then whisk in oil. Toss with the salad and serve.

Serves 6.

138 CALORIES PER SERVING: 2 G PROTEIN, 4 G FAT, 23 G CARBOHYDRATE; 306 MG SODIUM; 0 MG CHOLESTEROL.

PASTA, GRAINS, BEANS & POTATOES

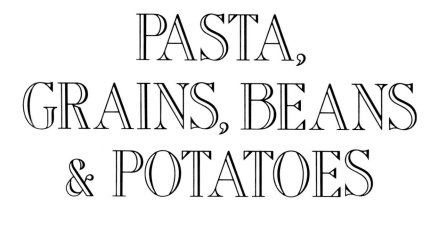

Spaghetti With Shrimp

Since both the shrimp and the pasta suffer when overcooked,
bring the pasta water to a boil and chop the sauce ingredients in advance.

1 Tbsp. olive oil
15 cloves garlic, minced
1 tsp. tomato paste
1¼ cups dry white wine
¼ cup Cognac (optional)
2-3 tsp. grated lemon zest

1½ lbs. medium-sized shrimp, peeled and
   deveined
¼ cup minced fresh parsley
salt and freshly ground black pepper to taste
1 lb. spaghetti
⅓ cup fresh bread crumbs, toasted *(page 242)*

In a large, deep saucepan, heat oil over low heat. Add garlic and tomato paste and sauté for 2 to 3 minutes, or until the garlic begins to stick to the bottom of the pan. Add wine, Cognac, if using, and lemon zest. Increase heat to medium and simmer, uncovered, for 5 minutes, or until garlic has softened. Add shrimp and cook for about 3 minutes longer, or just until shrimp are pink. Add parsley and season with salt and pepper.

Meanwhile, cook spaghetti in a large pot of boiling, salted water until it is tender but still firm. Drain the spaghetti in a colander and transfer it to a large, warm, shallow serving bowl. Toss with shrimp sauce. Taste and adjust seasonings. Sprinkle with toasted bread crumbs and serve immediately.

Serves 8 (as the sole entrée, serves 4).

300 CALORIES PER SERVING: 19 G PROTEIN, 4 G FAT, 46 G CARBOHYDRATE; 128 MG SODIUM; 87 MG CHOLESTEROL.

Spaghetti With Shrimp

Spaghetti With Eggplant & Tomato Sauce

*This dish comes from Sicily, where eggplant is abundant. There the
eggplant is fried in a lot of oil and then cooked in tomato sauce. Here it is baked
separately to avoid using so much oil and mixed into the tomato sauce after it is cooked.*

1 lb. eggplant, peeled and cut in ½" dice
1 tsp. salt
2 Tbsp. olive oil
4 cloves garlic, minced, or more to taste
1 small onion, minced
3 lbs. tomatoes, peeled, seeded and chopped
  or two 28-oz. cans plus one 15-oz. can,
  well-drained and chopped

3 Tbsp. tomato paste
pinch sugar (optional)
2-3 Tbsp. chopped fresh basil or ½ tsp. dried
  mixed with 2 Tbsp. fresh parsley
salt and freshly ground black pepper to taste
¾ lb. spaghetti
¼ cup grated Parmesan

Preheat the oven to 450 degrees F. Dice eggplant, sprinkle with salt and let sit in a colander for 30 minutes. Rinse and shake dry in a kitchen towel. Place in a lightly oiled 9-by-13-inch baking dish and toss with 1 Tbsp. oil. Cover tightly and bake for 30 to 35 minutes, or until tender.

Meanwhile, make the tomato sauce: sauté garlic and onions in a Dutch oven in the remaining Tbsp. oil over low heat, about 9 minutes, or until onions just turn golden. Add tomatoes and tomato paste.

If the sauce tastes too acid, add sugar. Simmer uncovered over medium heat, stirring often, for 40 to 55 minutes, or until thickened. Stir in eggplant and basil. Season with salt and pepper. Heat through while the pasta cooks.

In a large pot of boiling water, cook the spaghetti until it is tender but still firm. Drain, toss with the sauce and serve with Parmesan, if using.

Serves 4 generously.

451 CALORIES PER SERVING: 17 G PROTEIN, 11 G FAT, 77 G CARBOHYDRATE; 204 MG SODIUM; 5 MG CHOLESTEROL.

Spaghetti With Eggplant & Tomato Sauce

Orecchiette With Vegetable Sauce

When friends and Romans lend an ear nowadays, it is likely to be in the form of the little ear-shaped orecchiette, the pasta of choice for this dish. (See Sources, page 242.)

1 Tbsp. olive oil
1 medium-sized onion, minced
2 cloves garlic, minced
4 ripe tomatoes, diced, or 28-oz. can, undrained
2 carrots, peeled and cut into bite-sized chunks
2 Tbsp. all-purpose white flour
1 tsp. salt
½ tsp. freshly ground black pepper

2 zucchini squash, cut into bite-sized chunks
1 red bell pepper, seeded and cut into bite-sized chunks
1 yellow bell pepper, seeded and cut into bite-sized chunks
1 lb. orecchiette or medium-sized shells
6 Tbsp. grated Parmesan (optional)
20 fresh basil leaves, minced, or 2 tsp. dried

Heat oil in a large saucepan over medium heat. Add onions and garlic and sauté for 1 to 2 minutes, or until onions begin to soften. Add tomatoes and carrots and cook for 5 minutes, or until tomatoes soften. Sprinkle vegetables with flour and stir to coat evenly. Add 1½ cups water, salt and pepper. Bring to a boil, stirring. Cover pot and simmer, stirring occasionally, for 15 minutes. Add zucchini and peppers and cook for 20 minutes longer, or until the sauce has thickened slightly and vegetables are tender. *(The sauce can be made up to 2 days ahead and refrigerated. Reheat in a saucepan on low heat or in a covered casserole dish in a 325-degree-F oven for 20 to 25 minutes, or until heated through.)*

Meanwhile, cook pasta in a large pot of boiling, salted water until it is tender but still firm. Drain thoroughly in a colander, transfer to a warm, shallow serving bowl and toss well with the sauce, cheese, if using, and basil. Taste and adjust seasonings.

Serves 4.

288 CALORIES PER SERVING: 11 G PROTEIN, 4 G FAT, 52 G CARBOHYDRATE; 371 MG SODIUM; 4 MG CHOLESTEROL.

Orecchiette With Vegetable Sauce

Pasta Primavera With Dijon Vinaigrette

This colorful salad tastes best warm.

¾ cup finely diced carrots

1 lb. macaroni

1 cup Italian Dressing *(recipe follows)*

4-5 Tbsp. Dijon Vinaigrette *(recipe follows)*

2 cups chopped scallions

½ cup chopped celery

2 large tomatoes, seeded and diced

2 Tbsp. chopped fresh basil

1 Tbsp. balsamic vinegar or to taste

salt and freshly ground black pepper

Steam carrots for 1 to 2 minutes. In a large pot of boiling salted water, cook macaroni until tender but still firm. Drain and transfer to a large bowl. Toss with Italian Dressing, Dijon Vinaigrette, carrots, scallions, celery, tomatoes, basil, balsamic vinegar, salt and pepper to taste.

Serves 8.

239 CALORIES PER SERVING: 8 G PROTEIN, 1 G FAT, 48 G CARBOHYDRATE; 179 MG SODIUM; 0 MG CHOLESTEROL.

Italian Dressing

2 Tbsp. cornstarch

7 Tbsp. plus 2 tsp. white-wine vinegar

¼ red bell pepper, seeded and minced

2 shallots, minced

2 cloves garlic, minced

2 Tbsp. Dijon mustard

1 Tbsp. honey

1 tsp. salt

½ tsp. minced fresh Italian parsley

½ tsp. paprika

⅛ tsp. freshly ground black pepper

In a small bowl, dissolve cornstarch in ¼ cup water. In a saucepan, bring 1¾ cups water to a boil. Add the cornstarch mixture and whisk until thickened and clear. Let cool and stir in remaining ingredients. *(The dressing may be stored in the refrigerator for several days.)*

Makes 3 cups.

4 CALORIES PER TABLESPOON: 0 G PROTEIN, 0 G FAT, 1 G CARBOHYDRATE; 53 MG SODIUM; 0 MG CHOLESTEROL.

Dijon Vinaigrette

¼ cup Dijon mustard
3 Tbsp. red-wine vinegar
3 Tbsp. soft (silken) tofu
1 Tbsp. white-wine vinegar
1 Tbsp. grated onion

2 cloves garlic, minced
½ tsp. dried basil
¼-½ tsp. salt
⅛ tsp. freshly ground black pepper
2 drops hot-pepper sauce

Combine all ingredients in a jar or bowl and shake or whisk until blended. *(The dressing may be refrigerated for several days. Shake before using.)*
Makes ¾ cup.

12 CALORIES PER TABLESPOON: 1 G PROTEIN, 1 G FAT, 1 G CARBOHYDRATE; 114 MG SODIUM; 0 MG CHOLESTEROL.

Mushroom Lasagna

Those who like their lasagna covered with melted cheese can add a thin layer of part-skim mozzarella to this dish, and it will still be low in fat. Farmer's cheese is excellent for baking. If you can't find it, use cottage cheese and drain off the excess moisture.

1 lb. farmer's cheese
½ lb. low-fat or part-skim ricotta
2 egg whites
2 Tbsp. grated Parmesan
1 Tbsp. minced fresh chives
1 Tbsp. minced fresh parsley

¼ tsp. freshly ground black pepper
8 oz. lasagna noodles, uncooked
1 large onion, minced (1 cup)
¼ cup dry red wine
1½ lbs. mushrooms, cleaned and sliced
4 cups Red Sauce *(page 185)*

Puree farmer's cheese, ricotta, egg whites and Parmesan. Blend in chives, parsley and pepper by hand. In a large pot of lightly salted boiling water, cook lasagna noodles until just tender but not mushy, about 10 minutes. Remove noodles with a slotted spoon, dip into cold water and lay out flat on clean kitchen towels (not paper).

In a skillet, simmer onions in wine for about 5 minutes until very soft. Stir frequently, but keep the pot covered in between stirrings. Add mushrooms and cook until they are soft and half their original volume, about 5 minutes. Drain the vegetables.

Preheat oven to 375 degrees F. Combine cheese mixture and all but ¼ cup of the mushroom mixture. Spread 2 cups Red Sauce in the bottom of a 9-by-14-inch baking pan. Alternate layers of noodles, cheese, noodles, cheese, ending with a final layer of noodles. Cover with remaining sauce. Distribute reserved mushrooms over the top.

Bake, covered, for 1 hour. Uncover and bake for 5 minutes longer. Remove from the oven and let sit for 10 minutes before cutting.
Serves 9.

235 CALORIES PER SERVING: 22 G PROTEIN, 4 G FAT, 29 G CARBOHYDRATE; 523 MG SODIUM; 13 MG CHOLESTEROL.

Pappardelle With Squab

*This is a cherished dish in Tuscany, where cooks are particularly partial to game.
Pappardelle—wide noodles that can be up to 15 inches long—are also typical of
the region (see Sources, page 242). Or use the broadest fettuccine you can find.
Do not add cheese to this dish; it will blot out the delicate balance of flavors.*

2 squabs or Cornish game hens (1-1½ lbs.
  each)
1 Tbsp. olive oil
1 stalk celery, minced
1 medium-sized onion, minced
1 medium-sized carrot, minced

2 oz. prosciutto, minced
½ tsp. chopped fresh sage or pinch dried
1 cup Chianti or other dry red wine
1 16-oz. can tomatoes, with juice, pureed
salt and freshly ground black pepper to taste
1 lb. fresh or dried pappardelle or fettuccine

Remove skin and excess fat from squabs or hens.
Cut each one into quarters. In a Dutch oven, heat
oil over medium heat and add celery, onions, carrots,
prosciutto and sage. After 3 to 5 minutes, add squabs
or hens, and sauté 5 to 7 minutes, turning the pieces
to brown evenly. Add wine and simmer over medium
heat for about 15 minutes until wine is nearly evaporated. Add tomato puree, cover, reduce heat to low
and simmer for another 45 to 60 minutes, or until
the meat is very tender and juices run clear when the
thigh is pierced with a skewer. If you find that the
sauce is becoming too thick, add a little hot water.

Adjust seasoning with salt and pepper. *(The sauce can
be made up to 2 days ahead and refrigerated. Reheat in
a covered casserole dish in a 325-degree-F oven for 20 to
25 minutes, or until heated through.)*

Meanwhile, cook the pappardelle or fettuccine in
a large pot of boiling, salted water. When the pasta
is tender but still firm, drain it thoroughly in a colander and transfer it to a warm, shallow serving bowl.
Arrange the pieces of squab or hen over the pasta
and spoon the sauce over top.

Serves 4.

337 CALORIES PER SERVING: 25 G PROTEIN, 5 G FAT, 47 G CARBOHYDRATE; 253 MG SODIUM; 45 MG CHOLESTEROL.

Pappardelle With Squab

Pan-Fried Egg Noodles With Chicken & Broccoli

These crisp pan-fried noodles are sometimes referred to as "two-sides-brown"
in Canton, China, since the noodle cake is fried until golden on both sides before
being garnished with meat and vegetables in sauce. (For noodles, see Sources, page 242.)

SAUCE
1½ cups defatted chicken stock
4 Tbsp. oyster sauce
4 tsp. soy sauce
4 tsp. rice wine
½ tsp. sesame oil
2 Tbsp. cornstarch
½ tsp. sugar
NOODLES, CHICKEN & BROCCOLI
½ lb. thin Oriental egg noodles (Chinese
    dan mian, Japanese ramen) or vermicelli
3 Tbsp. plus 1½ tsp. corn or safflower oil

2 Tbsp. soy sauce
1 Tbsp. rice wine
1 tsp. sesame oil
1 tsp. sugar
2 tsp. minced garlic
1 tsp. cornstarch
1½ lbs. boneless chicken breast meat or
    turkey cutlets, skin and fat removed
1 lb. broccoli, head separated into florets and
    stems peeled and cut diagonally into 1" pieces
3 Tbsp. minced scallions
1 Tbsp. peeled, minced gingerroot

Combine sauce ingredients (chicken stock, oyster sauce, soy sauce, rice wine, sesame oil, cornstarch and sugar) in a small bowl and set aside.

In a large pot containing 4 qts. boiling water, cook noodles until just tender, about 3 to 5 minutes. Drain in a colander and toss with 1½ tsp. corn or safflower oil. Place noodles on a 9-inch round plate or cake pan, flatten to form a thin cake and let cool.

In a medium-sized bowl, combine soy sauce, rice wine, sesame oil, sugar, garlic, cornstarch and 1 Tbsp. water. Cut chicken or turkey diagonally across the grain into thin slices. Cut the slices into pieces 1½ inches long. Place meat in the bowl, toss lightly and let sit for 20 minutes.

Preheat oven to 200 degrees F. Steam or boil broccoli stems for ½ minute. Add florets and cook for 2½ minutes, or just until the broccoli is tender. Refresh broccoli immediately in cold water. Drain. Heat a heavy-bottomed, nonstick skillet over medium heat and add 1 Tbsp. oil. Slide the noodle cake into the skillet and cook until the bottom of the cake is golden

brown, about 10 minutes, shaking the pan from time to time in a circular motion to prevent the noodles from sticking. Slide noodle cake back onto a plate.

Place another plate over the top of the noodles and invert the cake onto it. Slide the cake back into the skillet and cook the other side for 10 minutes, or until it, too, is golden brown. Remove from the skillet and place on an ovenproof serving platter. Keep warm in the oven.

Heat a nonstick skillet or wok and add 1 Tbsp. oil. When it is hot, add half the chicken or turkey slices and cook, stirring, for 3 to 4 minutes, or until the pieces are no longer pink. Remove with a slotted spoon and drain. Add remaining 1 Tbsp. oil to the wok. Add remaining chicken or turkey and cook, stirring, until no longer pink. Remove and drain.

Reheat the pan, add scallions and ginger and stir-fry until fragrant, about 10 seconds. Pour in the sauce mixture, stirring constantly, and just before the mixture reaches a boil (about 2 minutes), add the broccoli. Cook, stirring constantly, for about 30 seconds.

Add cooked chicken or turkey and toss to coat. Cut the noodle cake into wedges, portion the meat mixture over the noodles and serve immediately. Serves 6.

310 CALORIES PER SERVING: 27 G PROTEIN, 16 G FAT, 16 G CARBOHYDRATE; 808 MG SODIUM; 61 MG CHOLESTEROL.

Pad Thai (Thai Fried Rice Noodles)

Once cooked, flat rice sticks turn translucent and somewhat gelatinous—a wonderful contrast to the tender shrimp and crunchy bean sprouts. Place all ingredients (except those for the topping) near the stove before beginning. (For noodles, see Sources, page 242.)

¾ lb. flat rice sticks (Thai *jantaboon*,
  Vietnamese *banh pho*)
½ cup fish sauce
½ cup tomato sauce
¼ cup sugar
2 Tbsp. corn oil
¾ lb. medium-sized shelled shrimp, peeled
  and deveined
1 Tbsp. minced garlic
1 egg plus 2 egg whites, beaten together

TOPPING
1½ cups bean sprouts, rinsed and drained
3 Tbsp. chopped peanuts
2 Tbsp. minced scallions, green tops only
½ tsp. red-pepper flakes
2 Tbsp. coarsely chopped fresh cilantro leaves
2 limes, cut into wedges

In a large bowl, cover rice sticks with cold water and let soften for 30 minutes. Drain thoroughly. Combine fish sauce, tomato sauce, sugar and 1¾ cups water.

In a wok or deep skillet, heat 1 Tbsp. oil until quite hot. Add shrimp and stir-fry until pink and firm to the touch, about 3 minutes. Remove with a slotted spoon and set aside. Add remaining 1 Tbsp. oil. When it is hot, add garlic and cook briefly, stirring, for about 15 seconds, then add egg and egg whites and cook, stirring to scramble, for about 30 seconds. Stir in fish sauce mixture and noodles.

Cook for about 4 to 8 minutes, until the noodles are tender and the sauce has been reduced to a coating consistency. Add the shrimp, toss lightly to coat and remove to a serving platter. Sprinkle the top of the noodles with bean sprouts, peanuts, scallions, red-pepper flakes and cilantro and toss lightly. Serve hot, with lime wedges on the side.

Serves 6.

403 CALORIES PER SERVING: 21 G PROTEIN, 9 G FAT, 61 G CARBOHYDRATE; 299 MG SODIUM; 146 MG CHOLESTEROL.

Cold Soba Noodles

*Japanese soba noodles, made from buckwheat flour and water, can be served as
a light lunch or supper. They are traditionally served cold. (See Sources, page 242.)*

¾ lb. dried buckwheat noodles (soba)
2 eggs, lightly beaten (optional)
2 cups julienne carrots (3-4 medium-sized)
2 cups julienne snow peas, tough strings and
   ends removed (½ lb.)
1½ cups julienne red bell pepper
   (1 medium-sized)

½ cup reduced-sodium soy sauce
6 Tbsp. rice vinegar
¼ cup sesame oil
3 Tbsp. minced scallions, green tops only
2 Tbsp. rice wine
2 Tbsp. sugar
1½ Tbsp. peeled, minced gingerroot

In a large pot cook buckwheat noodles in 3 qts. boiling water for 5 to 6 minutes, or until just tender. Drain the noodles, plunge them into cold water, then rinse them quickly to remove any starch. Drain thoroughly and place in a large bowl.

If using eggs, heat a small nonstick skillet until a drop of water dances when sprinkled on the surface. Add ⅓ of the beaten eggs and rotate the pan so the egg coats it evenly and forms a thin omelet. Cook until set, flip and cook briefly. Repeat twice with remaining eggs and cut the omelets into thin strips.

Add to the noodles along with carrots, snow peas and peppers.

Combine soy sauce, rice vinegar, sesame oil, scallions, rice wine, sugar and ginger, stirring until sugar dissolves. Pour the dressing over the noodles and toss gently to combine. *(The noodles are best served immediately, but they can be held, covered, in the refrigerator for up to 8 hours. Toss the noodles again before serving if they have been refrigerated.)*
Serves 6.

377 CALORIES PER SERVING: 12 G PROTEIN, 12 G FAT, 55 G CARBOHYDRATE; 1,411 MG SODIUM; 71 MG CHOLESTEROL.

Vegetarian Jambalaya

*This one-dish supper, a specialty of Bill Neal's Crook's Corner restaurant in
Carrboro, North Carolina, is as full-flavored as traditional meaty renditions of jambalaya.*

2 green bell peppers
1 cup chopped celery
1½ cups chopped onion
4 cloves garlic, peeled and chopped
1 28-oz. can Italian tomatoes, chopped
   (juice reserved)
1 tsp. salt
1 tsp. freshly ground black pepper
1 tsp. hot-pepper sauce
1 tsp. dried basil
1 tsp. dried thyme
3 bay leaves

2½ cups uncooked long-grain rice, either
   white or brown
4 medium artichokes
3 cups shelled black-eyed peas (field peas),
   fresh or frozen
red-pepper flakes
SAUCE
1 16-oz. can Italian tomatoes, undrained
1 15-oz. can pimientos, drained
hot-pepper sauce
salt and freshly ground black pepper

Preheat oven to 350 degrees F. Combine peppers, celery, onions, garlic, tomatoes and juice, 4 cups water, salt, black pepper, hot-pepper sauce, basil, thyme and 2 bay leaves in a medium-sized saucepan. Simmer 10 minutes. Pour ½ of the mixture into a 3-qt. baking dish. Sprinkle rice over evenly. Pour remaining vegetable mixture over rice, cover and bake for about 30 minutes or until rice has absorbed all the liquid and is tender. (Brown rice may take up to an additional 30 minutes.) Discard bay leaves.

Meanwhile, break off tough outer leaves of artichokes. With a knife, slice off pointed tips of artichokes. With scissors, remove any thorns from remaining tips of leaves. Cut off the stems and discard. Cook artichokes in a large pot of boiling water for 25 to 35 minutes, or until the centers are tender. Drain, let cool slightly, then cut each artichoke into 6 wedges. Remove spiny choke and discard. Cook peas in a large pot of lightly salted water with a sprinkling of red-pepper flakes and remaining bay leaf until tender. Drain; discard bay leaf, and keep peas warm.

To make the sauce: Combine tomatoes and pimientos in a food processor or blender and puree until smooth. Transfer to a saucepan and simmer, uncovered, over low heat for 10 minutes. Season to taste with hot-pepper sauce, salt and pepper. Rub sauce through a strainer to remove any coarse pieces.

To serve: Warm dinner plates. Put a large mound of the rice mixture slightly off the center of the plate. Place 2 or 3 artichoke wedges next to the rice mound. Spoon peas over the rice. Fill in the bottom of the plate with some of the sauce. Pass the rest of the sauce at the table.

Serves 8 generously.

388 CALORIES PER SERVING: 13 G PROTEIN, 2 G FAT, 83 G CARBOHYDRATE; 587 MG SODIUM; 0 MG CHOLESTEROL.

Seafood Risotto

*Made with the readily available long-grain rice instead of Italian
short-grain, this dish does not require constant stirring as does traditional risotto.*

4 cups defatted chicken stock
½ cup chopped onions
1⅓ cups uncooked long-grain rice
¼ cup dry white wine
pinch saffron

¾ lb. fresh or frozen seafood (bay scallops
  and/or tiny shrimp)
½ cup frozen peas
¼ cup chopped pimiento
salt and freshly ground black pepper to taste

Place ¼ cup chicken stock in a heavy-bottomed saucepan, add onions and cook for 3 minutes, or until soft. Add the remaining 3¾ cups stock, rice, wine and saffron. Bring to a boil. Cover and simmer over low heat for 20 to 25 minutes, until rice is tender.

(The risotto should have a creamy consistency.) Stir in the seafood, peas and pimiento. Cover and cook for 3 to 5 minutes, or until the seafood is opaque. Season with salt and pepper.
Serves 6.

241 CALORIES PER SERVING: 18 G PROTEIN, 1 G FAT, 38 G CARBOHYDRATE; 117 MG SODIUM; 19 MG CHOLESTEROL.

Wild Rice Pilaf

The chewy qualities of wild rice make it especially appropriate for this pilaf.

1 cup uncooked wild rice
2 tsp. vegetable oil
1 medium-sized onion, finely chopped
2½ cups defatted chicken stock, heated to
  boiling

¼ tsp. freshly ground black pepper
½ cup raisins
¼ cup pine nuts, toasted *(page 242)*
1 tsp. grated orange zest

Wash rice in a colander until the water runs clear. In a heavy-bottomed pot with a tight-fitting lid, heat oil over low heat. Add onions and cook, stirring, until translucent, about 5 minutes. Add the rice and stir briefly over the heat. Add chicken stock and pepper,

and when the liquid reaches a boil, cover tightly and simmer over low heat about 1½ hours, or until the liquid has evaporated and the rice is tender.
Toss rice with raisins, pine nuts and orange zest.
Serves 6.

192 CALORIES PER SERVING: 6 G PROTEIN, 4 G FAT, 35 G CARBOHYDRATE; 5 MG SODIUM; 0 MG CHOLESTEROL.

Spicy Rice

From the Deep South comes this spicy rice full of vegetables and chicken.
Feel free to adjust the amount of Tabasco and cayenne pepper according to taste.

1 Tbsp. vegetable oil

3 cloves garlic, minced

1 lb. boneless, skinless chicken breasts,
   trimmed and cut into 1" chunks

5 scallions, trimmed and chopped

2 stalks celery, chopped

1 red bell pepper, seeded and chopped

½ green bell pepper, seeded and chopped

1⅛ cups uncooked long-grain rice

2 cups defatted chicken stock

1 16-oz. can tomatoes, chopped, with juice

1 Tbsp. chili powder

1 tsp. Tabasco Sauce

1 tsp. dried basil

1 tsp. dried oregano

½ tsp. cayenne pepper

½ tsp. ground cumin

⅔ cup frozen peas

salt to taste

Heat oil in a 4-qt. saucepan over medium-high heat. Add garlic and sauté for 30 seconds. Add chicken and sauté for 3 minutes, or until flesh is opaque. Transfer chicken to a plate and set aside.

Add scallions, celery and red and green peppers and sauté for 2 minutes, or until softened. Add rice and stir for 1 minute. Add chicken stock, tomatoes and their juice, chili powder, Tabasco, basil, oregano, cayenne and cumin. Bring to a boil, stirring. Reduce heat to low, cover and simmer for 25 minutes. Add the frozen peas and chicken and cook for 1 minute, or until heated through. Season with salt.
   Serves 6.

306 CALORIES PER SERVING: 27 G PROTEIN, 5 G FAT, 37 G CARBOHYDRATE; 220 MG SODIUM; 54 MG CHOLESTEROL.

Sticky Rice *(Xoi)*

This rice, which is sold variously as sweet, sticky or glutinous rice,
has a delicious, slightly sweet taste. It can be dipped in sauces or eaten in place of plain rice.
In Vietnam, it is frequently prepared with peanuts, which are mixed into the rice before cooking.
(See Sources, page 242.) Note: *If you are cooking a large quantity of rice, you can divide*
the rice between 2 bamboo steamers and stack them. The cooking time may increase by 5 minutes.

1 cup uncooked long- or short-grain sticky rice

Soak rice in 2 cups warm water for 2 hours, or in 2 cups cold water for 8 hours or overnight. Drain rice and place in a steamer basket lined with cheesecloth. Set the steamer basket over several inches of boiling water in a wok or saucepan. Cover and steam for 20 to 25 minutes, or until rice is tender, shiny and slightly sticky. Make sure that the pot doesn't run dry.
   Serves 4.

168 CALORIES PER SERVING: 3 G PROTEIN, 0 G FAT, 37 G CARBOHYDRATE; 1 MG SODIUM; 0 MG CHOLESTEROL.

Refried Black Beans

Refried beans are always fried in lard or bacon drippings in Mexico and the Southwest. In this recipe by Martha Rose Shulman, their flavor comes from the cumin and chili, which are sautéed with them, and from the garlic, onion and cilantro, which are simmered with them in the boiling water.

1 lb. black beans, washed and picked over
1 Tbsp. plus 1 tsp. safflower or vegetable oil
1 large onion, chopped
4-6 large cloves garlic, minced
3 Tbsp. chopped fresh cilantro

approximately 1½ tsp. salt
4 tsp. mild chili powder
1 Tbsp. ground cumin
low-fat yogurt for garnish

Soak beans overnight in 8 cups water. (Use bottled water if your water is very hard.) Drain. Heat 1 tsp. oil in a large, nonstick, heavy-bottomed saucepan, bean pot or Dutch oven, and sauté onions and 4 cloves garlic over medium heat until tender, about 8 to 10 minutes. Add beans and 8 cups fresh water and bring to a boil. Reduce the heat, and simmer 1 hour, uncovered. Add more garlic, if you wish, cilantro and 1 tsp. salt, and continue to simmer, adding water as needed, until the beans are soft and the liquid is thick and aromatic and barely covers the beans, about 45 minutes longer. Remove from the heat.

Allow the beans to cool. Mash them coarsely in batches in a food processor or blender or with a potato masher. Make sure not to puree until smooth; you want texture.

Heat remaining 1 Tbsp. oil in a large, heavy-bottomed, nonstick frying pan and add chili powder and cumin. Sauté for 1 minute over medium heat and add the mashed beans (this can be done in batches, depending on the size of your skillet). Taste for salt, adding ½ tsp. more if desired, and fry the beans, stirring often, until they begin to get crusty and aromatic. If they seem too dry, add some water. Mash and stir as they cook. There should be enough liquid so that they bubble as they cook, while at the same time a thin crust forms on the bottom. Cook for about 10 to 20 minutes and either serve immediately topped with a dollop of yogurt, or transfer to an oiled serving dish if you plan to reheat the beans later. *(The dish will hold for about 3 days in the refrigerator.)*

Reheat for 20 to 30 minutes, covered, in a 325-degree-F oven. If the beans seem dry, moisten them with water before reheating.

Serves 6 to 8.

255 CALORIES FOR EACH OF 6 SERVINGS: 15 G PROTEIN, 4 G FAT, 41 G CARBOHYDRATE; 566 MG SODIUM; 0 MG CHOLESTEROL.

Pueblo Pumpkin Stew

A sweet and spicy vegetarian dish that can be served over rice as a main dish. Garam masala, an Indian spice mix, can be found in Asian food stores or it can be prepared at home in small batches.

8 New Mexican (Anaheim) chilies
1 Tbsp. canola oil
1 large onion, sliced
1 Tbsp. peeled, minced gingerroot
2 serrano chilies, chopped
4 large tomatoes, chopped
2 tsp. ground cumin

2 tsp. garam masala *(recipe follows)*
½ tsp. ground turmeric
5 cups cubed pumpkin or acorn squash
1 cup cooked pinto beans
2 Tbsp. freshly grated Parmesan
salt

Preheat broiler. Place Anaheim chilies on a foil-lined baking sheet and broil until skin is black, turning so that the sides are evenly charred. Put chilies in a paper bag, close and let cool. Hold chilies under cool running water while you slip off the skins. Cut chilies open and remove seeds, stems and ribs. Chop and set aside.

In a large saucepan, heat oil over medium heat. Add onions, ginger and Anaheim and serrano chilies and sauté for 4 minutes, or until softened. Add tomatoes, cumin, garam masala and turmeric and cook for 5 minutes, stirring often. Add 2 cups water and squash. Bring to a boil. Reduce heat to low, cover and simmer for 30 minutes, or until squash is tender. Stir in pinto beans and heat through. Stir in Parmesan. Add salt to taste.

Serves 8.

112 CALORIES PER SERVING: 5 G PROTEIN, 3 G FAT, 19 G CARBOHYDRATE; 38 MG SODIUM; 0 MG CHOLESTEROL.

Garam Masala

5 tsp. coriander seeds
1 Tbsp. cumin seeds
1 Tbsp. black peppercorns

1 tsp. whole cloves
1 tsp. cinnamon
1 tsp. green cardamom pods

In a small, dry, heavy-bottomed skillet over medium heat, toast coriander and cumin seeds for 3 to 5 minutes. Combine with other ingredients and grind in a mortar and pestle or a blender until smooth. Store in a bottle or well-sealed container for up to 6 months.

Makes about ¼ cup.

Bulgur Pilaf With Currants & Pine Nuts

This family favorite can be the "star" of a meatless meal. It is also marvelous with chicken or lamb.

1 tsp. olive oil
1 small onion, finely chopped
1 cup medium or coarse bulgur
2 cups hot defatted chicken stock

¼ cup currants
2 Tbsp. pine nuts, toasted *(page 242)*
salt to taste

Preheat oven to 350 degrees F. In a heavy 2½- or 3-qt. saucepan, heat oil over moderate heat. Add onions and sauté, stirring, until soft but not brown, about 2 to 4 minutes. Add bulgur and sauté 1 minute, stirring constantly, until the grains are coated with the oil.

Add stock and currants and bring to a boil, stirring. Cover and bake in the oven for 40 to 45 minutes, or until all the liquid has been absorbed and the bulgur is tender. Do not stir during this time. Fluff the pilaf by tossing it briefly with two forks. Stir pine nuts into the pilaf. Taste and adjust seasonings, adding salt if necessary.

Serves 4.

160 CALORIES PER SERVING: 5 G PROTEIN, 4 G FAT, 29 G CARBOHYDRATE; 2 MG SODIUM; 0 MG CHOLESTEROL.

Barley-Scallion-Pine Nut Casserole

Try this when you need a starchy side or main dish; it's a nice change from rice.

1 cup pearl barley
2 tsp. butter
1 medium-sized onion, chopped
3 cups hot defatted chicken stock

¼ cup finely chopped scallions
⅓ cup finely chopped fresh parsley
2 Tbsp. pine nuts, toasted *(page 242)*
salt and freshly ground black pepper to taste

Preheat oven to 350 degrees F. Rinse barley, drain and set aside. Melt butter in a 1½-qt. flameproof casserole dish over medium heat. Add onions and cook until softened, about 2 minutes. Add barley and continue cooking, stirring constantly, until the barley is coated with butter, about 1 minute. Stir in stock and scallions. Mix well, bring to a boil, cover and bake for 1 hour, or until barley is tender and liquid is absorbed. Add parsley and pine nuts. Taste and adjust seasonings. Fluff with two forks and turn out into a warm serving dish.

Serves 6.

171 CALORIES PER SERVING: 7 G PROTEIN, 4 G FAT, 29 G CARBOHYDRATE; 19 MG SODIUM; 3 MG CHOLESTEROL.

Athenian Orzo

*Orzo, a rice-shaped pasta found in supermarkets, makes a delightful
base for an authentically Greek combination of shrimp, tomatoes and feta.
To serve as a side dish, omit the shrimp and drain the tomatoes before adding them.*

1½ tsp. olive oil
1 small onion, chopped
4 cloves garlic, minced
¼ cup dry white wine
1 28-oz. can tomatoes, chopped, with juice
3 Tbsp. chopped fresh parsley
1 Tbsp. capers
½ tsp. dried oregano

½ tsp. dried basil
½ tsp. salt
¼ tsp. freshly ground black pepper
pinch red-pepper flakes
1 lb. medium-sized shrimp, peeled
1 cup orzo
½ cup crumbled feta cheese

In a 2-qt. saucepan, heat oil over medium heat. Add onions and garlic and sauté for 3½ minutes, or until softened. Add wine and boil for about 1 minute. Stir in tomatoes, 1½ Tbsp. parsley, capers, oregano, basil, salt, pepper and red-pepper flakes and cook for 5 minutes. Drop in the shrimp and cook, stirring, for 2½ minutes, or just until shrimp are pink.

Preheat oven to 450 degrees F. Cook orzo in a large pot of boiling, salted water for 10 minutes, or until tender but still firm. Drain in a colander and transfer it to a 2-qt. casserole dish. Toss with the tomato-shrimp sauce. Sprinkle with remaining 1½ Tbsp. parsley and feta cheese. Bake for 10 minutes, or until feta is bubbly.

Serves 4 to 6.

212 CALORIES FOR EACH OF 6 SERVINGS: 20 G PROTEIN, 5 G FAT, 20 G CARBOHYDRATE; 620 MG SODIUM; 124 MG CHOLESTEROL.

Italian Potato Salad

In Italy, this potato salad is known as Russian salad.
It has a thousand versions, most of them bound with plain or garlic mayonnaise.
In this one, lightly steamed vegetables are splashed with vinegar while still hot,
so they absorb the pungent aroma and flavor. A lemony vinaigrette binds the vegetables
together. This salad looks especially pretty when made with red-skinned new potatoes and
served in a cupped leaf of red radicchio. Butter lettuce or ruffled kale makes a nice presentation too.

1 Tbsp. olive oil
1 clove garlic, minced
½ tsp. finely grated lemon zest
2 lbs. new potatoes, preferably red-skinned, well-scrubbed and cut into quarters or eighths (about 20 potatoes)
½ lb. young carrots, cut into coins (about 12 carrots)
½ lb. snap beans, ends removed, and cut into 1" lengths

2 small zucchini squash, cut into ½" chunks
1 crookneck or summer squash, cut into ½" chunks
1 bunch scallions, including tops, chopped
¼ cup red-wine vinegar, diluted with 1 Tbsp. water
½ tsp. salt
¼ tsp. freshly ground black pepper
6 leaves radicchio, butterhead lettuce or ruffled kale

In a measuring cup, combine oil, garlic and lemon zest; set aside. Arrange potatoes in a steamer basket. Add carrots and steam for 8 minutes. Add beans, zucchini and summer squash, and steam for 3 to 5 minutes longer, or just until tender-crisp. Do not overcook. Lift out steamer and transfer vegetables to a large bowl. Add scallions and splash vegetables with 2 Tbsp. of the vinegar mixture. Toss gently, and let sit until cooled, about 15 minutes. Combine remaining vinegar mixture with oil mixture and drizzle over salad. Season with salt and pepper and serve on lettuce leaves.

Serves 6.

198 CALORIES PER SERVING: 5 G PROTEIN, 3 G FAT, 41 G CARBOHYDRATE; 23 MG SODIUM; 0 MG CHOLESTEROL.

Italian Potato Salad

Zesty Dill Potato Salad

Red potatoes are a perfect choice of potato because they keep their shape when sliced and they add color. Leftover meat or chicken may be added to this salad for a main dish.

1 lb. medium-sized red potatoes, scrubbed
salt to taste
2 Tbsp. balsamic vinegar
1 Tbsp. white-wine vinegar
1 Tbsp. extra-virgin olive oil

¼ cup diced red bell pepper
¼ cup diced green bell pepper
¼ cup chopped scallions
1 Tbsp. chopped fresh dill
white or freshly ground black pepper to taste

In a saucepan, boil potatoes in salted water for 20 minutes, or until tender. Drain and let stand until cool enough to handle. Cut potatoes in half lengthwise, then cut in approximately ½ inch slices. Place them in a serving bowl. Sprinkle the potatoes with vinegars and oil, tossing gently to coat. Add remaining ingredients and toss gently to mix. Taste and adjust seasonings. Serve at room temperature.

Serves 4.

134 CALORIES PER SERVING: 2 G PROTEIN, 4 G FAT, 24 G CARBOHYDRATE; 6 MG SODIUM; 0 MG CHOLESTEROL.

Roasted Potatoes With Rosemary & Garlic

There is no bad way to cook potatoes, but roasting makes them crunchy outside and tender inside, like French fries without the fat. The garlic must be added last or it will scorch.

8 red-skinned potatoes, about 2" long,
    unpeeled, scrubbed
1 Tbsp. fresh rosemary, chopped (1 tsp.
    crumbled dried)

1 Tbsp. olive oil
1 tsp. kosher salt
freshly ground black pepper to taste
2 large cloves garlic, coarsely chopped

Preheat oven to 450 degrees F. Cut potatoes in quarters. Place them in a bowl and add 1½ tsp. fresh rosemary or ½ tsp. dried. Pour 2½ tsp. olive oil over them. Using a rubber spatula, toss them until they are well coated and the rosemary is well distributed. Place them in a single layer on a heavy baking sheet and sprinkle them with salt and pepper. Roast for 15 minutes, turning every 5 minutes.

In a small bowl, mix garlic with remaining ½ tsp. oil. Add it to the potatoes and continue roasting for 10 to 15 minutes, or until the potatoes are crisp and browned and easily pierced with a fork. Transfer to a serving dish, season with more fresh pepper and remaining 1½ tsp. fresh rosemary or ½ tsp. dried.

Serves 4.

323 CALORIES PER SERVING: 6 G PROTEIN, 4 G FAT, 68 G CARBOHYDRATE; 550 MG SODIUM; 0 MG CHOLESTEROL.

Potato Gratin

A favorite dish in France is gratin dauphinois, *a layered potato-and-cheese casserole that is usually very rich. Martha Rose Shulman's low-fat version, which calls for skim milk instead of whole milk, no crème fraîche and very little cheese, is just as luscious as any potato gratin in France.*

2 large cloves garlic, cut in half lengthwise
3 lbs. russet or new potatoes, unpeeled or
  peeled, scrubbed and thinly sliced
  (9 medium-sized)
3⅓ cups skim milk

2 large eggs, lightly beaten
about 1 tsp. salt
freshly ground black pepper
6 Tbsp. freshly grated Parmesan

Preheat oven to 400 degrees F. Rub the inside of a large (about 14-by-9-by-2-inch) oval gratin dish all over with the cut side of the garlic. Slice the garlic into thin slivers and toss with potatoes. Layer potatoes and garlic evenly in the gratin dish. Mix together milk, eggs and salt and pour over potatoes. Add a generous amount of pepper.

Bake for about 1 to 1¼ hours. Every 15 minutes or so, remove the casserole from the oven and, using a knife or wooden spoon, break up the top layer of potatoes, which is drying up and getting crusty and fold it into the rest of the potatoes.

When the gratin is golden and the potatoes tender, sprinkle on Parmesan and return to the heat. Bake another 15 to 20 minutes, until a golden-brown crust has formed on the top.

Serves 6 to 8.

215 CALORIES FOR EACH OF 6 SERVINGS: 10 G PROTEIN, 3 G FAT, 36 G CARBOHYDRATE; 444 MG SODIUM; 74 MG CHOLESTEROL.

New Potatoes & Peas

If you are using large potatoes, cut them into ¾-inch-diameter pieces.
Use only the lightest seasoning: butter for richness, mint for sweetness, and pepper.

1 lb. new potatoes, scrubbed, unpeeled
12 new onions or scallions, bulbs whole, tops
  chopped (optional)
2 cups fresh or frozen peas

2 tsp. butter
½ tsp. coarsely ground black pepper
2 Tbsp. chopped fresh mint or more to taste

Place potatoes and onions or scallions (if using) in a small saucepan, barely cover with water and bring to a boil. Cook over medium heat for 5 to 6 minutes, or just until tender. Add peas, cover and cook for 1 minute, or until tender. Drain, add butter, pepper and mint. Heat for 1 minute and toss gently.

Serves 6.

122 CALORIES PER SERVING: 4 G PROTEIN, 2 G FAT, 24 G CARBOHYDRATE; 63 MG SODIUM; 3 MG CHOLESTEROL.

POULTRY & GAME

~

Lacquered Cornish Game Hens

*To achieve the lacquerlike finish,
the hens are baked on a rack and basted
frequently with an orange juice-wine-honey mixture.*

3 Cornish game hens (about 1½ lbs. apiece)
3 small onions, cut in quarters
6 cloves garlic, crushed
salt and freshly ground black pepper
1 cup orange juice
1 cup red wine
¼ cup honey
2 Tbsp. soy sauce

(Recipe continues on next page)

Blot Cornish hens dry inside and outside with a paper towel. Remove any excess fat. Place 4 quarters of onion and 2 garlic cloves in each cavity and sprinkle the inside with salt and pepper. Preheat oven to 400 degrees F. Tie the legs together and arrange the hens on a rack in a roasting pan, breast-side up.

Combine orange juice, red wine, honey and soy sauce and spoon some of the mixture over the hens. Bake 15 minutes, then spoon more of the mixture onto the hens. Continue cooking for another 50 minutes, basting the hens with additional glaze every 10 to 15 minutes, until skin is crisp and dark brown and juices run clear when thigh is pierced with a skewer. (About 1½ cups of glaze will be left; reserve for sauce.) Remove hens from pan and allow to cool for 10 minutes. Pour pan juices into a saucepan, along with remaining glaze. Bring to a boil and skim fat.

Cut each hen in half with poultry shears or a knife, removing string, backbone, onions and garlic. Place skin-side up on a serving platter and serve with the sauce.

Serves 6.

449 CALORIES PER SERVING: 52 G PROTEIN, 13 G FAT, 22 G CARBOHYDRATE; 494 MG SODIUM; 144 MG CHOLESTEROL.

Quick-Roasted Chicken With Chili Essence

Chicken can be roasted plain, but adding seasonings under the skin gives intense flavor with little effort. Even though the skin is removed after roasting, coating it with the seasonings makes for a moister result. The bed of kosher salt placed beneath the chicken absorbs fat and prevents splattering.

1 whole chicken, about 3½-4 lbs.
1 Tbsp. chili powder
1 tsp. dried thyme
1 tsp. dried oregano
1 tsp. celery salt
½ tsp. dried sage

½ tsp. minced garlic
½ tsp. freshly ground black pepper
2 tsp. olive oil
1 shallot, peeled and thinly sliced
1 sprig fresh thyme (optional)
2 cups kosher salt

Preheat oven to 500 degrees F. Rinse chicken and pat completely dry. Cut off any interior fat deposits. Lift skin at the neck and carefully slide your fingers between the flesh and the skin on both sides of the breast, loosening the skin, to make a pocket extending all the way to the legs. Take care not to break the skin.

In a small bowl, combine chili powder, thyme, oregano, celery salt, sage, garlic and pepper. Lift skin and pat a little of the seasoning mixture directly onto the chicken's flesh. Smooth the skin with your fingers, then lift and pat on more seasoning. Repeat until the flesh is fairly well coated, reserving about 2 tsp. for the skin. Rub the bird all over with olive oil, then sprinkle remaining seasoning over the skin.

Insert shallots and fresh thyme, if using, into the cavity. Tuck the wings under the body and tie the legs together. Pour kosher salt into a deep, heavy-bottomed roasting pan or into a cast-iron skillet. Lay the bird over the salt and place it in the hot oven. Roast for 15 minutes, lower heat to 450 degrees F and continue roasting about 30 more minutes, or until the juices run clear when the thigh is pierced with a skewer. Let stand 10 minutes. Remove string and skin before carving.

Serves 4.

360 CALORIES PER SERVING: 62 G PROTEIN, 10 G FAT, 3 G CARBOHYDRATE; 699 MG SODIUM; 169 MG CHOLESTEROL.

Glenn's Easy Pollo Cubano

The fresh flavor of tarragon enhances poached chicken breasts in this simple preparation.

4 boneless, skinless chicken breasts (1 lb. total)
½ cup fresh lime juice (about 4 large limes)
2 shallots, minced
2½ Tbsp. chopped fresh tarragon
2½ Tbsp. chopped fresh cilantro

½ tsp. salt
¼ tsp. freshly ground black pepper
½ cup dry sherry
1 Tbsp. red-pepper flakes
3 bay leaves

Place chicken breasts in a shallow nonaluminum dish and add ¼ cup lime juice. Toss lightly, cover and marinate for 30 minutes in the refrigerator. Drain and reserve marinade.

In a small bowl, combine shallots, ½ Tbsp. tarragon, ½ Tbsp. cilantro, ¼ tsp. salt and black pepper. Spread 2 tsp. of the mixture at the base of each breast and roll the breasts up. Using two pieces of butcher's string, one running horizontally and one vertically, tie each breast into a package.

In a poacher or straight-sided skillet, combine 1 qt. water, remaining ¼ cup lime juice, reserved marinade, remaining 2 Tbsp. tarragon, remaining 2 Tbsp. cilantro, sherry, red-pepper flakes, bay leaves and remaining ¼ tsp. salt. Bring to a boil, reduce heat to low, add chicken breasts, cover and poach gently for 20 to 25 minutes, or until the breasts are no longer pink inside.

Serves 4.

216 CALORIES PER SERVING: 31 G PROTEIN, 4 G FAT, 7 G CARBOHYDRATE; 346 MG SODIUM; 82 MG CHOLESTEROL.

Apple-Cider Chicken

This dish is served like a stew and is especially good ladled over rice or pasta.

¼ cup all-purpose white flour
½ tsp. salt
½ tsp. freshly ground black pepper
1½ lbs. skinless, boneless chicken breast, cubed
1-3 tsp. corn oil for sautéing

1 medium-sized onion, quartered and sliced
1 cup apple cider
2 fresh tomatoes, peeled and chopped, or 14-oz. can, drained
1 Tbsp. chopped fresh basil or 1 tsp. dried
1 tsp. grated orange zest

Combine flour, salt and pepper in a plastic bag. Shake chicken, a few pieces at a time, in the flour until lightly coated. In a Dutch oven or heavy-bottomed, nonstick pan, heat oil and brown chicken on medium heat until the flesh turns from pink to white on all sides. Do not crowd the chicken. (You may have to do this in several batches.)

Remove the chicken and set aside. Sauté onions in the same pan. If needed, add a little cider.

Add tomatoes and apple cider to the pan. Bring to a simmer, return the chicken to the pan and simmer, covered, for 20 minutes. Add basil and orange zest and simmer, uncovered, for 10 minutes more.

Serves 6.

206 CALORIES PER SERVING: 24 G PROTEIN, 4 G FAT, 18 G CARBOHYDRATE; 330 MG SODIUM; 61 MG CHOLESTEROL.

Baked Chicken With 40 Cloves of Garlic

*This is a lusty, beautiful dish. The chicken becomes succulent and ever so fragrant
as it bakes slowly in white wine with the unpeeled cloves of garlic. The garlic becomes
mild, sweet and soft as it cooks, and you eat it like butter on croutons. Most authentic French
versions of this dish include more olive oil, as well as some butter, but the results here are heavenly.*

1 Tbsp. olive oil
4 lbs. bone-in chicken pieces, skinned
salt and freshly ground black pepper
40 large cloves garlic, unpeeled (about 4 heads)
1¾ cups dry white wine

4 sprigs thyme or ¼ tsp. dried
1 sprig rosemary or ¼ tsp. dried
2 Tbsp. Cognac
chopped fresh parsley
12 ½"-thick slices coarse bread

Preheat oven to 350 degrees F.

Heat oil over medium heat in a heavy-bottomed, flameproof casserole dish wide enough to accommodate the chicken in a single layer. Add chicken and season with salt and pepper. Sauté for 5 minutes, then turn over and sauté another 5 minutes. If the bottom of the pot scorches a little, don't worry; it won't affect the flavor of the dish. Remove chicken pieces from the pot.

Add garlic, reserving 1 clove, and sauté, stirring, for 3 to 5 minutes, until beginning to brown. Again, don't worry about scorching. Spread cloves in a single layer and return the chicken pieces to the pot. Add wine, thyme and rosemary, and cover tightly.

Place casserole in the oven and bake 45 minutes. After 45 minutes, check the chicken. It should be tender and fragrant. If it isn't quite cooked through or very tender, bake another 15 minutes.

Remove casserole from oven. Heat Cognac in a small saucepan and light with a match. Pour over the chicken and shake the casserole until the flames die down. Taste the sauce in the pot, adjust seasonings and sprinkle with parsley.

Toast the bread slices in an oven preheated to 350 degrees F until they begin to color, about 10 minutes, then rub both sides with the cut side of the reserved garlic clove.

To serve, place a couple of garlic croutons on each plate and top them with a piece or two of chicken, some of the sauce in the pot and several garlic cloves, which your guests should squeeze out onto the croutons.

Serves 6.

431 CALORIES PER SERVING: 47 G PROTEIN, 7 G FAT, 41 G CARBOHYDRATE; 448 MG SODIUM; 109 MG CHOLESTEROL.

Chicken Sauté With Citrus Sauce

*Using whole, fresh fruit and marmalade makes this
sauce thicker and sweeter than it would be with just the juice.*

1 medium-sized orange
1 small pink grapefruit
¼ cup all-purpose white flour
salt and freshly ground black pepper
4 boneless, skinless chicken breasts, trimmed
   (1 lb. total)

1 Tbsp. vegetable oil
1 leek, trimmed, cleaned and sliced
¼ cup dry vermouth
2 Tbsp. orange marmalade
2 Tbsp. chopped fresh mint or ½ tsp. dried

Using a sharp knife, remove skin and white pith from the orange and grapefruit and discard. Cut the segments away from their surrounding membranes into a bowl (discard seeds). Squeeze any remaining juice from the membranes into the bowl. Drain the segments and measure the juice. Add enough water, if necessary, to make ½ cup and set the juice and fruit aside.

Combine flour, ½ tsp. salt and ½ tsp. pepper in a shallow dish. Dredge chicken breasts lightly in the flour mixture. Heat 2 tsp. oil in a nonstick skillet over medium-high heat. Add chicken and cook for 3 to 4 minutes per side, or until golden on the outside and no longer pink inside. (Reduce heat to medium if the chicken is browning too quickly.) Remove and keep warm. Add remaining 1 tsp. oil to the skillet. Add leeks and cook, stirring, for about 3 minutes, or until softened. Add reserved fruit juices and vermouth and bring to a boil. Boil for about 3 minutes, or until reduced by half. Reduce heat to low and add marmalade, reserved fruit, mint and salt and pepper to taste. Return the chicken to the skillet and reheat gently.

Serves 4.

311 CALORIES PER SERVING: 32 G PROTEIN, 7 G FAT, 26 G CARBOHYDRATE; 79 MG SODIUM; 82 MG CHOLESTEROL.

Chicken Forestière

*This healthful version of a classic chicken sauté
with mushroom sauce is rich-tasting even without the cream.*

3 Tbsp. all-purpose white flour
salt and freshly ground black pepper
2 boneless, skinless chicken breasts, trimmed
   (½ lb. total)
1 Tbsp. vegetable oil

2 Tbsp. minced shallots or onions
2 cups sliced mushrooms (¼ lb.)
¾ cup defatted chicken stock
½ cup dry white wine
1 Tbsp. chopped fresh parsley or chives

Combine 2 Tbsp. flour, ¼ tsp. salt and ¼ tsp. pepper in a shallow dish. Dredge chicken breasts in the flour mixture. Heat 2 tsp. oil in a nonstick skillet over medium heat. Add chicken and cook for 3 to 4 minutes per side, or until golden on the outside and no longer pink inside. (Reduce heat to medium if chicken is browning too quickly.) Remove and keep warm. Add remaining 1 tsp. oil to the skillet. Add shallots or onions and cook, stirring, for 10 to 20 seconds.

Add mushrooms and sauté for 1 to 2 minutes, or until softened and browned. Add remaining 1 Tbsp. flour and cook, stirring for 30 seconds. Pour in stock and wine and bring to a boil, stirring. Cook for 5 minutes, or until slightly thickened. Reduce heat to low and stir in parsley or chives. Season with salt and pepper to taste. Return the chicken to the pan and heat gently.

Serves 2.

301 CALORIES PER SERVING: 35 G PROTEIN, 11 G FAT, 14 G CARBOHYDRATE; 115 MG SODIUM; 82 MG CHOLESTEROL.

Chicken Curry With Yogurt

The addition of apricot preserves makes this curry taste faintly of chutney.
Serve it with brown rice seasoned with curry powder.

2 cloves garlic, minced
1 medium-sized onion, chopped
1 Tbsp. olive oil
2 boneless chicken breasts, skinned, halved
   and cubed (½ lb. total)
1½ tsp. ground coriander
1 tsp. ground ginger
¾ tsp. ground cumin

½ tsp. ground cardamom
⅛ tsp. cayenne pepper or more to taste
½ cup golden raisins
¼ cup apricot preserves
2 cups low-fat or nonfat yogurt
2 Tbsp. cornstarch
salt and pepper

In a large skillet, sauté garlic and onions in oil until golden. Add chicken and sauté until browned. Add ¼ cup water, coriander, ginger, cumin, cardamom, cayenne, raisin, and apricot preserves. Simmer uncovered for 15 to 20 minutes, stirring occasionally until chicken is cooked. The liquid will be mostly absorbed. Gradually stir yogurt into cornstarch until dissolved. Stir mixture into skillet. Simmer gently, stirring constantly, until sauce thickens and no taste of cornstarch remains. Do not boil. Season with salt and pepper.

Serves 4.

379 CALORIES PER SERVING: 34 G PROTEIN, 8 G FAT, 42 G CARBOHYDRATE; 149 MG SODIUM; 80 MG CHOLESTEROL.

Crusty Herbed Chicken

A crunchy crust of crumbs and minced herbs seals in the natural juices.

1 lemon (3 Tbsp. juice)
2 Tbsp. olive oil
2 tsp. black peppercorns, cracked with a
    hammer or heavy-bottomed pot
2 cloves garlic, crushed
6-10 pieces chicken with bone, skinned
    (about 4 lbs.)

2 cups fresh whole-wheat bread crumbs,
    toasted *(page 242)*
⅔ cup minced fresh herbs (approximately
    6 Tbsp. chopped scallions or chives,
    1 Tbsp. rosemary, 1 Tbsp. sage)

Using a vegetable peeler, remove half the rind from the lemon and cut it into strips. Juice the lemon. Combine lemon rind, juice, oil, pepper and garlic, and place the mixture in a large plastic bag. Shake to blend seasonings. Add chicken, squeeze out excess air, seal and marinate in the refrigerator until cooking time, or for at least 2 hours.

Prepare a charcoal fire or preheat a gas grill. In a large, shallow dish, combine crumbs and chopped herbs. Remove chicken from the marinade, brush off lemon rind and peppercorns, and roll each piece in the herbed-crumb mixture. Coat each piece as thickly and evenly as possible. Cook at once on a greased grill over medium-hot coals, turning every 10 to 15 minutes, until juices run clear, about 30 to 40 minutes.

Serves 6.

435 CALORIES PER SERVING: 49 G PROTEIN, 14 G FAT, 27 G CARBOHYDRATE; 369 MG SODIUM; 134 MG CHOLESTEROL.

Grilled Mustard Chicken

A distinctive blend of three mustards keeps these chicken breasts moist and tasty.

¼ cup Dijon mustard
¼ cup coarse-grain (stone-ground) mustard
¼ cup German mustard
¼ cup white vinegar
⅓ cup apple juice
1½ Tbsp. fresh lemon juice

¼ tsp. grated lemon zest
1 shallot, peeled and thinly sliced
1 clove garlic, minced
freshly ground black pepper
vegetable oil for brushing grill
4 boneless, skinless chicken breasts (1 lb. total)

In a shallow nonaluminum dish, combine mustards, vinegar, juices, zest, shallots, garlic and pepper. Add chicken and turn to coat. Cover and marinate for 2 to 4 hours in the refrigerator, turning occasionally. Shortly before serving, prepare a charcoal fire or preheat a gas grill. Remove chicken from marinade, discard marinade, and cook chicken on a lightly oiled grill for about 3 to 4 minutes per side, or until no longer pink inside.

Serves 4.

164 CALORIES PER SERVING: 30 G PROTEIN, 4 G FAT, 1 G CARBOHYDRATE; 123 MG SODIUM; 82 MG CHOLESTEROL.

Crusty Herbed Chicken

Chicken & Pasta

The real heart of this Greek dish is its ample gravy. It is equally delicious without the chicken.

1 Tbsp. olive oil
1 large chicken, cut into 8 pieces, skinned
   (about 5 lbs.)
2 large onions, finely chopped
2-3 cloves garlic, finely chopped
2 lbs. ripe tomatoes, peeled, seeded and
   chopped (about 5 medium-sized)
½ cup dry red wine

1 Tbsp. wine vinegar
3 whole cloves
2 bay leaves
pinch paprika
pinch cinnamon
1 lb. spaghetti or elbow macaroni
¼ cup freshly grated Parmesan
salt and freshly ground black pepper to taste

In a Dutch oven, heat oil and brown chicken in batches over medium-high heat for 3 to 4 minutes per side. Set aside. Discard all but 2 tsp. of the fat in the pan. Add onions and garlic and fry, stirring occasionally, for 2 to 3 minutes, or until softened. Add 1⅔ cups water, tomatoes, wine, vinegar, cloves, bay leaves, paprika and cinnamon. Bring to a boil and reduce heat. Add chicken, cover and simmer until chicken is tender and juices run clear, about 45 minutes. Remove chicken and keep warm. Remove bay leaves and cloves from the sauce; discard. Skim fat and set sauce aside.

In a large pot of lightly salted boiling water, cook spaghetti or macaroni for 5 minutes (it will still be quite firm). Drain, stir it into the sauce and simmer, uncovered, for about 5 minutes, or until tender, stirring occasionally. Taste and adjust seasonings. Serve with grated Parmesan, with the chicken as either a separate course or on the side.

Serves 8.

487 CALORIES PER SERVING: 48 G PROTEIN, 8 G FAT, 51 G CARBOHYDRATE; 172 MG SODIUM; 105 MG CHOLESTEROL.

Northern-Style Shredded Chicken With Tomatoes

Moist and delicate, this dish has a complexity of flavor that
belies its simple ingredients. Serve in corn or flour tortillas (page 44).
Quick-Cooked Tomatillo-Chili Sauce (page 187) complements this filling nicely.

¼ medium-sized onion, roughly chopped,
  plus 1 medium-sized onion
3 large chicken breast halves (about 1½ lbs.
  total, with bone)
½ tsp. mixed dried herbs (such as marjoram
  and thyme)
2 bay leaves
3 cloves garlic
1 Tbsp. vegetable oil

2 ripe tomatoes, roasted or boiled *(page 242)*,
  peeled and chopped, or one 15-oz. can
  tomatoes, drained and chopped
2 large scallions, root ends removed,
  chopped in ¼" pieces
2-3 fresh hot green chilies to taste (roughly
  2-3 serrano chilies or 1-2 jalapeños,
  stemmed, seeded and finely chopped)
salt to taste, about ½ tsp.

Place ¼ onion and 4 cups water in a 2-qt. saucepan and bring to a boil. Add chicken breasts (plus additional hot water to cover, if necessary). Skim off any foam that rises during the first minute of simmering, add herbs and bay leaves, partially cover and simmer over medium heat for 13 minutes, or until juices run clear when the flesh is pierced with a skewer. Remove the saucepan from the heat and let the chicken cool in the broth. Discard bay leaves and reserve broth. Skim off any fat. Skin and bone chicken, then shred the meat into small pieces.

Dice remaining onion and mince garlic. Heat oil in a large, heavy-bottomed, nonstick skillet over medium-high heat. When hot, add onions and stir frequently for 4 to 5 minutes, until lightly browned. Reduce heat to medium, add garlic, tomatoes, scallions and chilies, and cook, stirring frequently, until the tomatoes have softened, about 4 minutes. Stir in ⅔ cup of the reserved broth, then simmer until the liquid has almost evaporated, about 5 to 10 minutes. Add chicken, heat through, and season with salt.

Makes enough for 10 tacos. Serves 4 to 6 as a light main course.

172 CALORIES FOR EACH OF 4 SERVINGS: 22 G PROTEIN, 6 G FAT, 8 G CARBOHYDRATE; 323 MG SODIUM; 55 MG CHOLESTEROL.

Vietnamese Chicken Salad

*This delicate chicken salad can be eaten on its own as an appetizer,
with sticky rice (page 103) as a main course or, as the Vietnamese often do,
as a side dish to accompany Chicken & Cellophane-Noodle Soup (page 53).*

2 lbs. bone-in chicken pieces, excess fat
   removed
3 Tbsp. fresh lime juice
3 Tbsp. fish sauce
2 Tbsp. rice vinegar
1 Tbsp. sugar
2-3 "bird" or serrano chili peppers with
   seeds, finely chopped
2 large cloves garlic, finely chopped

1 large red onion, thinly sliced
1 cup bean sprouts
2 cups shredded Chinese cabbage (Napa)
⅔ cup fresh Vietnamese coriander or fresh
   basil or mint leaves, shredded, plus 10 to
   12 leaves for garnish
lettuce leaves
freshly ground black pepper

Poach chicken in lightly salted, simmering water for about 30 minutes, or until juices run clear when flesh is pierced with a skewer. Remove from the liquid and let cool. Discard skin. Remove the meat from the bones and shred. (There should be about 2 cups.)

In a small, nonaluminum bowl, stir together lime juice, fish sauce, rice vinegar, sugar, chili peppers and garlic. Stir in onions, cover and let steep at room temperature for 30 minutes, or until needed.

Blanch bean sprouts in boiling water for 1 minute. Drain and refresh with cold water. In a large bowl, combine chicken, bean sprouts, cabbage and Vietnamese coriander or basil or mint. Add sauce and toss to mix well. Line a serving platter with lettuce leaves and spoon chicken mixture over lettuce. Grind black pepper over top and garnish with Vietnamese coriander, basil or mint leaves.

Serves 6.

136 CALORIES PER SERVING: 21 G PROTEIN, 3 G FAT, 7 G CARBOHYDRATE; 83 MG SODIUM; 54 MG CHOLESTEROL.

Cold Chicken & Avocado With *Chile Chipotle*

Without the chiles chipotles *(smoky, hot jalapeños), this dish
loses many of its special qualities, though it can be made using pickled
jalapeños and chopped fresh cilantro. Serve with corn or flour tortillas (page 44).*

1 chicken leg-and-thigh quarter or 1 large
 bone-in breast half (½ lb. total)
½ tsp. salt
2 small boiling potatoes, preferably red-
 skinned ones, halved (about 6 oz. total)
2 medium-sized carrots, peeled and cut into
 1½" lengths (about 6 oz. total)
¼ cup cider vinegar
1 tsp. dried oregano
½ tsp. salt

2-4 canned *chiles chipotles*, seeded and
 minced, or substitute 1 Tbsp. chopped fresh
 cilantro plus 2 tsp. pickled jalapeños,
 seeded and chopped
¼ small onion, finely diced
4 large romaine lettuce leaves, sliced in ½"
 strips, plus several whole leaves for garnish
1 ripe avocado, peeled, pitted and diced
1 slice of onion, broken into rings, for garnish

Bring 2 cups water to a boil in a medium-sized saucepan, add chicken and salt, skim off the foam that rises as the water returns to a boil, partially cover and simmer over medium heat—20 to 23 minutes for the dark meat, 13 to 15 minutes for the breast. Cool the chicken in the broth.

Boil potatoes and carrots in salted water to cover until they are just tender, 12 to 15 minutes. Rinse for a moment under cold water, strip off the potato skins, if you wish, then cut potatoes and carrots into ½-inch dice. Place in a large mixing bowl.

Skin and bone chicken, then tear the meat into large shreds and add to the potatoes. Skim off all fat on top of the broth, then measure 3 Tbsp. of broth

into a small bowl. Stir in vinegar, oregano and salt. Pour the dressing over the chicken mixture and add *chiles chipotles* or cilantro-jalapeño mixture and diced onions. Stir, cover and let stand for 45 minutes, refrigerated.

Shortly before serving, mix sliced lettuce and diced avocado into the chicken mixture. Toss lightly. Taste for salt.

Line a serving platter with the remaining romaine leaves and pile on the chicken mixture. Decorate with onion rings.

Makes enough for 12 tacos. Serves 4 as a light main course.

175 CALORIES FOR EACH OF 4 SERVINGS: 9 G PROTEIN, 9 G FAT, 18 G CARBOHYDRATE; 603 MG SODIUM; 18 MG CHOLESTEROL.

Turkey Scallopini Marsala

Simple and elegant; serve with mashed potatoes.

¼ cup all-purpose white flour
½ tsp. salt
¼ tsp. freshly ground black pepper
1 lb. turkey cutlets
vegetable cooking spray

1 Tbsp. vegetable oil
½ lb. mushrooms, trimmed, cleaned and
   thinly sliced
½ cup Marsala
1 tsp. chopped fresh parsley

Shake flour with salt and pepper in a plastic bag, then turn out onto a piece of wax paper. Dip each cutlet into the flour until well coated. Fry in batches over medium heat in a nonstick skillet coated with vegetable cooking spray until lightly colored on both sides, about 2 minutes per side, turning once. (The cutlets will not be very brown, but will take on color from the sauce.) Transfer to a warm plate.

Heat oil in the same skillet. Sauté mushrooms over high heat until they are softened, about 2 to 3 minutes, keeping them moving with a wooden spoon.

Cover the skillet, reduce heat to low and cook until tender, about 4 to 6 minutes. Transfer to a warm plate.

Over high heat, add Marsala to the skillet, scraping up any brown bits. Stir until slightly thickened, for 1 to 2 minutes. Return cutlets and mushrooms to the skillet, lower the heat and heat through. Taste and adjust seasonings. Arrange on a platter and garnish with parsley.

Serves 4.

266 CALORIES PER SERVING: 27 G PROTEIN, 6 G FAT, 9 G CARBOHYDRATE; 325 MG SODIUM; 57 MG CHOLESTEROL.

Turkey Scallopini Marsala

Sweet-&-Sour Turkey Meatballs

Ground turkey makes tender meatballs. If you do not have Italian seasonings on hand,
substitute a mixture of ¼ tsp. dried oregano, ¼ tsp. thyme, ¼ tsp. marjoram and ¼ tsp. basil.

SAUCE
4 8-oz. cans tomato sauce
1 small onion, minced
½ red bell pepper, seeded and minced
½ green bell pepper, seeded and minced
¼ cup packed brown sugar
¼ cup fresh lemon juice
¼ cup minced fresh parsley
2 cloves garlic, minced
1 tsp. Italian seasonings
½ tsp. freshly ground black pepper

MEATBALLS
1 medium-sized red potato, peeled
1 small onion, cut into large chunks
2 egg whites
1 tsp. Italian seasonings
1 clove garlic
1 tsp. salt
½ tsp. freshly ground black pepper
2½ lbs. ground turkey

To make sauce: Combine all ingredients in a 4-qt. saucepan. Simmer over medium-low heat for 30 minutes.

To make meatballs: In a food processor or blender, puree potato, onions, egg whites, Italian seasonings, garlic, salt and pepper until smooth. Transfer to a large bowl. Add turkey and mix thoroughly. Shape the mixture into 1-inch balls.

Add meatballs to the sauce. Shake to coat meatballs with sauce. Partially cover and simmer on low heat for 30 minutes. (Refrain from stirring for the first 30 minutes, or until the meatballs are firm.) Remove cover and simmer for another 30 minutes until sauce thickens. Shake the pot several times during cooking to avoid sticking.

Makes 32 1-inch meatballs; serves 8 as a main course or 16 as an appetizer.

227 CALORIES FOR EACH OF 16 SERVINGS: 33 G PROTEIN, 5 G FAT, 11 G CARBOHYDRATE; 561 MG SODIUM; 81 MG CHOLESTEROL.

Peppers Stuffed With Turkey

Ground turkey makes a delicious, low-fat substitute for hamburger in stuffed peppers. When prepared in the microwave, this meal can be ready in 20 minutes.

4 large green bell peppers
1½ tsp. vegetable oil
1 medium-sized onion, chopped
1 clove garlic, minced
1 lb. ground turkey

1½ cups cooked rice
1 8-oz. can tomato sauce (1 cup)
1 Tbsp. chopped fresh parsley
1 tsp. salt (optional)
¼ tsp. freshly ground black pepper

Conventional cooking method: Cut out stem ends of peppers and discard. Scoop out seeds. In a large pot bring 8 cups water to a boil and blanch peppers for 1 minute, or until tender-crisp. Drain and cool under cold running water. Set aside.

In a large, nonstick skillet, heat oil over medium heat. Add onions and garlic and sauté for 3 minutes, or until softened. Add turkey and sauté for 2 minutes, or just until it loses its pink color. Drain fat.

Preheat oven to 350 degrees F. In a medium-sized bowl, mix the turkey mixture with rice, ½ cup tomato sauce, parsley, salt (if using) and pepper. Stuff the peppers with the mixture and place them in a 2-qt. casserole dish. Spoon remaining ½ cup tomato sauce over the peppers. Cover and bake for 30 to 35 minutes, or until peppers are tender and filling is heated through.

Microwave method: Place prepared peppers upright in a 2-qt. microwaveproof casserole. Pour ¼ cup water over the bottom of the dish and cook, covered, in a microwave oven at 100 percent power for 2 minutes. Drain, cool under cold running water and set aside.

Crumble turkey into a bowl and add onions and garlic. Cook, uncovered, at 100 percent power for 4½ minutes, stirring once, until the meat loses its pink color. Drain fat. In a medium-sized bowl, mix turkey, rice, ½ cup tomato sauce, parsley, salt (if using) and pepper. Stuff the peppers with this mixture and return them to the casserole dish. Spoon remaining ½ cup tomato sauce over peppers. Cover and cook at 100 percent power for 10 to 12 minutes, or until peppers are tender and the filling is heated through.

Serves 4.

289 CALORIES PER SERVING: 28 G PROTEIN, 6 G FAT, 29 G CARBOHYDRATE; 436 MG SODIUM; 65 MG CHOLESTEROL.

Turkey Chili

Serve this basic, low-fat chili by itself or over baked potatoes, garnished with chopped scallions.

1 lb. ground turkey
1 large onion, finely chopped
1 green bell pepper, seeded and finely
　chopped
1 clove garlic, minced
1 15-oz. can red kidney beans, with juice

1 15-oz. can tomato sauce
1 14½-oz. can Mexican-style tomatoes,
　chopped, with juice
2 Tbsp. chili powder
1 tsp. ground cumin
salt and freshly ground black pepper to taste

In a nonstick Dutch oven or large skillet, sauté ground turkey, onions, peppers and garlic over medium-high heat for 10 minutes, or until meat is brown and vegetables are tender. Drain fat. Add remaining ingredients, reduce heat to low and simmer, uncovered, for 30 minutes. Taste and adjust seasonings.

Serves 6.

217 CALORIES PER SERVING: 23 G PROTEIN, 4 G FAT, 24 G CARBOHYDRATE; 839 MG SODIUM; 43 MG CHOLESTEROL.

Turkey Scallopini With Apricot Sauce

*This sweet-and-sour sauce with chunks of dried apricot
and flecks of mint is a nice way to season lean turkey cutlets.*

2 Tbsp. all-purpose white flour
salt and freshly ground black pepper
½ lb. turkey cutlets
2 tsp. vegetable oil
1½ Tbsp. minced shallots or onions
1½ tsp. peeled, minced gingerroot
⅓ cup apricot or peach nectar

⅓ cup defatted chicken stock
1 Tbsp. cider or wine vinegar
½ tsp. brown sugar
1 Tbsp. chopped dried apricots
1 Tbsp. currants
1 tsp. chopped fresh mint or ¼ tsp. dried

Combine flour, ¼ tsp. salt and ¼ tsp. pepper in a shallow dish. Dredge turkey lightly in the flour mixture. Heat oil in a nonstick skillet over medium-high heat. Add turkey and cook for 2 to 3 minutes per side, or until golden on the outside and no longer pink inside. Transfer to plates and keep warm. Add shallots or onions and ginger to the skillet and cook, stirring, for 10 to 20 seconds. Add nectar, chicken stock, vinegar and sugar and bring to a boil, stirring. Add apricots and currants and cook for several minutes, or until they are tender and the sauce has been reduced slightly. Remove from heat and stir in mint. Taste and adjust seasonings with salt and pepper to taste. Spoon the sauce over the turkey.

Serves 2.

259 CALORIES PER SERVING: 29 G PROTEIN, 6 G FAT, 21 G CARBOHYDRATE; 76 MG SODIUM; 68 MG CHOLESTEROL.

Rabbit Marinated in Cider & Peppercorns

Moist and faintly spicy, the rabbit is garnished with buttery-tasting apple slices.
The recipe is from Campagne restaurant in Seattle, Washington.

1 2-lb. rabbit, cut into 6 serving pieces
1 cup apple cider
2 Tbsp. Dijon mustard
2 Tbsp. green peppercorns
1½ Tbsp. chopped fresh thyme leaves plus
   more for garnish or 1 tsp. dried
1 Tbsp. crushed black peppercorns

½ tsp. red-pepper flakes
2 tsp. olive oil plus more for oiling
   roasting rack
1 firm apple, unpeeled
1 Tbsp. fresh lemon juice
2 tsp. butter
1 Tbsp. brown sugar

Place rabbit pieces in a nonaluminum shallow dish. In a small bowl, whisk together cider, mustard, green peppercorns, thyme, black peppercorns and red-pepper flakes and pour over the rabbit, turning to coat well. Cover and marinate in the refrigerator for 24 hours, turning occasionally.

Preheat oven to 450 degrees F. Brush marinade off the rabbit pieces, reserving it. Heat oil in a non-stick skillet over medium-high heat, and sear the rabbit pieces for 1 to 2 minutes per side, or until lightly browned. Place them on a lightly oiled rack in a roast-ing pan. Roast for 35 to 40 minutes, basting occasionally with the reserved marinade, until the juices run clear when the rabbit is pierced with a skewer.

Meanwhile, core and slice apple into ½-inch slices. Toss with lemon juice. Heat butter in a nonstick skillet over medium heat. Add apples, sprinkle with brown sugar and cook for 3 to 4 minutes, or until golden, turning once. Arrange rabbit on a serving platter and garnish with apple slices and fresh thyme, if using.

Serves 4.

251 CALORIES PER SERVING: 26 G PROTEIN, 11 G FAT, 11 G CARBOHYDRATE; 168 MG SODIUM; 78 MG CHOLESTEROL.

FISH & SHELLFISH

~

Grilled Salmon Steaks With Black-Bean Sauce

*Cusk, swordfish and halibut
are also excellent with this sauce.*

SAUCE
- ¾ cup Chinese Chicken Stock *(recipe follows)* or canned reduced-sodium chicken stock, defatted
- 3 Tbsp. rice wine or sake
- 1½ Tbsp. reduced-sodium soy sauce
- 4 tsp. cornstarch
- 2 tsp. sugar
- 2 tsp. canola or corn oil
- 3 Tbsp. fermented black beans, rinsed and drained
- 1½ Tbsp. minced garlic

(Recipe continues on next page)

Grilled Salmon Steaks With Black-Bean Sauce

SALMON
6 6-oz. salmon steaks, about ¾" thick
2 Tbsp. rice wine or sake
3 scallions, white and light green parts only,
  smashed lightly

2 slices gingerroot, about the size of a
  quarter, smashed lightly
1 tsp. sesame oil
canola or corn oil for greasing grill

To make sauce: In a small bowl, combine chicken stock, rice wine or sake, soy sauce, cornstarch and sugar. In a wok or heavy skillet, heat canola or corn oil over high heat. Add beans and garlic and stir-fry for 10 to 15 seconds, or until fragrant. Add the chicken-stock mixture and cook, stirring, until thickened, for 2 to 3 minutes. *(The sauce can be held in the refrigerator for up to 2 days. Reheat before serving.)*

To prepare salmon: Rinse salmon steaks and pat dry. Place them in a shallow nonaluminum dish. In a small bowl, combine rice wine or sake, smashed scallions and ginger. Press down on the scallions and ginger with the back of a spoon or a pestle for several minutes to extract their flavors. Stir in sesame oil. Pour the marinade over the salmon steaks. Turn to coat, cover and marinate at room temperature for 20 minutes or for 1 hour in the refrigerator.

Prepare a charcoal fire or preheat a gas grill. Brush the grill lightly with oil. Discard the scallions and ginger and grill the steaks about 3 inches from medium-hot coals for 3½ to 4½ minutes per side, or until the flesh is opaque. Reheat sauce and serve it with the salmon.

Serves 6.

291 CALORIES PER SERVING: 37 G PROTEIN, 12 G FAT, 6 G CARBOHYDRATE; 211 MG SODIUM; 63 MG CHOLESTEROL.

Chinese Chicken Stock

2 lbs. chicken wings (about 10)
⅓ cup rice wine or sake

3 slices gingerroot

Place all ingredients in a large saucepan and cover with 4 cups water. Bring to a boil, reduce heat to low and simmer, uncovered, for 1 hour, skimming any foam. Strain and discard solids. Chill and skim off fat. *(The stock can be stored in the refrigerator for up to 3 days or in the freezer for up to 6 months.)*

Makes about 2½ cups.

Roasted Salmon With Mustard Crust

Roasting salmon is as easy as broiling it, but the fish cooks more evenly and tastes richer this way.

4 6-oz. salmon steaks, about 1" thick, rinsed
   and patted dry
salt and freshly ground black pepper
3 Tbsp. Provençal, green peppercorn or
   other flavored mustard

fresh lemon juice
2 tsp. chopped fresh dill, basil or parsley
   for garnish

Preheat oven to 500 degrees F. Place a large cast-iron skillet or other heavy-bottomed ovenproof skillet over high heat and heat until smoking. Season salmon steaks with salt and pepper and spread them with 1½ Tbsp. mustard.

Place the steaks, mustard-side down, into the dry, smoking skillet and cook them for 2 minutes without turning or touching. Meanwhile, spread remaining 1½ Tbsp. mustard on the top sides of the steaks. Carefully flip them and transfer the entire skillet to the oven. Bake for 6 to 8 minutes, or until flesh is opaque. Remove the skillet from the oven and transfer the steaks to serving plates. Squeeze lemon juice over the steaks and sprinkle them with fresh herbs.

Serves 4.

245 CALORIES PER SERVING: 36 G PROTEIN, 10 G FAT, 1 G CARBOHYDRATE; 229 MG SODIUM; 63 MG CHOLESTEROL.

Peppered Salmon Steaks With Yogurt-Lime Marinade

The yogurt marinade, with hints of lime and ginger, makes the salmon wonderfully succulent.

½ cup low-fat yogurt
1 Tbsp. canola or safflower oil
1 Tbsp. fresh lime juice
1 tsp. honey
1 Tbsp. peeled, minced gingerroot

1 clove garlic, minced
¼ tsp. salt
freshly ground black pepper
4 salmon steaks, 1" thick
lime wedges

In a shallow nonaluminum dish, whisk together yogurt, oil, lime juice, honey, ginger, garlic, salt and ½ tsp. pepper. Add fish steaks and turn to coat with marinade. Cover and marinate in the refrigerator for at least 30 minutes or up to 1 hour, turning once. Prepare a charcoal fire or preheat a gas grill.

Coarsely grind pepper onto steaks and gently press in. Place steaks on a lightly oiled grill, and grill for 10 minutes per inch of thickness, turning once and brushing with any additional marinade, until the fish flesh is opaque. Serve immediately with lime wedges.

Serves 4.

371 CALORIES PER SERVING: 48 G PROTEIN, 17 G FAT, 4 G CARBOHYDRATE; 254 MG SODIUM; 86 MG CHOLESTEROL.

Broiled Salmon With Papaya-Mango Relish

*This relish yields enough for 8 to 12 servings, so you may want to double the
amount of salmon or save the remaining relish to serve with grilled chicken. If you make
the relish well in advance, add the avocado at the last minute to prevent it from turning brown.*

1 small papaya, peeled, seeded and diced
1 small mango, peeled, pitted and diced
1 green bell pepper, seeded and diced
1 red bell pepper, seeded and diced
1 yellow bell pepper, seeded and diced
1 jalapeño or serrano chili or to taste, seeded
    and minced

½ avocado, peeled, pitted and diced
4½ tsp. extra-virgin olive oil
3 Tbsp. fresh lime juice or to taste
2 Tbsp. balsamic vinegar or to taste
salt and freshly ground black pepper to taste
6 6-oz. salmon steaks

In a nonaluminum bowl, combine papayas, mangoes, peppers, chilies, avocados, 1 Tbsp. oil, 1 Tbsp. lime juice, vinegar and a pinch salt. Let marinate for at least 15 minutes at room temperature. Taste and adjust seasonings, adding a few grindings of black pepper, if desired. *(The relish can be made up to 8 hours in advance and refrigerated, but bring it to room temperature before serving.)*

Season salmon steaks with a little salt and remaining 2 Tbsp. lime juice. Let sit for 10 minutes. Pat salmon steaks dry and brush them lightly with remaining 1½ tsp. oil. Preheat the broiler. Heat a heavy-bottomed, ovenproof skillet, preferably cast iron, until very hot. Place the steaks in the skillet and place the skillet under the broiler. Broil for 2 to 3 minutes on each side, or until fish flesh is opaque. Remove the skin from each steak before serving and serve with relish.

Serves 6.

293 CALORIES PER SERVING: 36 G PROTEIN, 13 G FAT, 7 G CARBOHYDRATE; 78 MG SODIUM; 63 MG CHOLESTEROL.

Broiled Salmon With Papaya-Mango Relish

Thin Salmon Scallops With Herb Dressing

*This creation by French chef Michel Guérard is an
elegant meal. The sauce makes a good dip or salad dressing as well.*

¼ cup fromage blanc or low-fat yogurt
1 Tbsp. fresh lemon juice
2½ tsp. olive oil
1½ tsp. red-wine vinegar or to taste
¼ tsp. Worcestershire sauce
1½ tsp. chopped fresh parsley
1½ tsp. chopped fresh chervil or dill

½ tsp. finely chopped fresh basil or ¼ tsp.
   dried
¼ tsp. finely chopped fresh tarragon or
   pinch dried
salt and freshly ground black pepper
1 lb. fillet of salmon, skinned
sprigs fresh tarragon, dill or chervil

In a small bowl, whisk together fromage blanc or yogurt, 2 Tbsp. warm water, lemon juice, 1½ tsp. oil, red-wine vinegar, Worcestershire sauce, herbs, and salt and pepper to taste. *(The sauce can be made ahead, covered and refrigerated for up to 8 hours.)*

Preheat oven to 500 degrees F. Line a baking sheet with aluminum foil and brush with remaining 1 tsp. oil. Place salmon on a cutting board. With a sharp knife, slice across the grain into ¼-inch-thick slices.

Lay salmon slices on the baking sheet, making sure that they don't overlap, and season lightly with salt and pepper.

Bake the salmon for 1½ to 2 minutes, or just until fish flesh is opaque. Divide salmon scallops evenly among 4 plates. Place 1 Tbsp. sauce over each serving, spreading it out with the back of a spoon. Garnish with sprigs of fresh tarragon, dill or chervil.

Serves 4.

201 CALORIES PER SERVING: 25 G PROTEIN, 10 G FAT, 2 G CARBOHYDRATE; 66 MG SODIUM; 45 MG CHOLESTEROL.

ⓦ

Thin Salmon Scallops With Herb Dressing

Poached Cod With "Melted" Tomatoes

*This French sauce of tomatoes cooked until they "melt" is delicious with any
mild fish: hake, pollack, red snapper, black sea bass, grouper, tilapia, ocean perch
or orange roughy. It also goes well with shrimp, scallops and even chicken and veal.*

1 tsp. olive oil
2 Tbsp. minced shallots
2 tsp. minced garlic
2 Tbsp. dry white vermouth
2 cups peeled, diced tomatoes, fresh or canned
2 Tbsp. chopped black olives, preferably
    oil-cured

1 tsp. extra-virgin olive oil
salt and freshly ground black pepper
pinch sugar (optional)
1 tsp. white-wine vinegar or rice-wine vinegar
4 4-oz. cod fillets or other white-fleshed fish
lime or lemon wedges

Heat oil in a heavy-bottomed saucepan over low heat and add shallots and garlic. Cook, stirring often, until softened and slightly golden, about 5 minutes. Add vermouth, increase the heat to medium and simmer for 1 minute, until reduced by half. Add tomatoes and simmer 5 minutes, just until warmed through. Add olives, extra-virgin olive oil and salt and pepper to taste. Add sugar, if needed, to balance the acidity.

In a pan wide enough to hold the fillets in a single layer, combine 5 cups water, 1 Tbsp. salt and vinegar. Bring water to a simmer, then reduce heat to low. Lower the fillets into the water (they should be generously covered), and regulate the heat so that there is no more than an occasional shiver on the surface of the water. Cook fillets for 8 to 10 minutes per inch of thickness, or until fish flesh is opaque. When the fillets are done, remove them to plates with a spatula and spoon tomato sauce over them. Garnish with lime or lemon wedges.

Serves 4.

153 CALORIES PER SERVING: 21 G PROTEIN, 4 G FAT, 7 G CARBOHYDRATE; 292 MG SODIUM; 47 MG CHOLESTEROL.

Grilled Swordfish With Spicy Hot-&-Sour Sauce

When properly cooked, swordfish has a firm, sweet flavor
that lends itself nicely to this sauce. The fish may also be broiled.

SAUCE
1 cup Chinese Chicken Stock *(page 136)*
    or canned reduced-sodium chicken stock,
    defatted
3½ Tbsp. reduced-sodium soy sauce
2½ Tbsp. rice wine or sake
4 tsp. sugar
1 Tbsp. cornstarch
1 Tbsp. Chinese black vinegar or 1½ tsp.
    Worcestershire sauce
½ tsp. sesame oil
¼ tsp. freshly ground black pepper
1½ tsp. canola or corn oil
2 Tbsp. minced garlic

3 Tbsp. minced scallions, white and light
    green parts only
1 Tbsp. peeled, minced gingerroot
1½ tsp. chili paste or to taste
SWORDFISH
6 6-oz. swordfish steaks, ¾-1" thick
2 Tbsp. rice wine or sake
4 slices gingerroot, smashed lightly
4 scallions, white and light green parts only,
    smashed lightly, plus 1 Tbsp. minced green
    tops
1 tsp. sesame oil
canola or corn oil for greasing grill

To make sauce: In a small bowl, combine chicken stock, soy sauce, rice wine or sake, sugar, cornstarch, black vinegar or Worcestershire sauce, sesame oil and pepper. In a wok or a heavy skillet, heat canola or corn oil over high heat. Add garlic, scallions, ginger and chili paste and stir-fry until fragrant, about 10 to 15 seconds. Add the chicken-stock mixture and cook, stirring, until thickened, for 2 to 3 minutes. *(The sauce can be prepared ahead and held in the refrigerator for up to 2 days. Reheat before serving.)*

To prepare swordfish: Rinse swordfish steaks and pat dry. Place in a shallow nonaluminum dish. In a small bowl, combine rice wine or sake, ginger and 4 scallions. Press down on the scallions and ginger

with the back of a spoon or a pestle for several minutes to extract their flavors. Stir in sesame oil and pour over swordfish steaks. Turn to coat, cover and marinate for 20 minutes at room temperature or for 1 hour in the refrigerator.

Prepare a charcoal fire or preheat a gas grill. Brush the grill lightly with oil. Discard ginger and scallions and grill the steaks about 3 inches from medium-hot coals for 3 to 5 minutes per side, or until flesh is opaque. Meanwhile, reheat sauce. Place fish on platter, spoon some of the sauce over the fish and sprinkle with minced green tops of scallions. Pass remaining sauce separately.

Serves 6.

250 CALORIES PER SERVING: 34 G PROTEIN, 8 G FAT, 6 G CARBOHYDRATE; 478 MG SODIUM; 65 MG CHOLESTEROL.

Teriyaki-Grilled Swordfish

This recipe is also good with tuna or salmon steaks.

⅔ cup reduced-sodium soy sauce
½ cup medium-dry sherry
1 Tbsp. sugar

1 clove garlic, crushed
2 tsp. peeled, minced gingerroot
1½ lbs. swordfish steaks, at least ¾" thick

In a small saucepan, combine soy sauce, sherry, sugar, garlic and ginger. Bring to a boil over moderate heat, then strain into a shallow nonaluminum pan. Let cool. Marinate fish steaks in this mixture for about 30 minutes, turning several times. Preheat broiler or prepare a charcoal or gas grill. Broil swordfish on a foil-covered baking sheet, or grill on a greased grill over medium-hot coals, for 10 minutes per inch of thickness, or until fish is opaque, brushing with the marinade. Turn once halfway through the cooking. If desired, the remaining marinade may be used as a dipping sauce. (Boil it before serving.) Cut steaks into serving-sized portions. Serves 6.

154 CALORIES PER SERVING: 23 G PROTEIN, 5 G FAT, 4 G CARBOHYDRATE; 275 MG SODIUM; 44 MG CHOLESTEROL.

Grilled Orange Roughy Margarita

Red snapper, grouper and sea trout also taste good made this way.

1½ lbs. orange roughy fillets
⅓ cup white or gold tequila
½ cup triple sec
¾ cup fresh lime juice
1 tsp. salt plus more to taste
2 large cloves garlic, crushed
1 Tbsp. vegetable oil

3 medium-sized tomatoes, diced
1 medium-sized onion, finely chopped
1 Tbsp. minced jalapeño or serrano chilies or
   to taste
2 Tbsp. chopped fresh cilantro
pinch sugar
freshly ground black pepper

Place fish in a nonaluminum dish just large enough to hold it in a single layer. Combine tequila, triple sec, lime juice, 1 tsp. salt, garlic and 2 tsp. oil and pour over fish, rubbing it all over. Cover and marinate for ½ hour at room temperature or up to 3 hours in the refrigerator, turning and basting occasionally.

Shortly before serving time, combine tomatoes, onions, chilies, cilantro, sugar and salt to taste. Heat the grill to very hot. Remove fish from the marinade (reserve marinade), pat dry and brush lightly with remaining 1 tsp. oil and grind pepper over the surface. Cook on a greased grill for about 4 minutes per side or until fish flesh is opaque. Meanwhile, boil marinade in a saucepan for about 2 minutes, remove and discard garlic cloves. Arrange fish on plates and spoon a little marinade over each portion. Spoon the tomato salsa alongside. Serves 6.

226 CALORIES PER SERVING: 22 G PROTEIN, 4 G FAT, 14 G CARBOHYDRATE; 454 MG SODIUM; 41 MG CHOLESTEROL.

Teriyaki-Grilled Swordfish and Japanese Spinach Salad With Sesame Seeds

Halibut With Lemon & Caper Sauce

If using fish steaks, chill them in the freezer for ½ to 1 hour so
they will be easy to slice. Fillets of sole, orange roughy, ocean perch or
catfish are delicious cooked this way but do not need to be sliced before cooking.

½ lemon or more to taste
¼ cup all-purpose white flour
½ tsp. salt
½ tsp. freshly ground black pepper
1 lb. fillet of halibut, monkfish or swordfish
   (about 1½" thick), cut into ¼"-thick
   diagonal slices

2 tsp. olive oil
1 clove garlic, minced
⅓ cup fish or defatted chicken stock
1 Tbsp. capers (optional)
2 tsp. butter
1 Tbsp. chopped fresh parsley

With a sharp knife, remove skin and white pith from lemon and discard. Cut the segments of the fruit away from their surrounding membranes into a bowl (discard seeds). Strain and reserve juice. Chop fruit coarsely.

Combine flour, salt and pepper in a shallow dish. Dredge fish lightly in the flour mixture. Heat oil in a large, nonstick skillet over medium-high heat. Cook the fish for 1 to 3 minutes per side, or until the out-side is golden brown and the interior is opaque. Transfer to plates or a platter and keep warm. Add garlic to the skillet and cook, stirring, for several seconds. Add fish or chicken stock and bring to a boil, stirring. Add lemon and juice, capers (if using) and butter, swirling the skillet until the butter has melted. Spoon the sauce over the fish. Sprinkle with parsley and grind more pepper over top.

Serves 4.

191 CALORIES PER SERVING: 24 G PROTEIN, 7 G FAT, 7 G CARBOHYDRATE; 348 MG SODIUM; 41 MG CHOLESTEROL.

Braised Tuna Milanese-Style

This dish is also delicious with swordfish. To save time, chop the vegetables in a food processor.

1½ lbs. tuna
1 cup dry white wine
2 tsp. olive oil
1 tsp. minced garlic
1 bay leaf
¼ tsp. dried leaf thyme
2 tsp. salt
1 tsp. freshly ground black pepper
1½ cups finely chopped onions
½ cup finely diced carrots
½ cup finely diced celery
1 16-oz. can tomatoes, with juice, coarsely
  crushed or chopped

1 cup fish or defatted chicken stock
¼ cup chopped fresh basil (optional)
GREMOLATA
2 Tbsp. finely chopped fresh parsley
1 tsp. minced garlic
2 tsp. grated lemon zest or a combination
  lemon and orange zest

2 tsp. olive or vegetable oil
about ¼ cup all-purpose white flour for
  dredging
2 tsp. butter
salt

Cut tuna into 6 uniform chunks. In a nonaluminum bowl, combine white wine, 2 tsp. olive oil, 1 tsp. garlic, bay leaf, thyme, 2 tsp. salt and black pepper. Add tuna and marinate, turning and basting occasionally, for 30 minutes or up to 6 hours in the refrigerator. Meanwhile, combine onions, carrots and celery in one bowl and tomatoes, stock and basil (if using) in another.

Make gremolata by combining parsley, 1 tsp. garlic and lemon and/or orange zest.

Remove tuna from marinade (reserve marinade) and wipe chunks dry with paper towels. In a heavy, nonaluminum skillet or flameproof casserole dish large enough to hold the tuna in a single layer, heat 2 tsp. oil over medium-high heat. Dredge tuna lightly in flour, shaking off the excess. Brown it lightly on all sides in the oil for about 1 to 2 minutes per side. Remove to a platter and blot off the oil with paper towels. Refrigerate.

Add butter to pan, add diced vegetable mixture and sauté over low heat until tender, about 5 to 10 minutes. Add half the gremolata and cook briefly, about 1 minute. Add the tomato mixture and the reserved marinade. Bring to a boil, lower the heat and simmer gently, covered, for about 1 hour, stirring occasionally. Discard bay leaf.

Add tuna to the sauce in a single layer and baste. Cook, uncovered, over low heat for 10 to 15 minutes, basting several times, or just until the inside of the flesh is slightly pink. Remove tuna to a serving platter. Boil the sauce over high heat for 5 to 10 minutes to reduce it. Pour sauce over tuna. Season with salt and pepper to taste and sprinkle on remaining gremolata.

Serves 6.

262 CALORIES PER SERVING: 37 G PROTEIN, 4 G FAT, 12 G CARBOHYDRATE; 937 MG SODIUM; 54 MG CHOLESTEROL.

Stir-Fried Monkfish & Asparagus

*New York's neighborhood Chinese restaurants celebrate
spring with a menu that features asparagus. Here is one variation.*

1½ lbs. monkfish fillets, trimmed of dark
    flesh and cut into 1" cubes
salt
1¼ tsp. sugar
3 large dried mushrooms, preferably shiitake
1¼ lbs. medium-sized asparagus, trimmed
    and cut into diagonal ½" long slices
3 Tbsp. rice wine or dry sherry
2 Tbsp. sodium-reduced soy sauce
2 Tbsp. Chinese chili sauce or to taste
2 Tbsp. hoisin sauce

1 Tbsp. ketchup
½ tsp. dark sesame oil
1 tsp. cornstarch, mixed with 1 Tbsp. cold
    water
2 tsp. peanut oil
1 Tbsp. minced garlic
1 Tbsp. peeled, minced gingerroot
1 large red bell pepper, seeded and thinly
    sliced
3 scallions, trimmed and thinly sliced

In a nonaluminum bowl, toss monkfish with ½ tsp. salt and ¼ tsp. sugar. Soak mushrooms for 20 minutes in hot water until softened, drain, remove and discard stems and slice caps, if whole. Blanch asparagus in boiling, salted water for 30 seconds. Drain and refresh in cold water. Combine rice wine or sherry, soy sauce, chili sauce, hoisin, ketchup, remaining 1 tsp. sugar and sesame oil and taste for seasoning.

Stir cornstarch mixture into the fish by hand, gently but thoroughly. In a wok, heat ½ tsp. peanut oil over high heat. Stir-fry the fish in batches, cooking half at a time and using 1 tsp. oil in all. Cook 4 to 5 minutes, or until fish flesh is opaque. Set aside. Add the remaining 1 tsp. peanut oil, garlic and ginger and stir-fry for about 30 seconds. Add asparagus, peppers, mushrooms and the soy-sauce mixture and toss well. Return the fish to the wok and toss in scallions.
Serves 6.

165 CALORIES PER SERVING: 19 G PROTEIN, 4 G FAT, 12 G CARBOHYDRATE; 376 MG SODIUM; 28 MG CHOLESTEROL.

Oven-Steamed Flounder With Cantonese Flavors

Black sea bass, red snapper, walleye (yellow pike) and sole are also delicious prepared this way.

4 scallions, trimmed and cut into 2" julienne
    strips
2" piece gingerroot, peeled and cut into
    julienne strips
4 4-oz. flounder fillets
2 Tbsp. light or reduced-sodium soy sauce

2 Tbsp. dry sherry
1 tsp. sesame oil
½ tsp. sugar
dash hot chili oil or large pinch white pepper
cilantro for garnish (optional)

Preheat oven to 375 degrees F. Scatter about ⅓ of the scallions and ginger into a 9-by-13-inch baking dish. Place fillets in the dish, with the side that has silvery connective tissue facing down, folding any thin tail ends under to create a uniform thickness. Scatter on remaining ginger and most of the remaining scallions, reserving a few for the garnish. In a small bowl, combine soy sauce, sherry, sesame oil, sugar and chili oil or pepper and pour the mixture evenly over the fish. Let marinate for 15 minutes.

Seal the baking dish with foil and place it in the oven. Bake for 15 minutes, or until the fish flesh is opaque. Garnish with remaining scallions and cilantro (if using).

Serves 4.

137 CALORIES PER SERVING: 23 G PROTEIN, 3 G FAT, 2 G CARBOHYDRATE; 393 MG SODIUM; 40 MG CHOLESTEROL.

↜

Stir-Fried Scallops With Walnuts & Snow Peas

*Scallops are extraordinarily low in fat, and much of
the fat they do have is from healthful omega-3 fatty acids.*

1 Tbsp. cornstarch
½ cup defatted, reduced-sodium chicken
    stock, cooled
2 Tbsp. dry sherry
2 Tbsp. reduced-sodium soy sauce
1 tsp. peeled, minced gingerroot
¼ tsp. red-pepper flakes or to taste
1 Tbsp. vegetable oil

1 Tbsp. minced garlic
8 scallions, including green tops, sliced
    diagonally into 1" lengths
1½ cups snow peas, strings removed (⅓ lb.)
1¼ lbs. sea scallops, halved or quartered,
    patted dry
3 Tbsp. coarsely chopped walnut halves,
    toasted *(page 242)*

Preheat oven to 350 degrees F. Place cornstarch in a small bowl and slowly whisk in chicken stock. Whisk in sherry, soy sauce, ginger and red-pepper flakes.

Place 1½ tsp. oil in a wok or nonstick skillet over high heat. When the oil is hot, add garlic, scallions and snow peas and stir-fry for 2 minutes, until the peas are tender-crisp. Remove from the wok. Add remaining 1½ tsp. oil and scallops and stir-fry for 1 minute. Stir in the chicken-stock mixture and cook until slightly thickened, about 1 minute. Add scallions, snow peas, garlic and walnuts. Cook to heat through for 1 minute longer, but do not overcook the scallops.

Serves 4.

242 CALORIES PER SERVING: 28 G PROTEIN, 8 G FAT, 12 G CARBOHYDRATE; 492 MG SODIUM; 47 MG CHOLESTEROL.

Catfish en Papillote With Lime & Chives

Because farm-raised catfish has a sweet, clean flavor, it has become something of an all-purpose fish. Feel free to vary the herbs called for according to availability and taste. Any white-fleshed fish can be fixed this way. If you don't have parchment paper, use aluminum foil.

1 4-oz. catfish fillet
salt and freshly ground black pepper
1 tsp. butter, softened
2 tsp. chopped fresh chives or scallion tops
½ tsp. fresh thyme or lemon thyme leaves or ¼ tsp. dried
1 sprig flat-leaved parsley
3 thin lime slices

Preheat oven to 400 degrees F. Cut a round of parchment paper or aluminum foil to a diameter at least 3 inches greater than the length of the fillet. Season fillet lightly on both sides with salt and pepper and place it, with the side that has silvery connective tissue facing down, on one half of the parchment. If the fillet has a thin tail end, fold it under so that the fish has a uniform thickness. Spread butter over the surface of the fillet and sprinkle with chives or scallions, thyme and parsley. Arrange lime slices over it.

Fold the parchment or foil over the fish and seal: starting at one end, make a series of small, overlapping folds, pressing each one flat to make a border all around, pressing out excess air as you reach the end.

Place the packet on a baking sheet and bake for 15 minutes, or until the paper is puffed and lightly browned. Transfer the packet to a plate and cut it open at the table, folding the cut edges under.

Serves 1.

174 CALORIES PER SERVING: 21 G PROTEIN, 9 G FAT, 2 G CARBOHYDRATE; 113 MG SODIUM; 76 MG CHOLESTEROL.

Catfish Meunière

Fish made meunière-style is lightly dusted with flour and flash-sautéed. Despite—or perhaps because of—its simplicity, the taste is wonderful. Here, catfish takes the place of the usual sole.

¼ cup low-fat milk
1 egg
⅓ cup all-purpose white flour
½ tsp. salt
½ tsp. cayenne pepper
4 catfish fillets (about 1 lb. total)

2 tsp. vegetable oil
1 Tbsp. butter
2 Tbsp. fresh lemon juice
2 Tbsp. chopped fresh parsley
½ tsp. Worcestershire sauce
parsley sprigs and lemon wedges for garnish

In a shallow pan, beat together milk and egg. In another shallow pan, combine flour, salt and cayenne pepper. Dip fillets in milk mixture and then in flour mixture, shaking off excess. Heat oil in a large non-stick skillet over medium heat, add fillets and cook until golden brown, turning only once, cooking about 2 to 3 minutes per side, or until fish flesh is opaque.

Meanwhile, melt butter in a small saucepan. Stir in lemon juice, parsley and Worcestershire sauce. Transfer catfish to a serving plate and spoon butter sauce over catfish. Garnish with parsley sprigs and lemon wedges.
Serves 4.

244 CALORIES PER SERVING: 24 G PROTEIN, 11 G FAT, 10 G CARBOHYDRATE; 398 MG SODIUM; 127 MG CHOLESTEROL.

Baked Bluefish au Poivre

The pepper forms a nice crust in this dish, which distinguishes itself by its simplicity and savor. Red snapper, black sea bass, grouper, sea trout and tilefish would also work here.

4 4-oz. bluefish fillets, skinned
4 Tbsp. fresh lemon juice
1-2 large cloves garlic, smashed
1 tsp. olive oil

salt to taste
1 Tbsp. cracked black peppercorns
4 parsley sprigs plus more for garnish
lemon slices for garnish

Preheat oven to 450 degrees F. Place fillets in a 9-by-13-inch baking dish. Spoon 2 Tbsp. lemon juice over the fillets and rub with garlic and ½ tsp. oil. Season lightly with salt and press 1½ tsp. peppercorns into them. Turn over and repeat on the other side, using the remaining 2 Tbsp. lemon juice, garlic, ½ tsp. oil, salt and 1½ tsp. peppercorns. Place a sprig

of parsley and a piece of the garlic under each fillet.
Bake for 8 to 10 minutes per inch of thickness, or until the fish flesh is opaque. Transfer to a platter and spoon on any pan juices. Garnish with lemon slices and parsley sprigs.
Serves 4.

153 CALORIES PER SERVING: 23 G PROTEIN, 6 G FAT, 3 G CARBOHYDRATE; 90 MG SODIUM; 44 MG CHOLESTEROL.

Catfish Meunière

Shrimp With Lime Dressing & Crunchy Vegetables

With warm tortillas or good bread and a salad, this shrimp dish makes a very good summer supper.

1 lime, halved
½ tsp. peppercorns, very coarsely ground
¼ tsp. allspice berries, very coarsely ground
3 bay leaves
12 oz. shrimp, in shells
½ small red onion, diced
1 ripe, medium-small tomato, cored and diced

5 radishes, finely diced
1½ Tbsp. finely chopped fresh cilantro
2½ Tbsp. fresh lime juice
3 Tbsp. olive oil
½ tsp. salt
2-3 leaves romaine or leaf lettuce, for garnish
sprigs of cilantro or radish roses, for garnish

Squeeze lime into a medium-sized saucepan, then add the two squeezed rinds, black pepper, allspice, bay leaves and 1 quart water. (To grind peppercorns and allspice, use a spice mill or crush with the bottom of a heavy saucepan). Cover and simmer over medium-low heat for 10 minutes.

Raise the heat to high, add shrimp, re-cover and let the liquid return to a full boil. Immediately remove the pan from the heat, hold the lid slightly askew and strain off all the liquid and discard. Re-cover tightly, set aside for 15 minutes, then rinse the shrimp under cold water to stop the cooking.

Peel the shrimp, then devein them by running a knife down the back to expose the dark intestinal tract and scraping it out under running water. If the shrimp are medium or larger, cut them into ½-inch bits; place in a bowl.

Add red onions, tomatoes, radishes and cilantro to the shrimp. In a small bowl or a jar with a tight-fitting lid, combine lime juice, oil and salt.

Shortly before serving, mix the dressing ingredients thoroughly, then pour over the shrimp mixture. Toss to coat everything well, cover, and refrigerate or set aside at room temperature.

Line a shallow serving bowl with lettuce leaves. Taste the shrimp mixture for salt, scoop it into the prepared bowl and serve, garnished with sprigs of cilantro or radish roses.

Makes enough for 12 tacos. Serves 4 as a main course.

194 CALORIES FOR EACH OF 4 SERVINGS: 19 G PROTEIN, 11 G FAT, 6 G CARBOHYDRATE; 462 MG SODIUM; 166 MG CHOLESTEROL.

Vietnamese Shrimp Rolls

*You can omit the rice papers and simply wrap the filling in lettuce leaves. The rolls can be assembled
ahead of time and served as an appetizer. Or the wrappers can be placed on the table (with
bowls of warm water for softening) with a platter of fillings, so that guests can make a meal of them.*

1 lb. medium-sized shrimp, unpeeled
2 cups bean sprouts
10 8" or 9" rice papers, cut into halves or
quarters *(see Sources, page 242)*
1 large head Boston, Bibb or leaf lettuce,
leaves separated and trimmed
½ fresh pineapple, peeled, eyes removed,

halved, cored and thinly sliced
2 tomatoes, thinly sliced
½ cup fresh cilantro leaves, coarsely chopped
½ cup fresh mint leaves, coarsely chopped
Nuoc Cham dipping sauce, with carrot shreds
(recipe follows)

Cook shrimp in salted, boiling water for 2 to 3 minutes, or until pink and firm to the touch. Drain and cool. Peel and devein shrimp, or serve them in their shells and let diners peel them at the table. Blanch bean sprouts in boiling water for 1 minute. Drain and refresh with cold water.

To assemble: Moisten rice papers in warm water for 10 to 20 seconds, or until softened. Place a lettuce leaf inside each piece of softened rice paper. Fill with a few shrimp, a little pineapple, bean sprouts, tomatoes, cilantro and/or mint. Roll up the bundles and serve with *Nuoc Cham*.

Serves 4 as a main course or 8 as an appetizer.

213 CALORIES FOR EACH OF 4 SERVINGS: 27 G PROTEIN, 2 G FAT, 21 G CARBOHYDRATE; 180 MG SODIUM; 173 MG CHOLESTEROL.

↙

Nuoc Cham

*This recipe for the classic Vietnamese dipping sauce is a guide; it will
produce a light yet tasty nuoc cham. Feel free to vary the proportions according to taste.*

3 cloves garlic, minced
1 small "bird" or serrano chili pepper with
seeds, minced
6 Tbsp. fish sauce

3-4 Tbsp. fresh lemon or lime juice
2 Tbsp. sugar
1 small julienne carrot (optional)

In a blender or food processor, combine garlic, chili peppers, fish sauce, lemon or lime juice, sugar and 6 Tbsp. water until quite smooth.

Alternatively, pound garlic and chili pepper in a mortar with a pestle until they are turned into a fine paste. Stir in fish sauce, lemon or lime juice, sugar

and 6 Tbsp. water. *(The sauce can be prepared ahead and stored, covered, in the refrigerator for up to 3 days.)*

Before serving, place in individual bowls for dipping and add several shreds of carrot (if using).

Makes ¾ cup.

13 CALORIES PER TABLESPOON: 0 G PROTEIN, 0 G FAT, 3 G CARBOHYDRATE; 19 MG SODIUM; 0 MG CHOLESTEROL.

Eight-Treasure Seafood Noodle Pot

Few dishes are as satisfying as this noodle pot with its fresh seafood, tender cabbage and translucent cellophane noodles. For a less authentic version, peel the shrimp before marinating them.

6 cups defatted chicken stock

¾ cup rice wine

2 tsp. salt

1½ tsp. corn or safflower oil

6 cups Chinese cabbage (Napa), stems removed and cut into 2" squares

2 cloves garlic, smashed

¾ lb. firm-fleshed fish fillet, such as haddock or scrod, skin removed, cut into slices 1½" long and 1" wide

½ lb. medium-sized shrimp, in their shells, rinsed and drained

½ lb. fresh scallops, sliced in half if large

4-6 slices gingerroot, about the size of a quarter, smashed

½ tsp. sesame oil

6 Chinese dried black mushrooms

1 oz. cellophane noodles (bean threads)

6 cups spinach, stems removed, rinsed and drained

In a bowl, combine chicken stock, ¼ cup rice wine and 1 tsp. salt. Heat a large Dutch oven and add oil. When oil is hot, add cabbage and garlic. Toss lightly and add several Tbsp. chicken stock mixture. Add remaining chicken stock mixture and heat until boiling. Reduce heat to low, partially cover and simmer for 30 minutes.

Place fish, shrimp and scallops in a bowl. In a separate bowl, mix remaining ½ cup rice wine, ginger, remaining 1 tsp. salt and sesame oil. Add rice wine mixture to seafood, toss lightly and marinate 20 minutes. Discard ginger.

Soak mushrooms for 20 minutes in hot water until soft; drain. Discard stems; halve caps. Soften cellophane noodles in hot water for 20 minutes, drain and cut into 2-inch lengths.

Preheat oven to 400 degrees F. Add mushrooms and noodles to the Dutch oven. Cover and bake 15 minutes. Drain seafood and add it to the Dutch oven. Lay spinach over the top. Cover and bake about 8 to 10 minutes, or until seafood is opaque and firm to the touch. Remove from the oven and taste for seasoning, adding a little more salt if desired. Ladle into bowls and serve immediately.

Serves 6.

210 CALORIES PER SERVING: 32 G PROTEIN, 4 G FAT, 8 G CARBOHYDRATE; 1,085 MG SODIUM; 127 MG CHOLESTEROL.

Eight-Treasure Seafood Noodle Pot

Shrimp & Grits, Crook's Corner Style

This is the most popular recipe at Bill Neal's restaurant, Crook's Corner, in North Carolina.

1 tsp. salt
1 cup hominy grits
1 tsp. butter
¼-¾ cup grated sharp Cheddar
hot-pepper sauce
freshly grated nutmeg
white pepper
3 slices bacon, diced

1 lb. medium-sized shrimp, peeled, deveined, rinsed and patted dry
2 cups sliced mushrooms
1 cup finely sliced scallions
1 large clove garlic, minced
4 tsp. fresh lemon juice
2 Tbsp. chopped fresh parsley
salt and freshly ground black pepper

In a heavy 3-qt. saucepan, combine 4½ cups water and salt; bring to a boil. Slowly sift grits through one hand into the water, stirring with a whisk in the other hand. When all grits have been added, continue stirring and reduce the heat to very low, until only an occasional bubble breaks the surface. Continue cooking for 30 to 40 minutes, stirring frequently to prevent scorching. Beat in butter and cheese. Season to taste with hot-pepper sauce, a very little nutmeg and white pepper. Cover and hold in a warm place or in the top of a double boiler over simmering water.

Sauté bacon lightly over medium-high heat in a skillet. The edges should brown, but the bacon should not become crisp. Remove bacon, discard fat and return bacon to the pan. When the pan is hot, add shrimp in an even layer. Turn shrimp as they begin to color, add mushrooms and sauté about 2 to 4 minutes, until shrimp are pink and just firm. Stir in scallions and garlic. Season with lemon juice, parsley and a dash or two of hot-pepper sauce. Add salt and pepper to taste.

Divide grits among 4 plates. Spoon shrimp over them and serve.

Serves 4.

339 CALORIES PER SERVING: 32 G PROTEIN, 8 G FAT, 35 G CARBOHYDRATE; 930 MG SODIUM; 236 MG CHOLESTEROL.

Mussels alla Marinara

Serve this half-soup, half-stew in bowls.

1 28-oz. can tomatoes, with juice
2 tsp. olive oil
2 carrots, peeled and sliced diagonally into
    ½" slices
1 onion, cut in eighths

4 cloves garlic, sliced
⅔ cup dry white wine
¾ tsp. salt or to taste
¼ tsp. freshly ground black pepper
2 lbs. mussels, scrubbed, beards removed

In a blender or food processor or by hand, coarsely chop tomatoes. (They should not be pureed.) Set aside. In a large saucepan or stockpot, heat oil over medium heat. Add carrots, onions and garlic and sauté for 3 to 4 minutes, or until softened. Add wine, tomatoes, salt and pepper and bring to a boil over high heat. Add mussels, cover and cook for 3 to 4 minutes, or until they have opened. (Discard any that do not open.)

Serves 2 as a main course or 4 as an appetizer.

453 CALORIES FOR EACH OF 2 SERVINGS: 38 G PROTEIN, 10 G FAT, 40 G CARBOHYDRATE; 1,371 MG SODIUM; 96 MG CHOLESTEROL.

BEEF, PORK & LAMB

~

Chinese Pepper Steak

*Not only does this stir-fry have vitamin-C-rich peppers, it has the added
appeal of Chinese black mushrooms known as tree-ear or wood-ear, which in ancient
Chinese medicine are considered "blood thinners" and may help protect against heart attacks.*

2 Tbsp. reduced-sodium soy sauce
2 Tbsp. rice wine or dry sherry
2 tsp. dark sesame oil
2 tsp. cornstarch
1 tsp. sugar
½ tsp. Tabasco Sauce
1 lb. lean sirloin steak, trimmed of fat, cut
   into ¼"-wide strips

6 dried Chinese black tree-ear mushrooms
1½ tsp. olive oil
1" piece gingerroot, peeled and minced
2 cloves garlic, minced
2 scallions, minced
1 green bell pepper, cut into 1" pieces
1 red bell pepper, cut into 1" pieces
1 yellow bell pepper, cut into 1" pieces

(Recipe continues on next page)

In a medium bowl, combine soy sauce, rice wine or sherry, sesame oil, cornstarch, sugar and Tabasco. Marinate steak in this mixture for 20 minutes. Meanwhile, pour boiling water over mushrooms and soak for 15 minutes. Drain, remove and discard stems and cut mushrooms into thin strips.

Shortly before serving, drain the meat, reserving the marinade. Heat 1 tsp. oil almost to smoking in a wok or large nonstick skillet. Add ginger, garlic and scallions and stir-fry for 30 seconds, or until fra-grant. Add the beef and stir-fry for 1 to 3 minutes, or until brown on the outside but still pink inside. Transfer to a bowl and keep warm.

Add remaining ½ tsp. oil to the wok. Add mushrooms and peppers and stir-fry for 1 minute. Return the beef mixture to the wok and add marinade. Stir-fry for 30 seconds, or until the sauce is heated through and slightly thickened.

Serves 4.

258 CALORIES PER SERVING: 29 G PROTEIN, 10 G FAT, 13 G CARBOHYDRATE; 315 MG SODIUM; 71 MG CHOLESTEROL.

Steak & Vegetable Kebabs

This light marinade of soy sauce, rice wine, minced garlic and a hint of sugar may be used for grilling chicken and fish. It may be served as an appetizer as well as a main course.

1½ lbs. beef sirloin, trimmed of fat
⅓ cup soy sauce
¼ cup rice wine or sake
2 Tbsp. sugar
1½ Tbsp. minced garlic
1 tsp. sesame oil

12 small white boiling onions (about ⅔ lb.)
12 large mushrooms, trimmed and cleaned (¾ lb.)
3 large bell peppers, red, yellow or a combination, seeded and cut into 1" squares
canola or corn oil for greasing grill

Cut beef into 24 1-to-1½-inch cubes and place in a shallow nonaluminum dish. In a small bowl, whisk together soy sauce, rice wine or sake, sugar, garlic and sesame oil, stirring until sugar has dissolved. Pour over meat and toss lightly. Cover and marinate in the refrigerator for 8 to 10 hours.

If using wooden skewers, about 1 hour before serving place 12 10-inch skewers in water to soak. Parboil onions for 3 to 5 minutes, or until barely ten-der. Drain, cool under cold water and slip off skins. Prepare a charcoal fire or preheat a gas grill. Drain the meat, reserving the marinade for basting. Alternate the meat, onions, mushrooms and peppers on the skewers. Brush the grill lightly with oil. Grill the kebabs about 3 inches from hot coals for about 3 to 4 minutes per side for medium-rare, basting occasionally with the reserved marinade.

Serves 12 as an appetizer or 6 as a main course.

126 CALORIES FOR EACH OF 12 SERVINGS: 14 G PROTEIN, 5 G FAT, 5 G CARBOHYDRATE; 116 MG SODIUM; 38 MG CHOLESTEROL.

Northern-Style Shredded Beef With Tomatoes

Mexican cooks boil and shred beef for snacks, though nowhere do they prepare it as frequently or as well seasoned as in Northern Mexico. Serve it as a filling for corn tortillas. (It can be made up to 4 days ahead, covered and refrigerated.)

1 lb. lean, boneless beef chuck, well trimmed and cut into 1½" pieces
1 medium-sized onion
3 cloves garlic
1 Tbsp. vegetable oil
2 large scallions, chopped in ¼" pieces

2 ripe tomatoes, roasted or boiled *(page 242)*, cored, peeled and chopped or one 15-oz. can tomatoes, drained and chopped
2-3 fresh hot green chilies to taste (roughly 2-3 serrano chilies or 1-2 jalapeño chilies), stemmed, seeded and finely chopped
salt to taste, about ½ tsp.

Bring 2 qts. water to a boil in a large saucepan, add meat, then skim off any grayish foam that rises during the first few minutes of simmering. Slice half of the onion and halve 1 clove of garlic; add to the meat. Partially cover and simmer over medium to medium-low heat until the meat is very tender, 1 to 1½ hours. Let the meat cool in the broth. Strain the liquid and spoon off all the fat that rises to the top; set aside. Finely shred the meat with your fingers, then dry with paper towels.

Dice remaining onion and mince remaining garlic. Heat oil in a large, heavy skillet over medium-high heat. When hot, add onions and shredded beef and cook, stirring frequently, for 8 to 10 minutes, until well browned. Reduce the heat to medium, add garlic, scallions, tomatoes and chilies, and cook, stirring frequently, until tomatoes have softened, about 4 minutes. Stir in ⅔ cup of the reserved broth, then simmer until the liquid has evaporated, 10 to 15 minutes. Season with salt.

Makes enough for 10 tacos. Serves 3 to 4 as a light main course.

336 CALORIES FOR EACH OF 3 SERVINGS: 37 G PROTEIN, 16 G FAT, 10 G CARBOHYDRATE; 439 MG SODIUM; 101 MG CHOLESTEROL.

Skillet Steak in Wild-Mushroom-&-Roasted-Garlic Sauce

This entrée of tender slices of steak in a glossy sauce with sweet roast garlic, woodsy mushrooms and thyme is a simple, elegant dinner. Accompany it with small, braised leeks.

16 medium cloves garlic, unpeeled
2 tsp. plus 4 Tbsp. olive oil
coarse salt and freshly ground black pepper
4 8-oz. boneless top-loin steaks (New York strip), about 1½" thick, trimmed of fat

½ lb. small wild mushrooms (chanterelles, cremini and shiitake), cleaned and trimmed
2 Tbsp. Scotch whisky
1 cup defatted beef stock
2 tsp. potato starch or arrowroot, mixed with a little stock
2 tsp. fresh thyme leaves

Preheat oven to 375 degrees F. Place garlic cloves on a large piece of aluminum foil, drizzle with 2 tsp. olive oil and sprinkle with salt and pepper. Fold edges of foil over garlic and crimp to enclose completely. Place the foil packet in the center of the oven and roast for 30 minutes. Open the foil and roast for an additional 10 minutes, or until lightly brown and tender. Remove from the oven and let cool. Carefully peel garlic, keeping the cloves whole, and set aside.

Dry steaks thoroughly on paper towels and set aside. In a large skillet, heat 2 Tbsp. olive oil over medium-high heat. Add mushrooms and sauté quickly until lightly browned. Season with salt and pepper. Transfer to a side dish and reserve. Add 2 more Tbsp. olive oil to the skillet and when almost smoking, add the steaks without crowding the pan. Sear steaks quickly on each side until nicely browned.

Season with salt and pepper, reduce heat and continue to cook, covered, for 3½ minutes per side for medium rare. Remove steaks to a side dish and keep warm.

Discard all fat from skillet, add Scotch and reduce to a glaze. Add stock, bring to a boil and reduce by a third. Whisk in just enough potato starch mixture to coat a spoon. Add the mushrooms, garlic and thyme and just heat through. Taste and correct the seasoning, adding a generous grinding of black pepper.

Slice each steak crosswise into thin slices and place on 6 individual warm serving plates in a decorative overlapping pattern. Spoon sauce onto plate beside the steak and serve at once.

Serves 6.

321 CALORIES PER SERVING: 36 G PROTEIN, 14 G FAT, 12 G CARBOHYDRATE; 223 MG SODIUM; 101 MG CHOLESTEROL.

Spicy Grilled Chili Steak

Serve with a bowl of chunky fresh tomato salsa, grilled corn in their husks and whole grilled scallions.

2 tsp. cumin seeds
2 large cloves garlic, mashed
1 medium-sized onion, thinly sliced
¼ cup finely minced fresh cilantro
1 Tbsp. chili powder
1 Tbsp. finely minced fresh oregano or
   1 tsp. dried
¼ cup olive oil

3 Tbsp. fresh lime juice
1 Tbsp. reduced-sodium soy sauce
1½ tsp. red-pepper flakes
2 lean shell steaks, about 1½" thick, trimmed
   of fat (3-3½ lbs. total)
oil for brushing grill
salt and freshly ground black pepper

Roast cumin seeds by placing them in a heavy-bottomed, dry skillet over medium heat. Shake the pan back and forth until the seeds become fragrant, about 1 minute. In a small bowl, combine cumin, garlic, onions, cilantro, chili powder, oregano, olive oil, lime juice, soy sauce and red-pepper flakes and whisk until well blended. Place steaks in a heavy plastic bag, pour the oil mixture over them and seal the bag. Place in the refrigerator and marinate overnight, turning the steaks several times in the mari-

nade by turning the bag over every few hours.

Prepare a charcoal grill. Remove the steaks from the bag, brushing off most of the marinade. When the coals are white-hot but not flaming, brush the grill with oil and place the steaks over the coals. Grill 4 minutes per side for medium-rare. When steaks are done, season with salt and pepper, transfer to a carving board and cut crosswise into thin slices.

Serves 8.

287 CALORIES PER SERVING: 39 G PROTEIN, 12 G FAT, 3 G CARBOHYDRATE; 143 MG SODIUM; 114 MG CHOLESTEROL.

Barbecued Beef & Lemon Grass

*There are a number of ways to prepare and eat Vietnamese beef with lemon grass—
all delicious. The beef can be over rice noodles, or you can also serve it in rice-paper wrappers.*
Note: *It is easiest to cut the meat into thin slices if it is partially frozen.*

BEEF & NOODLES
1 "bird" or serrano chili pepper, minced
2-3 cloves garlic, minced
2 stalks fresh lemon grass, trimmed and
  finely chopped, or 2 Tbsp. dried, soaked
  for 30 minutes
2 shallots, finely chopped
2 Tbsp. fish sauce
1 Tbsp. fresh lime juice
1 Tbsp. toasted sesame oil
¼ tsp. freshly ground black pepper
1 lb. rump roast or eye of round, trimmed
  of fat

2 Tbsp. sesame seeds, toasted *(page 242)*
¾ lb. thin rice sticks (noodles; *see Sources,*
  page 242)
ACCOMPANIMENTS
2 cups shredded leaf lettuce
1 cup diced cucumber
¼ cup fresh mint leaves
¼ cup fresh cilantro leaves
¼ cup unsalted peanuts, toasted *(page 242),*
  chopped (optional)
2 "bird" or serrano chili peppers, minced
Peanut Sauce *(recipe follows)*

To make the beef: In a blender or food processor, combine 1 chili pepper, garlic, lemon grass, shallots, fish sauce, lime juice, sesame oil, black pepper and 1 Tbsp. water. Blend until the mixture forms a thick paste. Cut beef across the grain into very thin slices. Place it in a shallow, nonaluminum bowl and spread chili-garlic paste over top. Mix well. Cover and marinate for ½ hour at room temperature, or for up to 8 hours in the refrigerator.

Prepare a charcoal or gas grill, or preheat the broiler. Lift the meat out of the marinade and pat it dry. Thread the pieces of meat onto thin skewers and sprinkle both sides with sesame seeds. Cook the beef on a lightly oiled grill or broiler pan for 1 to 2 minutes per side for rare or medium-rare. Let cool.

Meanwhile, soak rice sticks in warm water for 15 minutes. Drain and cook in boiling water for 1 minute, or until tender but still firm, stirring with chopsticks to keep the strands separated. Drain and rinse thoroughly with cold water.

To assemble: Place some noodles, lettuce, cucumber, mint and cilantro in each bowl. Divide the beef among the bowls and top with more mint, cilantro, peanuts (if using), and minced chili peppers. Arrange remaining lettuce, cucumber and herbs in piles on a platter and pass separately. Serve with individual bowls of Peanut Sauce.

Serves 4.

586 CALORIES PER SERVING: 33 G PROTEIN, 15 G FAT, 77 G CARBOHYDRATE; 88 MG SODIUM; 76 MG CHOLESTEROL.

Barbecued Beef & Lemon Grass

Peanut Sauce

There are many versions of Vietnamese peanut sauce, so you should feel free to experiment with proportions of chili, garlic, sugar and fish sauce. Note: If you cannot find soybean sauce, substitute 2 Tbsp. browned, lean ground pork, increase the fish sauce to ¼ cup and decrease the water to ½ cup. It is excellent with Barbecued Beef (page 166).

1 tsp. peanut oil
3 cloves garlic, minced
¼ cup soybean sauce (*tuong,* not soy sauce)
1 Tbsp. tomato paste
1 Tbsp. fish sauce
1 tsp. chili paste (optional)

1 Tbsp. peanut butter
½ Tbsp. sugar
1½ Tbsp. sesame seeds, toasted *(page 242)*
10-15 unsalted peanuts, toasted *(page 242),*
   coarsely chopped

Heat oil in a heavy-bottomed saucepan over medium heat. Add garlic and cook for 2 to 3 minutes, or until lightly browned. Reduce heat to low and stir in soybean sauce, tomato paste, fish sauce and chili paste (if using). If the soybean sauce has whole rather than mashed soybeans, mash the beans as you stir. In a small bowl, combine peanut butter, sugar and 1 cup water; stir into soybean mixture. Bring to a boil. Reduce heat to low and simmer for 2 minutes, stirring constantly. Pour the sauce into individual serving bowls and sprinkle sesame seeds and peanuts over top. Serve at room temperature.

Makes 1 to 1½ cups.

25 CALORIES PER TABLESPOON: 1 G PROTEIN, 2 G FAT, 2 G CARBOHYDRATE; 16 MG SODIUM; 0 MG CHOLESTEROL.

Saucy Chinese Noodles

This dish contrasts smooth-textured noodles with crunchy vegetables and tender beef pieces—all coated in a pungent sweet-bean sauce. Note: *Don't confuse the sweet-bean sauce called for below with sweetened red-bean paste. Sweet-bean sauce is made with ground soybeans mixed with sugar. Red-bean paste, made with adzuki beans, will ruin this dish. Hoisin sauce may be substituted.* (For Asian ingredients, see Sources, page 242.)

BEEF & MARINADE

1 lb. flank steak or London broil, trimmed of fat
1 Tbsp. soy sauce
2 tsp. rice wine
½ tsp. sesame oil
2 tsp. cornstarch

SAUCE

¾ cup sweet-bean sauce or hoisin sauce
3 Tbsp. rice wine
2 Tbsp. soy sauce
2½ Tbsp. sugar

NOODLES

¾ lb. fresh or dried flat white Chinese noodles or Japanese *kishimen*, udon or linguine
1½ tsp. sesame oil
2 Tbsp. safflower or corn oil
3 Tbsp. minced scallions
1 Tbsp. minced garlic
2 cups julienne carrots (3-4 medium-sized)
2 cups julienne, peeled, seedless cucumber (1 cucumber)
1½ cups bean sprouts, rinsed and drained thoroughly

To marinate beef: Cut beef into strips approximately ⅛ inch thick and 1½ inches long. Place in a bowl and add soy sauce, rice wine, sesame oil, 1 Tbsp. water and cornstarch. Toss lightly and marinate for 20 minutes.

To make sauce: Combine sweet bean or hoisin sauce, rice wine, soy sauce and sugar and set aside.

To make noodles and assemble: In a large pot containing 4 qts. boiling water, cook noodles until just tender, about 2 to 5 minutes. Drain in a colander and quickly rinse the noodles to remove the starch. Toss them lightly with sesame oil and arrange them in a deep serving bowl or in 6 individual dishes.

Heat a wok or deep skillet over high heat and add 1 Tbsp. safflower or corn oil, then add beef and stir-fry until meat changes color, about 3 minutes. Remove from wok. Add remaining 1 Tbsp. oil and stir-fry scallions and garlic until fragrant, about 15 seconds. Add sauce mixture and cook, stirring, for 3 to 5 minutes, or until sauce has thickened. Add beef and toss lightly to coat.

Spoon the mixture over the center of the noodles. Arrange carrots, cucumbers and bean sprouts in piles or concentric circles around the outside. Serve hot or at room temperature.

Serves 6.

497 CALORIES PER SERVING: 30 G PROTEIN, 15 G FAT, 60 G CARBOHYDRATE; 1,107 MG SODIUM; 51 MG CHOLESTEROL.

Curried Beef Ambrosia

The addition of mangoes and raisins makes this curried beef pleasantly sweet. Serve over rice.

1 lb. boneless blade steak, trimmed of fat,
    cut into 1" cubes
¾ cup dry red wine
1 Tbsp. olive oil
salt and freshly ground black pepper
1 small onion, chopped
3 Tbsp. curry powder

2 cups defatted beef or chicken stock
1 Tbsp. Worcestershire sauce
⅔ cup chopped dried or fresh pitted dates
4 ripe mangoes, peeled, pitted and cut into
    1" cubes, juice reserved
½ cup raisins

Place beef in a bowl, add red wine, 1½ tsp. oil, salt and pepper and toss lightly. Cover and marinate for 3 to 4 hours in the refrigerator. In a 4-qt. saucepan, heat remaining 1½ tsp. oil over medium heat. Add onions and curry powder and sauté for 5 minutes, or until onions have softened. Drain beef, reserving marinade. Add beef to pan and sauté for 3 to 5 minutes, or until browned. Stir in stock, marinade and Worcestershire sauce. Reduce heat to low and simmer for 5 minutes. Add dates and cook for 5 minutes. Add mangoes, juice and raisins and cook for 15 minutes.

Serves 6.

391 CALORIES PER SERVING: 34 G PROTEIN, 11 G FAT, 36 G CARBOHYDRATE; 108 MG SODIUM; 56 MG CHOLESTEROL.

⌇

Roasted Veal Chops With Gremolata

Gremolata, a mixture of minced fresh herbs, garlic and lemon zest, provides a finishing flourish for this fast supper. Note: *Six-oz. lamb chops work equally well. Roast them about 4 minutes longer.*

3 cloves garlic
4 8-oz. bone-in veal chops, about 1" thick,
    trimmed of fat
1 tsp. olive oil

salt and freshly ground black pepper
¼ cup minced fresh parsley
1 Tbsp. grated lemon zest

Preheat oven to 450 degrees F. Cut 1 clove garlic in half lengthwise. Rub veal chops with the garlic, then brush both sides of the chops lightly with olive oil. Season with salt and pepper.

Heat two cast-iron or other ovenproof heavy-bottomed skillets over high heat until they are nearly smoking. Place the chops in the pans and cook 2 minutes. Turn the chops over and transfer the skillets to the oven. Roast for 6 to 8 minutes, until the meat is cooked but still slightly pink inside.

Meanwhile, mince remaining 2 cloves garlic and combine with parsley and lemon zest. To serve, place the chops on individual serving plates and spoon 1 Tbsp. of the parsley mixture on top of each.

Serves 4.

273 CALORIES PER SERVING: 27 G PROTEIN, 17 G FAT, 1 G CARBOHYDRATE; 106 MG SODIUM; 125 MG CHOLESTEROL.

Stir-Fried Korean Noodles

This stir-fried noodle dish was inspired by a recipe given to Chinese-cooking expert Nina Simonds by J. Soon Cho, a talented native Korean cook and teacher.

SAUCE
¼ cup reduced-sodium soy sauce
1 tsp. sesame oil
1½ Tbsp. sugar
¾ tsp. freshly ground black pepper
PORK & NOODLES
1 lb. center-cut boneless pork loin, trimmed of fat
2 Tbsp. soy sauce
1 Tbsp. mirin (Japanese sweet rice wine)
1 tsp. sesame oil
1 tsp. peeled, minced gingerroot

8 Chinese dried black mushrooms
4 oz. potato-starch noodles (*dang myun*) or cellophane noodles
5 oz. fresh spinach (6 cups loosely packed), stems trimmed
1 egg, lightly beaten
2 Tbsp. corn oil
3 Tbsp. minced scallions
1 Tbsp. minced garlic
1 cup julienne carrots, plus 2 Tbsp. finely shredded
2 Tbsp. sesame seeds, toasted *(page 242)*

In a small bowl, combine sauce ingredients: soy sauce, ¼ cup water, sesame oil, sugar and black pepper. Set aside.

Cut pork across the grain into thin slices. Cut the slices into matchstick-size strips. Place pork in a bowl, add soy sauce, mirin, sesame oil and ginger, toss lightly and marinate for 20 minutes. Soak mushrooms for 20 minutes in hot water; drain. Remove and discard stems and slice caps. Soak potato-starch noodles in hot water for 5 minutes (if using cellophane noodles, soak them for 20 minutes), drain and cut into 6-inch sections. Blanch spinach in boiling water for about 10 seconds. Drain, refresh in cold water and drain again, squeezing out all moisture. Cut spinach into large pieces. Set aside.

Heat a small nonstick skillet until a drop of water dances when sprinkled on the surface. Pour in beaten egg so the egg coats the pan evenly and forms a thin omelet. Cook until set, turn and cook briefly. Remove from the pan and cut omelet into thin strips. Set aside.

Heat a wok or a large skillet and add 1 Tbsp. oil. When oil is hot, add pork loin and stir-fry until browned and no longer pink inside. Remove, set in a colander and drain. Reheat the pan and add remaining 1 Tbsp. oil. When the oil is hot, add scallions, garlic, black mushrooms and carrots and stir-fry about 1 to 2 minutes. Add noodles, pork, spinach and sauce mixture and cook until the noodles are transparent and have absorbed most of the liquid. Add sesame seeds, toss lightly and transfer to a serving platter. Garnish with omelet and shredded carrot.

Serves 6.

336 CALORIES PER SERVING: 23 G PROTEIN, 16 G FAT, 26 G CARBOHYDRATE; 1,287 MG SODIUM; 89 MG CHOLESTEROL.

Pork Chops With Pear-&-Ginger Sauce

*In this quick sauté, vinegar and sugar are quickly caramelized
in the skillet to coat the pork. Ginger and fruity flavors set off its mild taste.*

2 tsp. vegetable oil
4 ¾"-thick boneless, center-cut pork chops,
   trimmed of fat (1 lb. total)
salt and freshly ground black pepper
3 Tbsp. cider vinegar
2 Tbsp. sugar
⅔ cup dry white wine

⅔ cup defatted chicken stock
1 firm, ripe pear ('Anjou' or 'Bosc'), peeled,
   cored and cut lengthwise into eighths
1 2"-long piece gingerroot, peeled and cut
   into thin julienne strips
6 scallions, trimmed and sliced into ½" lengths
2 tsp. cornstarch

In a large, nonstick skillet, heat oil over medium-high heat. Add pork and cook for 3 to 5 minutes per side, or just until browned and the interior is no longer pink. Season lightly with salt and pepper. Remove and keep warm.

Add vinegar and sugar to the skillet, stirring to dissolve the sugar. Cook over medium-high heat for about 1 minute, or until the syrup turns dark amber. Pour in wine and chicken stock and cook, stirring, for about 30 seconds, or until caramel has dissolved.

Add pears and ginger and cook, uncovered, turning pears occasionally, for 3 minutes. Add scallions and cook about 2 minutes more, or until the pears are tender. Dissolve cornstarch in 2 tsp. water and whisk into the pear sauce. (The sauce will thicken almost immediately.) Reduce heat to low, and return the pork and any accumulated juices to the skillet. Simmer gently for about 1 minute, or until the pork is heated through.

Serves 4.

291 CALORIES PER SERVING: 25 G PROTEIN, 15 G FAT, 14 G CARBOHYDRATE; 89 MG SODIUM; 81 MG CHOLESTEROL.

Pork Medallions With Cumberland Sauce

Glossy and burgundy-colored, this traditional English
sweet-and-sour sauce turns a scrap of pork into an elegant entrée.

1 Tbsp. vegetable oil
1 lb. pork tenderloin, trimmed of fat and cut
　　into 1"-thick medallions
salt and freshly ground black pepper
2 Tbsp. minced onions or shallots
1 cup dry red wine

1 tsp. cornstarch
1 Tbsp. fresh lemon juice
2 Tbsp. red-currant jelly
1 tsp. brown sugar (optional)
1 tsp. Dijon mustard

Heat 2 tsp. oil in a nonstick skillet over medium-high heat. Season pork lightly with salt and pepper and cook for 3 to 4 minutes per side, or until brown on the outside and no longer pink but still juicy inside. Transfer to plates or a platter and keep warm. Add remaining 1 tsp. oil to the skillet. Add onions or shallots and cook, stirring, until softened, about 30 seconds. Add wine and bring to a boil, stirring.

Boil for 5 to 6 minutes, or until reduced to about ⅓ cup. Dissolve cornstarch in lemon juice and whisk into the sauce. Cook, stirring, until thickened and glossy. Remove from heat and stir in jelly, sugar (if using) and mustard. Taste and adjust seasonings with more salt and pepper, if needed. Spoon the sauce over the pork.

Serves 4.

208 CALORIES PER SERVING: 25 G PROTEIN, 8 G FAT, 9 G CARBOHYDRATE; 112 MG SODIUM; 79 MG CHOLESTEROL.

Broiled Lamb Chops or Medallions

Cracked peppercorns make a crunchy outer coating for the tender meat. The lamb may be grilled.

12 4-oz. loin or rib lamb chops, trimmed of
　　fat, approximately 1" thick, or 1"-thick
　　medallions, trimmed of fat (1½ lbs. total)
2 cloves garlic

1 tsp. olive oil
1 tsp. black peppercorns, crushed with the
　　underside of a heavy pot

Preheat broiler. Pat lamb chops or medallions dry. Insert slivers of garlic into each one, making small punctures with a paring knife and poking in the garlic. Brush the tops lightly with half the olive oil, then pat on half the cracked peppercorns. Repeat with the

other side of the lamb, using remaining oil and peppercorns. Broil for 3 to 4 minutes per side, until the lamb is browned but pink inside. Serve with Rhubarb Chutney Sauce *(page 180).*

Serves 6.

208 CALORIES PER SERVING: 24 G PROTEIN, 12 G FAT, 1 G CARBOHYDRATE; 73 MG SODIUM; 77 MG CHOLESTEROL.

Broiled Lamb Chops and Rhubarb Chutney Sauce

Tandoori Leg of Lamb With Fresh Mango Chutney

A spicy, yogurt-based marinade tenderizes the lamb,
which is accompanied by a sweet and gingery uncooked chutney.

1 5-lb. leg of lamb, trimmed of fat
1 cup nonfat yogurt
¼ cup fresh lime juice (2 limes)
2 Tbsp. peeled, minced gingerroot
3 cloves garlic, crushed
1½ tsp. salt
¼ tsp. freshly ground black pepper

1 Tbsp. ground coriander
½ tsp. cayenne pepper
½ tsp. cinnamon
½ tsp. ground cloves
½ tsp. ground cardamom
Fresh Mango Chutney *(recipe follows)*

With a sharp knife, make ¼-inch to ½-inch-deep gashes on all sides of lamb in a criss-cross pattern. Place the lamb in a plastic bag. In a small bowl, combine yogurt, lime juice, ginger, garlic, salt and pepper. Pour the yogurt mixture over the lamb, making sure it covers the meat. Tie the bag and marinate in the refrigerator overnight.

Preheat oven to 450 degrees F. Remove lamb from bag (some of the marinade should cling to the meat) and place it on a lightly oiled rack in a roasting pan. In a small bowl, combine coriander, cayenne, cinnamon, cloves and cardamom. Sprinkle evenly over the lamb. Roast for 15 minutes, reduce heat to 325 degrees F and continue roasting for 55 to 60 minutes for medium-rare, or until a meat thermometer registers 140 degrees F. Let stand for 10 minutes before carving. Serve with Fresh Mango Chutney. Serves 10.

243 CALORIES PER SERVING: 31 G PROTEIN, 8 G FAT, 10 G CARBOHYDRATE; 622 MG SODIUM; 91 MG CHOLESTEROL.

Fresh Mango Chutney

2 medium-firm mangoes, peeled, pitted and diced
2 Tbsp. minced fresh cilantro
1 Tbsp. peeled, minced gingerroot

1 Tbsp. peeled, finely chopped fresh coconut or flaked, unsweetened coconut
1 tsp. salt
⅛ tsp. cayenne pepper

In a small bowl combine all of the ingredients and mix well. Serve immediately or hold in the refrigerator for up to 8 hours.
Makes 1½ cups.

12 CALORIES PER TABLESPOON: 0 G PROTEIN, 0 G FAT, 3 G CARBOHYDRATE; 89 MG SODIUM; 0 MG CHOLESTEROL.

Rack of Lamb à la Provençal

In this classic preparation, a specialty of Campagne restaurant in Seattle, the lamb is covered with a mustard-and-herb crumb coating so it stays juicy during roasting. It is served with a fresh tomato compote flavored with Greek olives. Note: *Lamb racks can often be purchased with the chine bone already removed and the rib tips trimmed; you may want to ask your butcher to take care of this.*

LAMB
1 Tbsp. olive oil
½ cup fresh bread crumbs
1 clove garlic, minced
1 tsp. minced shallots
1 rack of lamb (8 ribs, about 2 lbs.)
salt and freshly ground black pepper
1½ Tbsp. Dijon mustard
½ tsp. chopped fresh oregano or pinch dried
½ tsp. chopped fresh thyme or pinch dried
½ tsp. chopped fresh Italian parsley

TOMATO COMPOTE
1 cup peeled, seeded, chopped tomatoes
2 Tbsp. chopped fresh Italian parsley
1 Tbsp. pitted, coarsely chopped Kalamata olives
1 Tbsp. extra-virgin olive oil
1½ tsp. fresh lemon juice
1 clove garlic, minced
½ tsp. minced shallots
salt and freshly ground black pepper

To roast lamb: Preheat oven to 450 degrees F. In a small nonstick skillet, heat 1 tsp. oil over medium heat. Add bread crumbs, garlic and shallots and sauté, stirring constantly, for about 2 minutes, or until just golden. Remove from skillet and set aside.

Using a cleaver or a sharp knife, cut chine bone away from lamb rack. Place the rack, ribs curved downward, on a cutting board. Make a vertical incision 2 inches from the tips, parallel to them, cutting down through the fat and meat to the bones. Cut and scrape away the fat and meat from the bones between the incision and the tips so that the ends are clean. Trim all visible fat from the rack.

In a large nonstick skillet, heat remaining 2 tsp. oil over medium-high heat. Season the lamb with salt and pepper and sear it for 2 to 3 minutes on each side. In a small bowl, combine mustard, oregano, thyme and parsley. Spread the mustard mixture over the top of lamb rack and cover with the bread-crumb mixture. Place the lamb rack on a rack over a roasting pan or baking sheet and roast it for 25 to 30 minutes, or until a meat thermometer registers 140 degrees F for medium-rare. Let stand for 5 minutes and carve into chops.

To make compote: While the lamb is roasting, combine all compote ingredients in a bowl and season with salt and pepper. Let stand at room temperature for up to 30 minutes. Arrange chops on plates with a dollop of compote. Garnish with sprigs of fresh herbs.

Serves 4.

332 CALORIES PER SERVING: 26 G PROTEIN, 19 G FAT, 13 G CARBOHYDRATE; 257 MG SODIUM; 77 MG CHOLESTEROL.

SAUCES, SALSAS & CHUTNEYS

Cranberry Chutney

This variation of the traditional cranberry sauce is excellent served with cold beef.

1 16-oz. can peeled tomatoes, with juice
4 cups fresh cranberries (1 lb.)
1 cup raisins
¾ cup sugar

1 tsp. salt
1 tsp. peeled, minced gingerroot or
    ½ tsp. ground ginger

Cut tomatoes into fairly large chunks. Combine tomatoes and their liquid with remaining ingredients in a large saucepan. Cover and bring to a boil over medium heat; simmer for 15 minutes.

Allow to cool to room temperature, then refrigerate in a tightly covered container for at least 2 days before serving.

Makes 5 cups.

64 CALORIES PER ¼ CUP: 1 G PROTEIN, 0 G FAT, 17 G CARBOHYDRATE; 147 MG SODIUM; 0 MG CHOLESTEROL.

Cranberry Chutney

Rhubarb Chutney Sauce

A thick, spunky sauce that is a standby—good with grilled lamb, chicken or halibut. It can be made with frozen rhubarb. This recipe makes a small batch, which you can adjust for heat and sweetness.

5-6 stalks rhubarb, cut into 1" pieces (about
    4 cups)
1 onion, chopped
⅓-½ cup honey
¼ cup cider vinegar
¼-½ cup golden raisins

1-3 jalapeño chilies, seeded or not
3 cloves garlic, chopped
8 whole cardamom pods (white or green),
    tied in a cheesecloth bag
1 cup chopped fresh cilantro

In a medium-sized saucepan, combine rhubarb, onions, ⅓ cup honey, vinegar, raisins, 1 chili, garlic and cardamom. Add ½ cup water, bring to a boil, cover and simmer for 15 minutes, or until rhubarb is very tender. Taste, adding more chilies and honey as desired. Cook, uncovered, for 5 more minutes, remove from heat, remove cheesecloth bag and stir in cilantro. Serve warm or cold. *(The chutney can be made ahead and stored in the refrigerator for up to 1 week.)* Makes 4 cups.

10 CALORIES PER TABLESPOON: 0 G PROTEIN, 0 G FAT, 3 G CARBOHYDRATE; 0 MG SODIUM; 0 MG CHOLESTEROL.

Plum-Nectarine Chutney

When made with ripe fruit, this is a sweet chutney; for a slightly tart flavor, use fruit that is a bit underripe. It goes well with duck or chicken.

1 Tbsp. vegetable oil
1 small onion, sliced
3 Tbsp. peeled, minced gingerroot
½ cup brown sugar
4 plums, pitted and coarsely chopped
4 nectarines, pitted and coarsely chopped

½ cup orange juice
¼ cup golden raisins
¼ cup cider vinegar
½ tsp. ground allspice
½ tsp. nutmeg
salt and coarsely ground black pepper to taste

In a heavy-bottomed saucepan, heat oil over medium-high heat until it is hot but not smoking. Add onion and ginger and cook for 3 to 5 minutes, stirring, until the onion slices are golden. Add the brown sugar and stir until fully dissolved. Add remaining ingredients and simmer over low heat, stirring, until the mixture is thickened, 20 to 25 minutes. *(This chutney will keep, covered and refrigerated, for up to 2 weeks.)* Makes about 5 cups.

14 CALORIES PER TABLESPOON: 0 G PROTEIN, 0 G FAT, 3 G CARBOHYDRATE; 1 MG SODIUM; 0 MG CHOLESTEROL.

Spicy Pear Chutney

With its tart spiciness, this chutney is a superb contrast to the rich meat of game hens or other poultry. Unlike some chutneys that require a substantial aging period, this one may be served immediately once it is cool. Tart apples may be substituted for pears.

¾ cup sugar
¾ cup cider vinegar
3 firm pears, such as Bosc, peeled, cored
    and diced (about 1¼ lbs. total)

2 tsp. minced garlic
1 tsp. peeled, minced gingerroot
¾ tsp. red-pepper flakes, or less if desired
½ tsp. mustard seed

Place sugar and vinegar in a 3-qt. saucepan and bring to a boil. Reduce heat and simmer about 10 minutes. Add pears, garlic, ginger, red-pepper flakes and mustard seed to the saucepan and bring to a boil. Lower the heat and simmer briskly, uncovered, for 45 minutes, or until the chutney thickens. Spoon into another container and refrigerate until well-chilled. *(The chutney can be made ahead and refrigerated for up to 2 weeks.)*

Makes 1½ cups.

37 CALORIES PER TABLESPOON: 0 G PROTEIN, 0 G FAT, 10 G CARBOHYDRATE; 1 MG SODIUM; 0 MG CHOLESTEROL.

Tomato & Peanut Salsa

This version of a classic salsa from the Bahia region of Brazil shows the strong influence of African cuisine. Add some tomato juice and a bit more chili pepper and you have a great dipping salsa. In Brazil, it is most often eaten as an accompaniment to vegetable dishes. It's great with green beans, lightly steamed zucchini or summer squash, or pork loin.

½ cup roasted, unsalted peanuts
2 large, ripe tomatoes, finely diced
½ large red onion, finely diced
2 jalapeño peppers, minced
2 Tbsp. chopped fresh cilantro
2 Tbsp. chopped fresh parsley

2 Tbsp. fresh lime juice (1 lime)
1 Tbsp. olive oil
1½ tsp. minced garlic
1½ tsp. sugar
1 tsp. salt or to taste
coarsely ground black pepper to taste

In a blender or food processor, grind peanuts coarsely. (They should have a slightly chunky, crumbly consistency.) In a medium-sized bowl, combine peanuts with remaining ingredients and mix well.

(This salsa will keep, covered and refrigerated, for up to 24 hours.)

Makes about 3 cups.

14 CALORIES PER TABLESPOON: 0 G PROTEIN, 1 G FAT, 1 G CARBOHYDRATE; 45 MG SODIUM; 0 MG CHOLESTEROL.

Avocado & Corn Salsa

The acidity of the lime juice balances the rich taste of the avocados.
This salsa is rich, so it goes well with plain tortillas or with grilled or roasted chicken.

3 ears corn, husked (about 2 cups)
2 firm, ripe avocados, peeled, pitted and
  coarsely diced
1 red onion, finely diced
1 red bell pepper, seeded and finely diced
2 Tbsp. olive oil
⅓ cup red-wine vinegar

1 Tbsp. minced garlic
1 Tbsp. ground cumin
1 tsp. red-pepper flakes
¼ cup chopped fresh oregano or 1 tsp. dried
¼ cup fresh lime juice (2 limes)
salt and coarsely ground black pepper to taste

Blanch corn in boiling water for 3 minutes. Drain and cool under cold water. Cut the kernels from the cobs and place them in a medium-sized bowl. Add remaining ingredients and mix well. *(This salsa is best served immediately, but it can be kept, covered and refrigerated, for up to 4 hours.)*

Makes about 4 cups.

19 CALORIES PER TABLESPOON: 0 G PROTEIN, 1 G FAT, 2 G CARBOHYDRATE; 1 MG SODIUM; 0 MG CHOLESTEROL.

Pineapple & Jalapeño Salsa

Try this tangy, peppery condiment with grilled or
broiled tuna, sautéed scallops, or chicken, turkey or ham.

1 small, fresh, juicy-ripe pineapple, diced
  (4 cups)
1 large jalapeño pepper, minced (2 Tbsp.)
1 scallion, including green top, minced (¼ cup)

3 Tbsp. chopped fresh cilantro
1 Tbsp. corn or vegetable oil
juice of 1 large lime (3 Tbsp.)
salt and freshly ground black pepper

Cut the top and skin off pineapple and remove the eyes and core. Finely dice the fruit and place it in a glass bowl. Remove the stem and seeds from jalapeño and mince the flesh, then add it to the pineapple. Add scallions, cilantro, oil and lime juice. Toss to mix completely. Season with salt (if desired) and fresh pepper. Chill at least 1 hour before serving to allow flavors to meld.

Makes about 4 cups.

7.3 CALORIES PER TABLESPOON: .07 G PROTEIN, .26 G FAT, 1.3 G CARBOHYDRATE; 4.3 MG SODIUM; 0 MG CHOLESTEROL.

Avocado & Corn Salsa

Cucumber-Pineapple Sambal

This hot Indonesian-inspired sambal contains a typical combination of fruit,
vegetables and spices. Serve it with seafood. It stands up particularly well to squid and monkfish.

2 cucumbers, peeled, seeded and diced

1 medium-sized pineapple, peeled, eyes
    removed, cored and diced

½ cup rice-wine vinegar or white vinegar

2 Tbsp. reduced-sodium soy sauce

2 Tbsp. brown sugar

2 Tbsp. peeled, minced gingerroot

1-2 tsp. minced red chili peppers, with seeds,
    or ½-1 tsp. red-pepper flakes

salt and coarsely ground black pepper to taste

In a medium bowl, combine all ingredients and mix well. *(This sambal will keep, covered and refrigerated, for up to 4 hours.)*

Makes about 5 cups.

5 CALORIES PER TABLESPOON: 0 G PROTEIN, 0 G FAT, 1 G CARBOHYDRATE; 18 MG SODIUM; 0 MG CHOLESTEROL.

Red Sauce

This basic spaghetti sauce contains no oil.

1 stalk celery, minced

¼ Spanish onion, or 1 small onion, minced

3 large cloves garlic, minced

⅓ cup dry red wine

3½ cups tomato puree (28-oz. can)

1½ cups canned whole peeled tomatoes,
    coarsely chopped, with juice

1 whole carrot, peeled

1 Tbsp. minced fresh parsley

1 Tbsp. dried basil

1 bay leaf

2 tsp. dried oregano

¼ tsp. dried rosemary

⅛ tsp. salt

Briefly sauté celery, onions and garlic in a little of the wine, then add remaining wine, cover, and simmer for 10 minutes. If more liquid is needed, use the juice from the canned tomatoes. Add remaining ingredients and continue simmering, uncovered, 30 to 45 minutes longer, or until sauce is thick and flavors have melded. If time permits, let the sauce sit overnight in the refrigerator. Before serving, discard bay leaf and carrot.

Makes 5 cups.

50 CALORIES PER ½ CUP: 2 G PROTEIN, 0 G FAT, 11 G CARBOHYDRATE; 411 MG SODIUM; 0 MG CHOLESTEROL.

Cucumber-Pineapple Sambal

Tomato-Herb Concassée

This sauce, which has a clean flavor, teams up well with
grilled swordfish or tuna, as well as sautéed chicken, pasta or veal.

2 cloves garlic, minced
1 Tbsp. olive oil
2 large ripe tomatoes, peeled, seeded and
   coarsely chopped

2 Tbsp. snipped fresh chives
1-2 Tbsp. snipped fresh dill
salt and freshly ground black pepper

Sauté garlic in oil in a medium-sized, nonaluminum skillet until it is just tender, about 1 minute. Add tomatoes and cook over medium-high heat just until most of the liquid evaporates, 5 minutes at most.

Stir in chives and dill. Season to taste with salt and pepper. Serve hot or cold.
Makes about 1½ cups.

8 CALORIES PER TABLESPOON: 0 G PROTEIN, 1 G FAT, 1 G CARBOHYDRATE; 12 MG SODIUM; 0 MG CHOLESTEROL.

Quick-Cooked Tomato-Chili Sauce

Many gastronomical commentators have singled out the tomato as
Mexico's most useful contribution to world cookery. Mexican cooks make this
fruit-of-the-groping-vine into all sorts of variations on this simple sauce. Serve it immediately,
alongside Mexican specialties, or within a couple of hours of preparation, or it will lose its brightness.

1½ lbs. pear-shaped ripe tomatoes (9-10),
   boiled or preferably roasted *(page 242)*
   or one 28-oz. can good-quality tomatoes,
   drained
fresh hot, green chilies to taste (3-5 serrano
   chilies or 2-3 jalapeño chilies), stemmed

½ small onion, chopped
1 large clove garlic, coarsely chopped
1 tsp. vegetable oil
salt to taste, about ¼ tsp.

If you want a more refined sauce, seed tomatoes by cutting them in half across the middle and squeezing out the seeds. Roughly chop the tomatoes and place them in a blender or food processor.

If you want a milder sauce, first seed chilies. Chop chilies into small bits and add them to the blender along with onions and garlic, stir to distribute ingredients evenly, then process the mixture until it is

pureed but still retains some texture.

Heat oil in a medium-large nonstick skillet over medium-high heat. When it is hot enough to make a drop of the puree sizzle, add the puree all at once and stir constantly for about 5 minutes as it sears and cooks into a thicker, more orange-colored sauce. Season with salt and remove from the heat.
Makes 1½ to 2 cups.

32 CALORIES PER ¼ CUP: 1 G PROTEIN, 1 G FAT, 6 G CARBOHYDRATE; 98 MG SODIUM; 0 MG CHOLESTEROL.

Quick-Cooked Tomatillo-Chili Sauce

This everyday Mexican salsa is green from a delicious native berry, the tomatillo. It makes a traditional sauce with an especially fresh, tart taste. The salsa keeps, covered and refrigerated, for up to 4 days. To blend ingredients of different consistencies into an even-textured puree, make sure that (1) harder items are chopped before blending, (2) the mixture is well stirred before blending, and (3) the blender is first pulsed, then turned on low. Blending should never take more than 30 seconds.

1 lb. fresh tomatillos, husked and washed
(11 medium), or two 13-oz. cans tomatillos
fresh hot, green chilies to taste (roughly 3
serrano chilies or 2 jalapeño chilies,
stemmed)
6 sprigs fresh cilantro, roughly chopped
(1 Tbsp.)

1 small onion, chopped
1 large clove garlic, coarsely chopped
1 tsp. vegetable oil
2 cups defatted chicken stock
salt to taste, about ¼ tsp. (depending on the
saltiness of the stock)

If using fresh tomatillos, cook them with chilies in boiling salted water until tender, about 5 minutes; drain. If using canned tomatillos, drain them.

Place tomatillos and chilies in a blender or food processor, along with cilantro, onion and garlic (if using a blender, stir well). Process until smooth, but still retaining a little texture.

Heat oil in a medium-large nonstick skillet set over medium-high heat. When oil is hot enough to make a drop of the puree sizzle sharply, pour the tomatillo mixture in all at once and stir constantly for 4 or 5 minutes, until mixture becomes darker and thicker. Add stock, return to a boil, reduce the heat to medium and simmer until thick enough to coat a spoon, about 10 to 15 minutes. Season with salt.

Makes about 2 cups.

26 CALORIES PER ¼ CUP: 1 G PROTEIN, 1 G FAT, 4 G CARBOHYDRATE; 99 MG SODIUM; 0 MG CHOLESTEROL.

⚘

Sweet Garlic Puree

The garlic-greedy like to spread this on grilled bread. Note: *It is important to use Rich Chicken Stock; when commercial stock is substituted, the result is too thin.*

3 medium-sized garlic heads, cloves separated,
smashed and peeled (about 6 oz.)

1 cup Rich Chicken Stock *(recipe follows)*

Combine garlic and stock in a medium-sized saucepan, cover with a lid and bring to a boil over moderate heat. Reduce heat to low and simmer, covered, for 25 minutes. Transfer garlic and stock to the food processor or blender and process until smooth. *(The puree may be stored, tightly covered, in the refrigerator for up to 2 days or frozen for up to 6 months.)*

Makes 1½ cups.

10 CALORIES PER TABLESPOON: 1 G PROTEIN, 0 G FAT, 2 G CARBOHYDRATE; 3 MG SODIUM; 0 MG CHOLESTEROL.

Rich Chicken Stock

If you don't have veal bones, substitute extra chicken bones.

3 lbs. chicken bones, trimmed of skin and fat
    and cut into 3" pieces
½ lb. veal bones, cut into 3" pieces

1 medium-sized onion, quartered
1 stalk celery, peeled and cut into 2" lengths
1 carrot, peeled and cut into 2" lengths

Place all ingredients and 8 cups cold water into a stockpot. Bring to a boil, reduce heat and simmer, partially covered, over low heat for 6 hours. Add water as needed during cooking to keep bones covered.

Strain stock through a fine sieve into a large bowl and discard solids. Chill thoroughly and skim all fat from the surface. *(The stock may be stored, tightly covered, in the refrigerator for up to 2 days or frozen for up to 6 months.)*

Makes 6 to 8 cups.

Barbara Kafka's Sweet Garlic "Mayonnaise"

This eggless version is worth the effort; by comparison,
store-bought mayonnaise lacks flavor, tastes sweet and is higher in fat.

½ cup Sweet Garlic Puree *(page 187)*
½-1 cup olive oil or olive and vegetable oils

salt, preferably kosher, and freshly ground
    black pepper to taste
fresh lemon juice
Dijon mustard

Place garlic puree in a blender or food processor. With the motor running, gradually add oil in a thin stream. When the mixture is fully combined, add salt and pepper. Stir in lemon juice and mustard. *(The sauce may be stored, tightly covered, in the refrigerator for up to 1 week.)*

Makes 1 to 1½ cups.

65 CALORIES PER TABLESPOON: 0 G PROTEIN, 7 G FAT, 1 G CARBOHYDRATE; 1 MG SODIUM; 0 MG CHOLESTEROL.

Barbara Kafka's Sweet Garlic "Mayonnaise"

garlic mayonnaise

Yogurt-Dill Rémoulade

This lively replacement for tartar sauce complements fish and seafood dishes.

1 cup low-fat yogurt
1 tsp. minced garlic
2 Tbsp. minced red onion

1½ Tbsp. chopped capers
1½ Tbsp. fresh lemon juice
1 Tbsp. chopped fresh dill

Place yogurt in a small bowl and stir in remaining ingredients.

Makes 1¼ cups.

21 CALORIES PER 2½ TABLESPOONS: 2 G PROTEIN, 0 G FAT, 3 G CARBOHYDRATE; 182 MG SODIUM; 2 MG CHOLESTEROL.

Roasted Shallot Sauce

A heady-tasting brown sauce, this is a good complement to
strong-flavored meats, such as beef or pork, as well as roast turkey or chicken.

16 medium-sized shallots
2 tsp. olive oil

1 cup defatted beef stock
salt and freshly ground black pepper

Preheat oven to 450 degrees F. Peel shallots and remove the ends. Place them in a glass dish and add oil, turning them until they are all lightly coated. Cover the dish tightly with aluminum foil and place in the oven. Roast about 30 minutes, turning them occasionally so that they don't burn, until shallots are dark, soft and caramelized.

Bring stock to a rolling boil, then place it in a blender or food processor. Add shallots and puree until thick and smooth. Season with salt (if desired) and freshly ground black pepper.

Makes about 1½ cups.

9 CALORIES PER TABLESPOON: 0 G PROTEIN, 0 G FAT, 1 G CARBOHYDRATE; 12 MG SODIUM; 0 MG CHOLESTEROL.

Mushroom Ragoût Gravy

This ragoût makes a great gravy for turkey at Thanksgiving or a sauce for pasta.

1 cup dried imported wild mushrooms, such
    as cèpes, porcini or chanterelles (1 oz.)
1 Tbsp. olive oil
1 medium-sized onion, minced
6 cups sliced fresh mushrooms (1 lb.)
3 cloves garlic, minced
½ cup dry red wine

2 cups defatted chicken stock
1 Tbsp. tomato paste
½ tsp. dried thyme
¼ tsp. crumbled dried rosemary
1 Tbsp. chopped fresh parsley
1 tsp. fresh lemon juice
salt and freshly ground pepper to taste

Place dried mushrooms in a bowl and cover them with 1½ cups boiling water. Let sit for 30 minutes. Drain mushrooms, reserving soaking liquid. Rinse under cold running water to remove any grit. Discard woody stems and chop caps finely. Strain soaking liquid through a cheesecloth or a sieve lined with filter paper, reserving 1 cup of the liquid.

Heat oil in a large nonstick skillet or wide, shallow pan and add onions. Cook over medium-low heat, stirring often, for about 5 minutes, or until softened. Add fresh mushrooms, increase the heat to medium high, and sauté for 3 to 5 minutes, until they begin to release their liquid. Add wild mushrooms and garlic and cook, stirring, for 1 minute. Add wine and bring to a boil, stirring. Add stock, reserved soaking liquid, tomato paste, thyme and rosemary. Bring to a boil, stirring. Cook, uncovered, over medium heat for 15 to 20 minutes. Remove a cupful of mushrooms and puree in a food processor or blender, then stir back into the ragoût. (The ragoût will be thick enough to coat a spoon.) Stir in parsley and lemon juice. Taste and adjust seasonings, with salt and pepper to taste.

Makes 3½ cups (4 to 6 servings).

119 CALORIES FOR EACH OF 4 SERVINGS: 4 G PROTEIN, 4 G FAT, 15 G CARBOHYDRATE; 58 MG SODIUM; 0 MG CHOLESTEROL.

DESSERTS

~

Frozen Lemon Mousse With Blackberry Sauce

Red or black raspberries can be substituted for blackberries. To serve, cut a wedge of mousse or fan out several thin slices. (For best results, see Egg-White Know-How, page 240.)

vegetable oil for brushing mold
3 large egg whites, free of yolk
¾ cup sugar
¼ cup light corn syrup
½ cup fresh orange juice, chilled
⅓ cup fresh lemon juice, chilled
2 tsp. finely grated lemon zest

¼ cup evaporated skim milk, chilled in the
  freezer for ½ hour
BLACKBERRY SAUCE
3 cups fresh blackberries
¼-⅓ cup sugar (use the smaller amount if
  berries are very sweet)
pinch lemon zest

(Recipe continues on next page)

Lightly brush a 6-to-8-cup ring mold or other decorative mold with oil. Place whites in a large grease-free mixing bowl and set the bowl in a larger bowl of hot tap water. Let stand for 10 minutes so they warm, stirring frequently.

Combine sugar, corn syrup and 2 Tbsp. water in a small saucepan, stirring until well blended. Bring to a simmer over medium-high heat. Cover and boil for 1½ minutes to allow the steam to wash any sugar crystals from the sides. Uncover and continue simmering, without stirring, for 2 to 3 minutes longer, or until the mixture reaches soft-ball stage (239 to 242 degrees F on a candy thermometer, or when a small bit of syrup forms a soft, pliable ball when dropped into ice water). Remove from the heat and set aside.

Immediately beat the whites with a mixer on medium speed until frothy and opaque. Raise speed to high and continue beating the whites just until they begin to form soft peaks. Return the hot syrup to the burner and reheat just to boiling. Beat the whites on high speed while pouring the hot syrup in a steady stream down the bowl sides and into the whites (not directly on the beaters). Pour rapidly so that all the syrup is incorporated in about 10 seconds. Continue beating on high speed until the mixture is stiffened, smooth, fluffy and cooled. Gently whisk in orange and lemon juices and lemon zest.

In a separate chilled mixing bowl with chilled beaters, beat evaporated skim milk until it forms firm, but not stiff, peaks. Whisk it into the beaten egg-white mixture until smooth. Turn out into the prepared mold. Cover and freeze for at least 8 hours or preferably overnight.

To make sauce: If desired, refrigerate a few perfect berries to use as a garnish. In a medium-sized saucepan, stir together sugar, lemon zest and remaining blackberries. Bring to a simmer over medium heat, stirring until the sugar dissolves. Cover and simmer about 5 minutes, until the berries are soft and the juices released. Press the berries through a fine sieve, forcing through as much juice and pulp as possible. Discard the seeds. Cover and refrigerate for at least 1½ hours or up to 48 hours.

To unmold and serve: Dip the mold in hot water for about 8 to 10 seconds. Run a knife around the edges to loosen the mousse and slide it out onto a platter. Return it to the freezer briefly to firm. Spoon sauce decoratively over the mousse. Cut into servings with a large knife wiped clean between each cut. Garnish with a few whole blackberries, if desired. Serve immediately, passing the remaining sauce separately.

Serves 8.

170 CALORIES PER SERVING: 2 G PROTEIN, 0 G FAT, 42 G CARBOHYDRATE; 38 MG SODIUM; 0 MG CHOLESTEROL.

Lemon-Yogurt Cheesecake

*This cheesecake invites guiltless indulgence. It is best chilled and served the same day.
If you don't have cherries, substitute an additional 1 cup blueberries.*

CRUST
1 cup graham-cracker crumbs
½ cup gingersnap crumbs
⅓ cup crushed walnuts
⅓ cup canola or corn oil
½ tsp. cinnamon
½ tsp. ground ginger
CHEESECAKE
2 cups yogurt cheese made from 48 oz. low-fat yogurt *(page 241)*
8 oz. low-fat cream cheese, softened

4 eggs at room temperature, well beaten
1 cup sugar
1 Tbsp. fresh lemon juice
1 Tbsp. grated lemon peel
1 cup low-fat yogurt (8 oz.)
MIXED FRUIT TOPPING
4 Tbsp. plus 1 tsp. honey
2 Tbsp. cornstarch
1 cup fresh blueberries
1 cup fresh cherries, pitted
12 strawberries, quartered lengthwise

To make crust: Butter and chill a 9-inch spring-form pan. Mix all ingredients together. Press into the bottom and 1½ inches up the sides of the pan. Chill at least 15 minutes.

To make cheesecake: Preheat oven to 300 degrees F. Beat together yogurt cheese, cream cheese, eggs, sugar, lemon juice and peel with an electric mixer. Stir in yogurt. Spoon mixture carefully into the crust-lined pan.

Bake for 1 hour and 20 minutes, or until the center sets. Cool in the oven with the door ajar for 1 hour. Refrigerate 3 hours or more and unmold.

To make topping: Combine 2 Tbsp. honey and 1 Tbsp. cornstarch in small saucepan. Blend well, add blueberries and boil gently 2 to 3 minutes until mixture clears. Remove from heat and cool.

In a separate saucepan, prepare cherries in the same manner, with the remaining 1 Tbsp. cornstarch and 2 Tbsp. honey. Spread a layer of cherries around the outside edge of cheesecake. Spread blueberries over the rest of cheesecake, leaving a circle in the center of cake bare. Arrange strawberries in a flower pattern in the center and brush lightly with 1 tsp. honey.
Serves 16.

262 CALORIES PER SERVING: 8 G PROTEIN, 13 G FAT, 31 G CARBOHYDRATE; 148 MG SODIUM; 69 MG CHOLESTEROL.

Pineapple Chiffon Cake

A delightful summer dessert alone or paired with fresh berries, this cake is most successful served fresh. (For best results, see Chiffon Basics, page 241).

½ cup vegetable oil plus extra for preparing
  pan
1½ cups sifted cake flour plus extra for
  preparing pan
1 cup sugar
2 tsp. baking powder
¼ tsp. salt
½ cup frozen pineapple-juice concentrate,
  at room temperature
1 tsp. vanilla extract

6 large egg whites at room temperature
  (page 240)
2 Tbsp. sifted confectioners' sugar
1 20-oz. can unsweetened crushed pineapple,
  very well drained
PINEAPPLE GLAZE
1½ cups sifted confectioners' sugar
4 Tbsp. frozen pineapple-juice concentrate,
  at room temperature
1 tsp. fresh lemon juice

Position rack in the center of the oven and preheat oven to 350 degrees F. Brush oil over the inside of a 9-inch Bundt or springform tube pan. Dust with flour and tap out the excess.

Sift together flour, sugar, baking powder and salt into a large mixing bowl. Make a well in the center of the dry ingredients and add oil, ½ cup pineapple-juice concentrate and vanilla. Do not mix.

In another large mixing bowl, beat egg whites until they are white and foamy. Add 2 Tbsp. confectioners' sugar and continue beating until stiff but not dry. Scrape off the beaters and, without washing them, place them in the flour-and-oil mixture and beat at low speed just until well blended. In four additions, gently fold the flour-and-oil mixture into the egg whites, adding a quarter of the crushed pineapple with each addition.

Turn the batter out into the prepared pan and smooth the top with a rubber spatula. Bake for 35 to 40 minutes, or until the cake top feels springy and a cake tester inserted in the center comes out clean. Cool the cake upright on a wire rack for 10 minutes. With a knife, loosen sides and center of cake from the pan. Invert onto the rack, lift off pan and cool cake to warm.

To make pineapple glaze: Combine 1½ cups confectioners' sugar, 4 Tbsp. pineapple-juice concentrate and lemon juice in a medium-sized bowl and beat until smooth. Adjust flavor and consistency by adding more sugar or juice if needed. Spread glaze on top of still-warm cake and let it drip down the sides. Serves 16.

215 CALORIES PER SERVING: 2 G PROTEIN, 7 G FAT, 37 G CARBOHYDRATE; 97 MG SODIUM; 0 MG CHOLESTEROL.

Pineapple Chiffon Cake

Cocoa Chiffon Cake

This low-fat chiffon cake has a light, soft crumb and a satisfying chocolate flavor. The egg yolk adds richness and moisture; it can be left out, but the cake will be slightly drier without it. For a 4-layer cake, bake the cake in two 8- or 9-inch layers, slice each layer horizontally and spread raspberry preserves between the layers. (For best results, see Chiffon Basics, page 241.)

½ cup vegetable oil plus extra for preparing pan

⅓ cup plus 1 Tbsp. sifted Dutch-process cocoa plus extra for preparing pan

1½ cups sifted cake flour

1¼ cups sugar

2 tsp. baking powder

¼ tsp. salt

¼ tsp. cinnamon

2 tsp. vanilla extract

1 large egg yolk

5 large egg whites at room temperature *(page 240)*

pinch cream of tartar

2 Tbsp. sifted confectioners' sugar plus extra for dusting cake

Position rack in the center of the oven and preheat oven to 350 degrees F. Brush the inside of a 9-inch Bundt or springform tube pan with oil and sift a little cocoa over the pan. Tap out the excess.

Sift together flour, ⅓ cup plus 1 Tbsp. cocoa, sugar, baking powder, salt and cinnamon into a large mixing bowl. Make a well in the center of the dry ingredients and add oil, ½ cup plus 2 Tbsp. warm water, vanilla and egg yolk. Do not mix.

Place egg whites in another large mixing bowl. Add cream of tartar and beat with an electric mixer until they are white and foamy. Add 2 Tbsp. confectioners' sugar and continue beating until stiff but not dry. Scrape off the beaters and, without washing them, place them in the flour-and-oil mixture and beat at low speed just until well blended. In four additions, gently fold this mixture into the egg whites.

Turn the batter out into the prepared pan and smooth the top with a rubber spatula. Rap the pan sharply on the counter once to remove any large air bubbles. Bake for 40 to 45 minutes, or until the top feels springy and a cake tester inserted in the center comes out clean. (The top of the cake will be cracked.)

Cool the cake upright on a wire rack for 10 minutes. With a knife, loosen sides and center of cake from the pan. Invert onto the rack, lift off pan and cool cake completely. Place on a serving platter and top with a light sifting of confectioners' sugar. Serves 16.

173 CALORIES PER SERVING: 3 G PROTEIN, 8 G FAT, 24 G CARBOHYDRATE; 94 MG SODIUM; 13 MG CHOLESTEROL.

૪

Chocolate Crepes With Orange-&-Chocolate Sauce

If you prefer, fill these chocolate crepes with vanilla frozen yogurt or fresh fruit instead of yogurt cheese.

CREPES
6 Tbsp. all-purpose white flour
2 Tbsp. unsweetened cocoa powder
1 Tbsp. sugar
pinch salt
¼ cup skim milk
1 large egg
2 tsp. vegetable oil

ORANGE SYRUP
½ cup sugar
zest from 2 oranges, cut into very thin strips
FILLING
1 cup yogurt cheese made from 3 cups plain
   low-fat yogurt *(page 241)*
2½ Tbsp. confectioners' sugar
1 tsp. vanilla extract
CHOCOLATE SAUCE *(recipe follows)*

To make crepes: In a food processor or blender, combine flour, cocoa, sugar, salt, milk, egg, 1 tsp. oil and ¼ cup water and blend until smooth. Transfer to a bowl and refrigerate for 1 hour or for up to 24 hours.

To make orange syrup: In a small saucepan, combine sugar and ½ cup water. Bring to a boil, add orange zest, reduce heat to low and simmer, uncovered, for 20 to 25 minutes, or until the syrup has thickened and the zest is tender. Several times during the cooking, brush the sides of the saucepan with a pastry brush dipped in cold water to keep sugar crystals from forming on the sides. Set aside to cool.

To make filling: In a small bowl, whisk together yogurt cheese, confectioners' sugar and vanilla until well blended. Cover and refrigerate until needed.

To cook and assemble crepes: If necessary, add 1 to 2 Tbsp. water to crepe batter so that it has the consistency of light cream. Heat an 8-inch nonstick skillet or crepe pan over medium heat until a drop of water sizzles when sprinkled on the surface. Reduce heat to medium low. Brush pan with a little of the remaining 1 tsp. oil as needed to prevent sticking. Pour about ⅛ cup batter on the skillet and swirl to coat the bottom evenly. Cook 30 to 40 seconds until the top of the crepe has a dull surface and the edges begin to curl. Flip and cook for 20 to 30 seconds, or until the crepe is firm. Remove to a plate and cover with a dry cloth. Repeat with remaining crepes. (The crepes may be stacked until served.)

Place a crepe on a dessert plate. Spread 2 Tbsp. of filling across the middle. Fold in half and spoon 1 Tbsp. Chocolate Sauce over top or beside it. Spoon 2 tsp. orange syrup and zest over the crepe. Repeat with remaining crepes.

Makes 8 crepes.

203 CALORIES PER ASSEMBLED CREPE: 6 G PROTEIN, 4 G FAT, 37 G CARBOHYDRATE; 93 MG SODIUM; 31 MG CHOLESTEROL.

Chocolate Sauce

This quick sauce is dark and delicious. Serve it over cake, ice milk or frozen yogurt.

3 Tbsp. unsweetened cocoa powder
1½ tsp. cornstarch
1½ tsp. sugar
3 Tbsp. skim milk

⅓ cup corn syrup
½ tsp. vegetable oil
½ tsp. vanilla extract

In a small saucepan, sift together cocoa, cornstarch and sugar. Gradually whisk in milk. Whisk in corn syrup. Bring to a boil, whisking. Reduce heat to low and simmer, stirring constantly, 1 to 2 minutes, or until thickened. Remove from heat and whisk in oil and vanilla.

Makes ½ cup.

58 CALORIES PER TABLESPOON: 1 G PROTEIN, 1 G FAT, 12 G CARBOHYDRATE; 13 MG SODIUM; 1 MG CHOLESTEROL.

Chocolate Cake

A simple, low-fat and—best of all—fast chocolate cake that is moist and dense.

1 Tbsp. vegetable oil plus extra for
  preparing pan
1 cup all-purpose white flour plus extra for
  preparing pan
1 cup sugar
2½ Tbsp. unsweetened cocoa powder
1 tsp. baking soda

½ tsp. salt
1 egg, lightly beaten
½ tsp. vanilla extract
1½ tsp. fresh lemon juice
½ cup skim milk
sifted confectioners' sugar for dusting cake
  (optional)

Position rack in the center of the oven and preheat oven to 325 degrees F. Brush the inside of an 8-inch square cake pan with oil and sprinkle flour over the pan. Tap out the excess.

Sift together sugar, flour, cocoa, baking soda, and salt into a large mixing bowl. In a small bowl whisk together egg, oil and vanilla. Stir lemon juice into milk. Add to the egg mixture. Stir in ½ cup hot water. Pour into the flour-cocoa mixture and stir until smooth.

Turn batter out into the prepared pan. Bake for 30 to 35 minutes, or until center springs back when pressed lightly and a toothpick inserted in the center comes out clean. Cool the cake upright on a wire rack for 10 minutes. With a knife, loosen the sides from the pan. Invert onto the rack, lift off pan and let cool completely. Place on a serving dish. Top with a light dusting of confectioners' sugar if desired.

Serves 12.

123 CALORIES PER SERVING: 2 G PROTEIN, 2 G FAT, 25 G CARBOHYDRATE; 169 MG SODIUM; 18 MG CHOLESTEROL.

Chocolate Potato Cake

The surprise ingredient in this cake, mashed potatoes, keeps it exceptionally moist.

1 cup sugar
½ cup vegetable oil
2 large eggs
½ cup cold, plain, mashed potatoes
1 cup all-purpose white flour
⅓ cup unsweetened cocoa powder
½ tsp. baking powder

½ tsp. cinnamon
¼ tsp. baking soda
pinch nutmeg
pinch salt
½ cup buttermilk
confectioners' sugar for dusting cake

Preheat oven to 350 degrees F. Lightly oil a 9-inch round cake pan and line the base with wax or parchment paper. Set aside. In a large mixing bowl, whisk together sugar, oil and eggs. Whisk in potatoes.

In another bowl, stir together flour, cocoa, baking powder, cinnamon, baking soda, nutmeg and salt. Using a spoon or rubber spatula, alternately add the dry ingredients and the buttermilk to the egg mixture, beginning and ending with the dry ingredients. Spoon the batter into the cake pan. Bake for 30 to 35 minutes, or until the top springs back when touched lightly. Let cool on a rack for 10 minutes. Invert the cake onto a rack and let cool thoroughly. Transfer to a plate and sift confectioners' sugar over top.

Makes one 9-inch cake; serves 12.

212 CALORIES PER SERVING: 3 G PROTEIN, 10 G FAT, 27 G CARBOHYDRATE; 102 MG SODIUM; 36 MG CHOLESTEROL.

Old-Fashioned Raisin-Spice Cake With Sea-Foam Frosting

A homey, easy cake served right from the baking pan. The billowy brown-sugar meringue complements it nicely. If you don't have whole-wheat pastry flour on hand, increase the unsifted cake flour to 2 cups. (For best results, see Egg-White Know-How, page 240.)

CAKE
⅓ cup dark seedless raisins, chopped
2 Tbsp. light or dark rum or orange juice
1 cup whole-wheat pastry flour
1 cup unsifted cake flour
1 tsp. baking powder
½ tsp. baking soda
1 tsp. ground cinnamon
½ tsp. ground nutmeg
½ tsp. ground cloves

⅛ tsp. salt
6 Tbsp. safflower or corn-oil margarine, slightly softened (do not use diet or tub margarine)
1 cup sugar
1 large egg
2½ tsp. vanilla extract
1 tsp. finely grated orange zest
1 cup buttermilk

FROSTING
2 large egg whites
3 Tbsp. light corn syrup
⅔ cup packed light brown sugar

pinch salt
½ tsp. vanilla extract
pinch finely grated orange zest

To prepare cake: Preheat oven to 350 degrees F. Lightly oil a 7-by-11-inch flat baking dish. Stir together raisins and rum or orange juice in a small bowl; set aside. Sift together flours, baking powder, baking soda, cinnamon, nutmeg, cloves and salt. In a large mixing bowl, with mixer on medium speed, beat margarine until softened. Add sugar and egg and continue beating until light and fluffy. Stir in vanilla and zest.

With mixer on low speed, alternately beat dry ingredients and buttermilk into the margarine mixture, beginning and ending with dry ingredients, until evenly blended. Do not overbeat. Fold in raisins and any unabsorbed liquid until blended.

Turn out batter into a prepared pan, spreading it evenly to the edges of the pan. Bake in the middle third of the oven for 30 to 35 minutes, or until top is lightly browned, center springs back when pressed and a toothpick inserted in the center comes out clean. Let cool on a rack.

To prepare frosting: Place egg whites in a large, grease-free mixing bowl. Set in a larger bowl of hot water and let stand 10 minutes, stirring occasionally. Combine corn syrup, 3½ Tbsp. water and brown sugar in a small saucepan, stirring until well blended.

Bring to a simmer over medium-high heat. Cover and boil for 2 minutes to allow steam to wash any sugar crystals from the sides. Uncover and continue simmering, without stirring, about 2 to 3 minutes longer, until the mixture bubbles loudly and reaches soft-ball stage (239 to 242 degrees F on a candy thermometer, or when a small bit forms a soft, pliable ball when dropped in ice water). Remove from heat and set aside.

With mixer on medium speed, beat egg whites until frothy and opaque. Add salt and increase speed to high, beating until whites just begin to stand in soft peaks. Return sugar syrup to burner and reheat just to boiling. With mixer on high, beat syrup into egg whites, rapidly pouring it down the sides of the bowl in a stream so that it is incorporated in about 10 seconds. (Avoid pouring syrup directly on the beaters or it will stick and spatter.) Continue beating until mixture is stiffened, fluffy and cooled, about 5 minutes. Beat in vanilla and orange zest. With a table knife or long-handled spatula, swirl icing over cooled cake. The cake is best when eaten promptly; particularly in humid weather, the icing loses its fluffiness within a few days.

Serves 12.

254 CALORIES PER SERVING: 4 G PROTEIN, 7 G FAT, 44 G CARBOHYDRATE; 197 MG SODIUM; 19 MG CHOLESTEROL.

Spiced Apple Chiffon Cake

With its chopped apples and spicy flavor from freshly grated gingerroot and orange zest, this chiffon fills the kitchen with the smell of old-fashioned coffee cake. (For best results, see Chiffon Basics, page 241.)

½ cup vegetable oil plus extra for preparing pan
1½ cups sifted cake flour plus extra for preparing pan
½ cup peeled, finely diced apples ('Granny Smith' or 'Greening')
2 tsp. baking powder
¼ tsp. baking soda
¼ tsp. salt
¾ cup plus 2 Tbsp. sugar
2 Tbsp. packed dark brown sugar
1 tsp. cinnamon
1 tsp. ground cardamom
½ tsp. nutmeg, preferably freshly grated

¼ tsp. ground cloves
2 tsp. grated orange zest or 1 tsp. dried ground orange peel
1 tsp. peeled, grated gingerroot
½ cup apple cider or apple juice
1 tsp. vanilla extract
5 large egg whites at room temperature *(page 240)*
2 Tbsp. sifted confectioners' sugar
MAPLE SYRUP GLAZE
5-6 Tbsp. maple syrup
approximately 1½ cups sifted confectioners' sugar
dash fresh lemon juice

Position rack in the center of the oven and preheat oven to 350 degrees F. Brush oil over the inside of a 9-inch Bundt or springform tube pan. Dust with flour and tap out the excess.

In a small bowl, toss apples with 2 Tbsp. flour. Sift together remaining flour, baking powder, baking soda and salt in a large mixing bowl. Add sugar, brown sugar, cinnamon, cardamom, nutmeg, cloves, orange zest or dried peel and ginger. Make a well in the center of the dry ingredients and add oil, apple cider or juice and vanilla. Do not mix.

In another large mixing bowl, beat egg whites until they are white and foamy. Add 2 Tbsp. confectioners' sugar and continue beating until stiff but not dry. Scrape off the beaters and, without washing them, place them in the flour mixture and beat at low speed just until well-blended. In four additions, gently fold the flour mixture into the whites. Fold in the apple mixture.

Turn the batter out into the prepared pan, smooth the top with a rubber spatula and bake for about 40 minutes, or until the top feels springy and a cake tester inserted in the center comes out clean. Cool the cake upright on a wire rack for 10 minutes. With a knife, loosen sides and center of cake from the pan. Invert onto the rack, lift off pan and cool cake to warm.

To make maple syrup glaze: In a small pan, warm 5 Tbsp. maple syrup slightly. Add 1½ cups confectioners' sugar and beat until smooth. Add lemon juice to taste. Adjust consistency by adding more confectioners' sugar or maple syrup until glaze is thick but pourable. Spoon over still-warm cake, letting it drip down the sides.

Serves 16.

207 CALORIES PER SERVING: 2 G PROTEIN, 7 G FAT, 35 G CARBOHYDRATE; 107 MG SODIUM; 0 MG CHOLESTEROL.

Strawberry-Raspberry Meringue Icebox Torte

This frozen torte, consisting of layers of meringue and raspberry-ripple ice milk topped with fresh strawberries, is a stunning company dessert. For greatest convenience, make it in the morning or the day before the dinner. (For best results, see Egg-White Know-How, page 240.)

4 large egg whites at room temperature, free of yolk
¼ tsp. cream of tartar
¾ cup sugar
1 tsp. vanilla extract
⅓ cup confectioners' sugar, sifted

1 10-oz. pkg. frozen red raspberries in syrup, thawed
2 tsp. cornstarch
4½-5 cups vanilla ice milk, slightly softened
1 qt. fresh strawberries, halved (about 4 cups)

Preheat oven to 275 degrees F and place the rack in the center of the oven. Line a 12-by-15-inch or larger baking sheet with aluminum foil, dull side up. Spacing them as far apart as possible, mark two circles on the sheet, tracing around an 8-inch cake pan or plate with the point of a knife.

In a grease-free large mixing bowl, beat egg whites with a mixer on low speed for 30 seconds. Gradually raise the speed to high and continue beating until the whites are frothy and opaque. Add cream of tartar and beat just until whites begin to form soft peaks. Immediately begin adding sugar a bit at a time. Beat in vanilla. Continue to beat until the meringue stands in stiff but not dry peaks. Fold in confectioners' sugar.

Spread half the meringue over one of the circles on the baking sheet, smoothing it so it is even. Repeat with the remaining meringue on the second circle. Immediately bake for 1 hour and 25 to 30 minutes, or until the meringue rounds are firm, dry and tinged with brown. Transfer to a rack and let meringues cool thoroughly. Gently peel the foil off the rounds. *(The meringues can be packed carefully in an airtight container and stored for up to 1 week.)*

Put raspberries and syrup in a fine sieve set over a small saucepan. Let stand 15 minutes until the juice has drained; do not press down on the berries. Set juice aside at room temperature. Set the drained raspberries over a bowl and press through as much of the pulp as possible, discarding the seeds. Cover and refrigerate.

Mix cornstarch and 1 Tbsp. cold water until smooth. Stir the cornstarch mixture into the reserved raspberry juice until well blended. Bring to a simmer over medium heat and cook, stirring, just until it thickens slightly and becomes clear, 1 to 2 minutes. Cover and refrigerate.

To assemble: Place one meringue, smooth-side down, in a 9-inch springform pan; trim the edges slightly, if necessary, to make the meringue fit. Swirl strained raspberries into ice milk. Spread ice milk evenly over the meringue layer in the springform pan. Place the remaining meringue layer over the ice milk, trimming the edges if necessary and pressing down firmly. Freeze at least 4 hours or up to 24 hours. Approximately 1 hour before serving, place the torte in the refrigerator so the ice milk softens slightly.

Toss together reserved raspberry sauce with strawberries. Run a knife around the pan to loosen the torte, release the sides of the pan and place the torte and the pan bottom on a large, rimmed serving plate.

Spoon raspberry-strawberry mixture over the torte. Cut into wedges with a serrated knife.

Serves 10.

235 CALORIES PER SERVING: 6 G PROTEIN, 2 G FAT, 50 G CARBOHYDRATE; 96 MG SODIUM; 6 MG CHOLESTEROL.

English Trifle

Store-bought angel food cake works fine here.
Note: *Be sure to cook the sugar syrup to the recommended temperature and*
follow the directions precisely when adding it to the egg whites so they will be properly cooked.

3 cups skim milk
4 eggs (2 whole, 1 yolk, 2 whites)
⅓ cup plus 2 Tbsp. sugar
¼ cup cornstarch
1 tsp. vanilla extract
1 small angel food cake (10 oz.)

⅓ cup raspberry preserves
⅓ cup medium-dry sherry
4 cups fresh fruit (oranges, grapes,
    strawberries, raspberries and/or kiwis)
¼ cup toasted slivered almonds
additional fresh fruit for garnish

Whisk together ¼ cup milk, 2 whole eggs, 1 egg yolk, 2 Tbsp. sugar and cornstarch. In a heavy-bottomed saucepan, heat remaining milk until steaming. Gradually whisk milk into the egg mixture. Return to the saucepan and cook over medium heat, whisking constantly, until custard boils and thickens, about 4 to 6 minutes. Remove from heat, stir in vanilla and transfer to a clean bowl. Place a piece of wax paper or plastic wrap directly on the surface of the custard to prevent a skin from forming and let cool.

In a small saucepan, combine remaining ⅓ cup sugar with ⅓ cup water. Bring to a boil, stirring occasionally. Continue cooking over medium-high heat, without stirring, for about 5 minutes, or until syrup registers 239 degrees F and is at the soft-ball stage (when a bit of syrup dropped into ice water forms a pliable ball). Remove syrup from heat. Set aside.

With an electric mixer, beat 2 egg whites just until soft peaks form. Return the syrup to the heat un-

til it boils. Gradually pour hot syrup into egg whites but not directly onto the beaters, beating constantly. Continue beating until egg whites are cool and very stiff, about 5 minutes. Whisk ¼ of the beaten egg whites into the warm custard. Fold in remaining egg whites. Cover and refrigerate for 40 minutes, or until chilled through.

Cut cake into 2-inch-thick slices and cut slices into 1-by-4-inch strips. Spread preserves over one side of each strip. Arrange half the cake, jam-side up, in the bottom of a 12-cup serving bowl. Sprinkle with half the sherry. Arrange half the fruit over the cake layer and spoon half the custard over the fruit. Repeat with remaining cake, sherry, fruit and custard. Cover and refrigerate for at least 4 hours or overnight. Just before serving, sprinkle almonds over the top and arrange fresh fruit decoratively in the center.
Serves 10.

237 CALORIES PER SERVING: 8 G PROTEIN, 3 G FAT, 43 G CARBOHYDRATE; 148 MG SODIUM; 65 MG CHOLESTEROL.

Frozen Framboise Chiffon Cake

Framboise is distilled raspberry brandy with a strong flavor. Chambord is raspberry liqueur, sweeter and slightly less flavorful than Framboise. (For best results, see Chiffon Basics, page 241.)

½ cup vegetable oil plus extra for preparing
   pans
1½ cups sifted cake flour plus extra for
   preparing pans
¾ cup sugar
2 tsp. baking powder
¼ tsp. salt
¼ cup Framboise or Chambord

1 tsp. vanilla extract
6 large egg whites at room temperature
   (page 240)
2 Tbsp. sifted confectioners' sugar
FROZEN YOGURT FILLING AND GARNISH
1 qt. low-fat frozen vanilla yogurt
2¼ cups fresh or frozen, thawed raspberries
3-4 Tbsp. Framboise or Chambord or to taste

Position rack in center of the oven and preheat oven to 350 degrees F. Brush the insides of two 9-inch round layer cake pans with oil. Dust with flour and shake out the excess. Line the bottom of each pan with a circle of baking parchment or wax paper.

Sift together flour, sugar, baking powder and salt into a large mixing bowl. Make a well in the center and add oil, Framboise or Chambord, ¼ cup water and vanilla. Do not mix.

In another large mixing bowl, beat egg whites until they are white and foamy. Add confectioners' sugar and continue beating until stiff but not dry. Scrape off the beaters and, without washing them, place them in the flour-and-oil mixture. Beat at low speed just until well-blended. Gently stir about 1½ cups beaten whites into the flour-oil batter, then fold in the remaining whites in three additions.

Divide the batter evenly between prepared pans and bake for 22 to 25 minutes, or until the tops of the cakes feel springy and a cake tester comes out clean. Cool the layers in their pans on a wire rack for 5 minutes. Invert onto a rack and remove pans. Peel off papers. Cool completely.

To fill and frost the cake: Transfer frozen yogurt to the refrigerator for 30 minutes, or until it is of spreading consistency. In a food processor or a blender, puree 1½ cups raspberries. Strain to remove seeds, if desired. Stir raspberry puree and Framboise or Chambord into softened frozen yogurt. Place 1 tsp. frozen yogurt in the middle of a 9-inch springform pan. Set down one cake layer. Top with about half the frozen yogurt, spreading it on top and down the sides to fill up the space between the cake and the pan sides. Set the second layer over top and spread the remaining frozen yogurt over top and down the sides. Smooth the cake top with a spatula. Cover with plastic, then with foil. Freeze for at least 4 hours, or overnight.

About 15 minutes before serving, soak a towel in hot water, wring it out and wrap it around the pan sides for about 5 seconds. Remove the side of the springform, leave the cake on the pan bottom and place it on serving platter. Arrange ¾ cup raspberries in a ring around the top edge of cake. Refrigerate the cake for 15 minutes, or until slightly softened. Serves 16.

222 CALORIES PER SERVING: 4 G PROTEIN, 8 G FAT, 30 G CARBOHYDRATE; 137 MG SODIUM; 3 MG CHOLESTEROL.

Frozen Framboise Chiffon Cake

Cranberry Dacquoise

A dacquoise is a tortelike dessert in which meringue layers enriched with ground nuts alternate
with layers of buttercream, or here, cranberry mousse. For a more sumptuous version, use heavy
cream. If using evaporated skim milk, which is lower in fat, chill the milk, beaters and mixing bowl
in the freezer ½ hour before beating. (For best results, see Egg-White Know-How, page 240).

DACQUOISE
1⅓ cups blanched almond slices, toasted
  (about 5 oz.) *(page 242)*
1½ cups sugar
3½ Tbsp. cornstarch
9 large egg whites at room temperature
½ tsp. cream of tartar
1 tsp. vanilla extract
⅛ tsp. almond extract

CRANBERRY MOUSSE
½ cup orange juice or cranberry-juice cocktail
1¼ tsp. unflavored gelatin
2½ cups fresh or frozen whole cranberries
  (about 10 oz.)
approximately 1 cup sugar
pinch cinnamon
½ cup evaporated skim milk or 1 cup heavy
  cream
1 Tbsp. confectioners' sugar for garnish
mint sprigs for garnish

To make dacquoise: Preheat oven to 325 degrees F. Line two 10-by-15-inch jelly-roll pans or large baking sheets with parchment paper. Make a circle pattern 8 inches in diameter and trace three circles on the parchment with a pencil, bearing down and leaving as much space as possible between them. Leave room for a fourth circle, but do not draw it. Turn over paper; lines will show through.

Reduce heat to 300 degrees F. In a food processor, grind almonds and ¾ cup sugar until powdery but not oily. Combine nut mixture and cornstarch in a small bowl, stirring until evenly incorporated. In a large, grease-free mixing bowl, with mixer on low speed, beat egg whites for about 30 seconds. Gradually raise speed to high, beating whites until frothy and opaque. Add cream of tartar and continue beating until whites just begin to stand in soft peaks. Gradually beat in remaining ¾ cup sugar. Add vanilla and almond extract. Continue beating until whites stand in stiff but not dry peaks. Using a rubber spatula, fold in about ⅓ of the almond mixture until thoroughly blended. Add remaining almond mixture to whites and continue folding in until ingredients are

thoroughly blended; do not overmix.

Spoon ¼ of the mixture onto the center of one of the circles on the pans. Working quickly, spread meringue evenly almost out to the perimeter, using a long-bladed spatula or table knife. Repeat the process to form the other two circles. In the remaining unused area, spread the rest of the meringue into a rough circle about 7½ inches in diameter. (This one will be broken into pieces later and added to the mousse.)

Place pans on separate racks in the center half of the oven. Bake for 45 to 55 minutes, or until rounds are just lightly browned, crisp on the edges and almost firm in the center. Reverse pans halfway through to ensure even baking. Cool meringues on a flat surface, paper still attached. Gently peel meringues off. (If rounds stick firmly or seem gummy in the center of their undersides, they are not done; return to the paper and bake at 300 degrees F for 10 minutes longer.) Don't worry if cracks form in the meringues; the mousse will hide them. Break the extra meringue into pieces, then crush into crumbs by hand or with a food processor. *(The layers can be stored in an air-*

tight container for up to 3 days, or wrapped and frozen for up to 2 weeks.)

To prepare mousse: Place 1½ Tbsp. orange juice or cranberry juice in a small cup and sprinkle gelatin over it. Set aside to soften for about 5 minutes. In a medium-sized saucepan, stir together cranberries, remaining orange or cranberry juice, 1 cup sugar and cinnamon. Bring mixture to a boil over medium-high heat. As soon as berries begin to pop and split, remove 8 or 10 perfect berries from the pan. Toss them with 1 tsp. sugar in a small cup until they are coated. Set aside in the refrigerator. Simmer remaining berries for about 5 minutes, stirring, until all berries are soft and split. Stir softened gelatin into berries. Remove from heat, stirring to dissolve all gelatin. Press as much juice and pulp as possible through a fine sieve into a bowl. Discard seeds and skins. Taste and stir in about 1 more Tbsp. sugar, if desired. The mixture should be slightly tart but not sour. Cover and set aside until cool. Stir or whisk briefly before using.

Beat evaporated skim milk or cream in a large bowl until firm but not in stiff peaks. Set bowl with cranberries over a larger pan of ice and stir gently for about 3 to 5 minutes, just until mixture begins to set. Immediately fold in whipped evaporated skim milk or cream until thoroughly blended. Fold in reserved meringue crumbs.

To assemble dacquoise: On a large sheet of wax paper, set aside the most even meringue layer to use for the top. Place a generous dab of mousse in the center of the serving plate to anchor the meringue. Place 1 meringue smooth-side down on the plate, fitting together any broken pieces. Spread some of the remaining mousse over the meringue. Repeat, alternating layers of meringue and mousse, reserving a bit of mousse for the top, and ending with the best meringue. Sift confectioners' sugar over the top. Place a dab of mousse in the center. Carefully cover and freeze at least 6 hours, or up to 48 hours.

Let stand 15 to 20 minutes before serving, or until partially thawed but still cold. Arrange reserved sugared cranberries over mousse in the center. Garnish with mint sprigs.

Serves 10.

329 CALORIES PER SERVING: 8 G PROTEIN, 8 G FAT, 60 G CARBOHYDRATE; 67 MG SODIUM; 1 MG CHOLESTEROL.

Summer Fruit Tart With Yogurt Custard

Strawberries, blueberries, peaches and kiwi fruit
make a particularly appealing and colorful combination.

1 Tbsp. vegetable oil plus additional for
    brushing pan
1 scant cup graham-cracker crumbs
1 Tbsp. butter, softened
1 envelope plus 2 tsp. unflavored gelatin
6 Tbsp. orange juice
¼ cup apricot preserves
6 oz. low-fat cream cheese (Neufchâtel),
    softened slightly and cut into chunks

2 cups nonfat vanilla yogurt
½ cup sugar
4 tsp. grated lemon zest
2½ tsp. vanilla extract
½-1 cup mixed fresh fruit: halved strawberries;
    halved seedless green or red grapes;
    peeled, sliced peaches tossed with 1 tsp.
    lemon juice; blueberries; raspberries or
    peeled, sliced kiwis

Preheat oven to 350 degrees F. Lightly brush an 11-inch fluted tart pan with a removable bottom with oil. (A 10-inch pie plate may be substituted.)

Place 1 Tbsp. oil, graham-cracker crumbs, butter and 2 tsp. water in a food processor and process until well blended and particles begin to hold together. (If you don't have a food processor, cut ingredients into crumbs with a fork.) Press the crumbs evenly into the prepared pan and into the flutes, extending ½ inch up the sides. Bake 8 to 10 minutes, until crust is crisp and lightly browned. Set aside on a wire rack until thoroughly cooled.

Sprinkle gelatin over orange juice in a small saucepan. Let stand for 5 minutes until softened. Heat over medium heat, stirring, until the gelatin dissolves. Remove 2 tsp. gelatin mixture and combine it with apricot preserves. Cover and set aside.

Place remaining gelatin mixture, cream cheese, yogurt, sugar, zest and vanilla in a blender. Process until smooth. Refrigerate, stirring occasionally, until it thickens slightly and begins to jell, about 10 minutes.

Immediately turn out the filling into the crust, smoothing the surface. Drain fruit and pat dry with paper towels. Working from the edge of the tart toward the center, arrange the fruits in tightly fitted or slightly overlapping concentric circles. Press down the fruit lightly to embed it in the custard.

Heat the reserved gelatin-apricot mixture in a small saucepan over medium heat until warm. Strain through a sieve into a small cup; discard pulp. Lightly brush the tops of the fruits with the apricot mixture. Refrigerate the tart for at least 1 hour or up to 4 hours. Lift the tart away from the sides, using the pan bottom, and transfer it to a serving plate (or serve directly from the pie plate, if using).

Serves 10.

200 CALORIES PER SERVING: 6 G PROTEIN, 8 G FAT, 28 G CARBOHYDRATE; 157 MG SODIUM; 17 MG CHOLESTEROL.

Lime Chiffon Angel Pie

Light and luscious, this chiffon pie is perfect on a sultry day.

MERINGUE PIE SHELL
vegetable oil for brushing foil
3 large egg whites at room temperature, free of yolk *(page 240)*
¼ tsp. cream of tartar
½ cup sugar
¾ tsp. vanilla extract
⅓ cup confectioners' sugar, sifted

CHIFFON FILLING
4 oz. light cream cheese (Neufchâtel), softened slightly and cut into chunks
1 cup sugar
5 Tbsp. fresh lime juice
1½ tsp. grated lime zest
1¼ tsp. vanilla extract
1 envelope plus 1 tsp. unflavored gelatin
1 cup nonfat yogurt
drop of green food coloring (optional)

To make meringue shell: Preheat oven to 275 degrees F. and place rack in the center of the oven. Line a 9-inch deep-dish pie plate with aluminum foil, dull side up. Lightly brush the foil with oil.

In a large, grease-free mixing bowl, beat egg whites with a mixer on low speed for 30 seconds. Gradually raise the speed to high and continue beating until the whites are frothy and opaque. Add cream of tartar and beat until the whites just begin to form soft peaks. Immediately begin adding sugar a bit at a time. Beat in vanilla. Continue to beat until the meringue stands in stiff but not dry peaks. Fold confectioners' sugar into the meringue evenly. Turn out the meringue into the pie plate. Using the back of a spoon, hollow out the center and spread the mixture up the sides to form a pie shell.

Immediately bake for 1 hour. Lower the heat to 250 degrees F and bake 30 to 40 minutes longer, or until the meringue is firm, dry and tinged with brown. Transfer the pie plate to a wire rack and let it cool thoroughly. Lift the meringue and foil off the pie plate and gently peel off the aluminum foil. *(Cooled meringue may be packed carefully in an airtight container and stored for up to 1 week.)*

To make chiffon filling: Combine cream cheese, sugar, lime juice, zest and vanilla in a food processor or blender and process until smooth. Transfer to a small bowl, place in the freezer and chill until very cold but not frozen, about 1 hour.

Sprinkle gelatin over ⅓ cup cold water in a small saucepan. Let stand for 5 minutes, until softened. Cook over medium heat, stirring until it dissolves. Immediately remove it from the heat and gradually whisk in a few Tbsp. yogurt. In a large mixing bowl, combine gelatin mixture, remaining yogurt and food coloring, if using. Beat with a mixer set on high speed for 4 to 5 minutes until lightened and greatly increased in volume.

Immediately stir the chilled cream-cheese mixture into the gelatin mixture by hand until smooth. Let the mixture stand a few minutes until thickened slightly but not set. Place meringue shell in the pie plate and spoon in the filling, piling it up in the center. Refrigerate for at least 1 hour longer or for up to 12 hours. (The shell gradually loses its crispness if stored longer, but it will taste fine.)

Serves 8.

219 CALORIES PER SERVING: 6 G PROTEIN, 3 G FAT, 44 G CARBOHYDRATE; 102 MG SODIUM; 12 MG CHOLESTEROL.

High-Summer Pudding

This great favorite of the British Isles can be served with frozen vanilla yogurt or by itself.

¼ cup cranberry or cranberry-raspberry-juice cocktail

2½ Tbsp. blackberry brandy or kirsch (cherry brandy) or orange juice

1 envelope plus 1½ tsp. unflavored gelatin

1 lb. red or black plums, pitted and chopped (about 5-6 medium-sized)

1 cup sugar

1¼ lbs. fresh peaches, peeled, pitted and chopped (about 4-5 medium-sized)

2½ cups fresh blackberries or black or red raspberries

1 Tbsp. finely grated lemon zest

⅛ tsp. cinnamon

14-15 slices thin-sliced homemade-style white bread (such as Pepperidge Farm), crusts removed

Line a 2-qt. bowl or mold with plastic wrap, carefully smoothing the wrap onto the bottom and sides so that the plastic hangs 1 inch over the sides. In a small bowl mix cranberry juice and brandy, kirsch or orange juice and sprinkle gelatin over the surface; let stand for 5 minutes until softened.

Combine plums, sugar and gelatin mixture in a medium-sized saucepan. Bring to a simmer over medium heat, stirring for 3 to 4 minutes until the gelatin dissolves. Reduce heat to low and simmer for 7 minutes. Add peaches and simmer for about 5 minutes longer, until the peaches are almost tender. Stir in blackberries, lemon zest and cinnamon and simmer 3 to 4 minutes longer, until the berries begin to release their juice. Refrigerate.

Arrange bread slices in the bottom of the bowl, cutting as needed and fitting them together tightly. Arrange more slices all around the sides of the bowl, fitting them together tightly and smoothly. Taking care not to dislodge the bread, spoon the fruit mixture into the center of the bowl, tilting the bowl to distribute the fruit evenly. If the bread extends more than ¼ inch above the layer of fruit, trim it with a knife. Cover the fruit with another layer of bread, patting it down firmly. Stack several saucers or small plates on the bread to weight down the pudding. Refrigerate for at least 8 hours or up to 24 hours.

To serve: Invert the bowl over a serving plate, tugging the overhanging plastic wrap to loosen the pudding. Center the pudding on the plate and peel off the plastic wrap. Serve immediately, cut into wedges. Serves 6.

370 CALORIES PER SERVING: 7 G PROTEIN, 2 G FAT, 85 G CARBOHYDRATE; 279 MG SODIUM; 0 MG CHOLESTEROL.

Brown Sugar-Pecan Meringue Cookies

These cookies, topped with grated chocolate and chopped nuts, are slightly
soft and chewy. (For best results, see Egg-White Know-How, page 240.)

1 cup finely chopped pecans, toasted
  (page 242)
2 Tbsp. all-purpose white flour
4 large egg whites at room temperature
¼ tsp. cream of tartar
⅛ tsp. salt

1⅔ cups packed light brown sugar
½ tsp. vanilla extract
1½ oz. bittersweet or semisweet chocolate
  (not unsweetened), grated or very finely
  chopped

Line two 12-by-15-inch or larger baking sheets with parchment paper.

Preheat oven to 275 degrees F. Stir ¾ cup pecans together with flour. In a large, grease-free mixing bowl, with mixer on low speed, beat egg whites for about 30 seconds. Gradually raise speed to high and beat until frothy and opaque. Add cream of tartar and salt and beat until soft peaks begin to form. Gradually beat in sugar. Add vanilla. Scraping down the sides of the bowl several times, continue to beat until the mixture stands in stiff but not dry peaks. Using a rubber spatula, quickly fold nut-flour mixture into whites.

Immediately drop batter by rounded teaspoonfuls onto baking sheets, spacing cookies about 1 inch apart. Using a table knife and working in a circular motion, smooth the tops slightly. Place pans on two racks in the center half of the oven and bake for 25 to 35 minutes, or until cookies are slightly firm on top. Reverse pans halfway through to ensure even baking. (A shorter baking time will yield softer cookies; longer baking, slightly crisper ones.) Remove pans from oven and sprinkle chocolate over cookies. Bake for about 30 seconds more to melt chocolate slightly. Sprinkle with remaining ¼ cup chopped pecans. Cool on a rack or flat surface, paper still attached. Let stand until chocolate sets, or put cookies in the refrigerator about 5 minutes to hasten setting. Peel cooled cookies off paper. *(Store in an airtight container, with wax paper between the layers, for up to 4 days.)*

Makes 35 to 40 cookies.

70 CALORIES PER COOKIE: 1 G PROTEIN, 3 G FAT, 12 G CARBOHYDRATE; 17 MG SODIUM; 0 MG CHOLESTEROL.

Chocolate Meringue Drop Cookies

Crunchy outside, gooey inside, these easy cookies contain hazelnuts. If you don't have hazelnuts, use almonds. (For best results, see Egg-White Know-How, page 240.)

¾ cup hazelnuts or blanched almond slivers, toasted *(page 242)*

1 oz. bittersweet or semisweet chocolate (not unsweetened), finely chopped

6 Tbsp. unsweetened American-style (not Dutch-process) cocoa powder

3 Tbsp. all-purpose white flour

3 large egg whites at room temperature

⅛ tsp. salt

1 tsp. instant coffee powder or granules

2 cups confectioners' sugar

½ tsp. vanilla extract

⅛ tsp. almond extract (increase to ¼ tsp. if almonds are used)

Line two large baking sheets with parchment paper. Coarsely chop nuts. Stir together nuts, chocolate, cocoa and flour; set aside.

Preheat oven to 275 degrees F. In a large, grease-free mixing bowl, with mixer on low speed, beat egg whites for about 30 seconds. Gradually raise speed to high and beat until whites are frothy and opaque. Add salt and coffee and continue beating until soft peaks begin to form. Gradually beat in confectioners' sugar. Scrape down the sides of the bowl several times. Add vanilla and almond extracts. Continue beating until mixture stands in very stiff but not dry peaks. Using a rubber spatula, fold about ⅓ of the nut mixture into the whites. Add remaining nuts to whites and continue folding them in, just until ingredients are thoroughly blended.

Immediately drop cookies by large teaspoonfuls about 1½ inches apart on baking pans. Place pans on separate racks in the center half of the oven and bake for 20 to 25 minutes, or until cookies are dry and firm on top when pressed. Reverse pans halfway through to ensure even baking. Cool on a rack or flat surface, paper still attached. Gently peel cookies off. *(Store in an airtight container for up to 1 week.)*

Makes about 30 cookies.

57 CALORIES PER COOKIE: 1 G PROTEIN, 2 G FAT, 9 G CARBOHYDRATE; 15 MG SODIUM; 0 MG CHOLESTEROL.

Almond Tuiles

*Tuiles is French for "tiles." These wafer-thin cookies are so
named because they are molded to a U-shape while still hot from the oven
and, when cool, are stacked on a serving tray so that they resemble curved, clay roof tiles.*

2 egg whites
½ cup sugar
⅓ cup all-purpose white flour
4 Tbsp. unsalted butter, melted

1 Tbsp. vanilla extract
½ tsp. ground cinnamon
¼ tsp. salt
½ cup sliced blanched almonds

Line 2 baking sheets with parchment paper. In a mixing bowl, whisk together egg whites, sugar, flour, butter, vanilla, cinnamon and salt until just blended. Stir in almonds with a rubber spatula. Cover with plastic wrap and refrigerate at least 1 hour.

Preheat oven to 325 degrees F. Drop scant teaspoonfuls of chilled batter onto the baking sheets, allowing 12 to a sheet. Using a long-bladed spatula or a table knife, gently smooth batter into thin circles. Bake, one baking sheet at a time, until the cookie edges are golden brown, about 10 to 12 minutes. While the cookies are still hot remove them from the pan one by one and curl each around a rolling pin or a broomstick. Let cool, stack on a platter and serve. *(The cookies can be stored in an airtight container for up to 2 days. If they lose their crispness, place them in a 275-degree-F oven for 1 minute.)*

Makes about 48 cookies.

55 CALORIES PER 2 COOKIES: 1 G PROTEIN, 3 G FAT, 6 G CARBOHYDRATE; 46 MG SODIUM; 5 MG CHOLESTEROL.

Lemon Meringue Kisses

*These tiny, subtly flavored meringues must be cooked slowly
so their outsides are powdery and crisp, yet the insides are chewy and yielding.
(For best results, see Egg-White Know-How, page 240.) Serve with sorbet.*

2 egg whites at room temperature
pinch salt
⅔ cup sugar, sifted

1 tsp. finely grated lemon zest
¼ tsp. vanilla extract

Preheat oven to 250 degrees F. Cover two baking sheets with parchment paper or aluminum foil. Beat egg whites with salt until soft peaks form. Add sugar very slowly, beating well between additions, until egg whites are stiff but not dry. Fold in lemon zest and vanilla. Drop by teaspoonfuls onto the baking sheets or pipe small kisses with a pastry bag, fitted with a ½-inch star tip. Bake until dry but not brown, 40 to 45 minutes. Cool 2 to 3 minutes before removing from the baking sheets. *(The meringues can be stored for up to 2 weeks in an airtight container.)*

Makes 50 kisses.

30 CALORIES EACH: 0 G PROTEIN, 0 G FAT, 8 G CARBOHYDRATE; 0 MG SODIUM; 0 MG CHOLESTEROL.

Biscotti

Crisp with nuts and whole wheat, these cookies are made to dunk in strong coffee.

vegetable oil for preparing baking sheet
1 cup all-purpose white flour plus extra for
   preparing pan
½ cup chopped walnuts, toasted *(page 242)*
½ cup chopped hazelnuts, toasted
½ cup whole-wheat pastry flour

1 tsp. baking soda
pinch salt
½ cup packed dark brown sugar
2 large eggs
1 tsp. vanilla extract
1½ tsp. finely grated orange rind

Lightly oil a baking sheet and dust it with flour, tapping out the excess. Set aside. In a food processor or blender, grind half the nuts until they are coarse meal but not powder. Chop remaining nuts coarsely.

In a large bowl, sift together flours, baking soda and salt. Stir in brown sugar and ground and chopped nuts. In a smaller bowl, beat together 1 whole egg and 1 egg yolk, reserving the second white. Stir in vanilla and grated orange rind. Make a well in the center of the dry ingredients, pour in egg mixture and mix thoroughly. Dough will be stiff.

Preheat oven to 375 degrees F. Shape dough into three 18-inch-long, ½-inch-thick ropes. Arrange the ropes on the baking sheet and brush them lightly with the reserved egg white. Bake them for 20 minutes. Cut the rolls into diagonal slices about ½ inch wide. Reduce the oven heat to 225 degrees F, and bake them again for 20 to 30 minutes or until the biscotti are crisp and browned. *(These cookies keep well in a tightly closed tin.)*

Makes about 50 biscotti.

79 CALORIES PER 2 BISCOTTI: 2 G PROTEIN, 3 G FAT, 11 G CARBOHYDRATE; 39 MG SODIUM; 17 MG CHOLESTEROL.

Meringue Hearts With Brandied Sour Cherries

Crisp meringue shells are filled with ice milk and sour cherry sauce. If you have a steady hand, pipe the meringue hearts freehand. (For best results, see Egg-White Know-How, page 240.)

MERINGUE SHELLS
3 large egg whites at room temperature
¼ tsp. cream of tartar
pinch salt
½ cup sugar
1 tsp. vanilla extract
⅓ cup confectioners' sugar

FILLING
1 1-lb. can unsweetened, pitted sour (pie) cherries, with juice
¼ cup frozen cranberry-juice cocktail concentrate, thawed
1 Tbsp. brandy or water
1 Tbsp. cornstarch
¼ cup sugar or to taste
pinch finely grated lemon zest
6 small scoops slightly softened vanilla ice milk

To make meringues: Preheat oven to 225 degrees F. Line a 12-by-15-inch or larger baking sheet with parchment paper or aluminum foil with dull side up. Make a round or heart-shaped pattern 3½ inches in diameter and trace 6 or 7 outlines on parchment paper with a pencil, bearing down. Space tracings about 2 inches apart. Turn paper over; outlines will show through. If using aluminum foil, trace around pattern with the point of a toothpick.

In a grease-free large mixing bowl, beat egg whites with mixer on low speed for 30 seconds. Gradually raise speed to high and continue beating until whites are frothy and opaque. Add cream of tartar and salt and beat until whites just begin to form soft peaks. Gradually beat in sugar. Add vanilla. Continue beating until meringue stands in stiff but not dry peaks. Fold in confectioners' sugar using a rubber spatula.

Put meringue mixture in a large pastry bag fitted with a ½-inch-diameter plain or open-star tip. Pipe mixture around outlines on parchment paper or foil to form the meringue shells. Build up the sides of the shells to about 1½ inches by continuing to pipe on meringue, forming a second outline directly on top of the first. Leave the interiors empty. *(A simpler al-*

ternative is to spoon dollops of the mixture 2 inches apart onto the parchment or foil, hollow out the centers and form them into rough rounds with the back of a spoon.)

Place a baking pan on a rack in the center of the oven and bake for about 2 hours, or until meringues are firm and dry, but not browned. Remove from oven and cool on a flat surface, paper or foil still attached. Gently peel meringues off. If the paper sticks, the meringues are not done. Return to a preheated 225-degree F oven and bake 15 minutes longer. *(Completely cooled meringues may be packed carefully in an airtight container and stored for up to 2 weeks.)*

To prepare filling: Carefully drain all juice from cherries and combine it in a 2-qt. saucepan with cranberry-juice concentrate. Boil over high heat for about 10 minutes, or until juice has been reduced to ¼ cup. As the juice evaporates, watch carefully to avoid scorching. Remove from heat. In a small bowl, stir together brandy or water and cornstarch until smooth. Add cherries and sugar to cooked juice. Return mixture to a boil over medium heat and stir in cornstarch mixture. Boil, stirring constantly, for a minute or two, or until mixture thickens slightly and

(Recipe continues on next page)

Meringue Hearts With Brandied Sour Cherries

becomes clear. Remove pan from heat and stir in zest. Cover and refrigerate until serving time. *(Cherries may be stored in the refrigerator for 3 or 4 days, if desired. Let them warm up slightly before serving.)*

To assemble meringues: Center meringue shells on individual dessert plates. Spoon a small scoop of softened ice milk into the center of each shell. Gently press down ice milk with a table knife to form an even surface. Carefully spoon some brandied cherries over the ice milk, dividing cherries equally among the desserts. Serve immediately.

Makes 6 meringues.

232 CALORIES PER SERVING: 3 G PROTEIN, 1 G FAT, 57 G CARBOHYDRATE; 48 MG SODIUM; 1 MG CHOLESTEROL.

Pumpkin Caramel Custard

With its silky texture and caramel topping, this dessert is a fitting finale for a holiday meal.

1 cup sugar
2 cups low-fat milk
½ cup pureed cooked pumpkin or canned
  pumpkin puree
½ cup sugar

4 eggs, lightly beaten
2 Tbsp. vanilla extract
1½ tsp. ground cinnamon
½ tsp. ground nutmeg
¼ tsp. ground ginger

In a heavy-bottomed saucepan, combine sugar and ½ cup water. Cook mixture over medium heat, washing down the sides with a brush dipped in water. Once the sugar has dissolved, gently swirl the pan from time to time and cook mixture, without stirring, over medium heat until it is a deep caramel color, about 15 minutes. Once the caramel has become golden, it can burn easily, so watch it carefully. Working quickly, divide the caramel among six ¾-cup ramekins and swirl the ramekins to coat them on the bottom and a little on their sides. Let cool. Preheat oven to 350 degrees F.

Scald milk in a heavy-bottomed saucepan. In a bowl, combine pumpkin, sugar, eggs, vanilla, cinna-mon, nutmeg and ginger. Whisk milk into the pumpkin mixture and portion the mixture into the ramekins. Place the ramekins in a baking dish, cover the tops with a piece of foil and pour hot water into the dish to reach halfway up the outsides of the ramekins. Bake for 45 to 50 minutes, or until custards have set. Remove from the baking dish and let custards cool on a rack. *(The custard can be made up to 2 days ahead and chilled. Before unmolding, place ramekins in a tray with ½ inch hot water and let sit for 5 minutes to melt the caramel.)* Run a knife around the sides, invert onto plates and serve warm or chilled.

Serves 6.

288 CALORIES PER SERVING: 7 G PROTEIN, 4 G FAT, 56 G CARBOHYDRATE; 85 MG SODIUM; 145 MG CHOLESTEROL.

Pumpkin Caramel Custard and Almond Tuiles

Hot Fudge Pudding

Serve this dense, fudgy pudding cake with vanilla frozen yogurt.

1 cup all-purpose white flour
⅓ cup sugar
¼ cup unsweetened cocoa powder
2 tsp. baking powder
½ tsp. salt
½ cup skim milk

1 large egg, lightly beaten
2 Tbsp. vegetable oil
1 tsp. vanilla extract
¼ cup shelled pecan halves, toasted *(page 242)*
¾ cup brown sugar
1⅓ cups hot, strong coffee

Preheat oven to 375 degrees F. In a large bowl, stir together flour, sugar, cocoa, baking powder and salt. In measuring cup, combine milk, egg, oil and vanilla. Make a well in center of dry ingredients and gradually pour in milk mixture, stirring until combined. Stir in pecans. Spoon into a lightly oiled 8-by-8-inch baking dish. Spread evenly. Dissolve brown sugar in coffee; spoon over batter. Bake for 25 minutes, or until a toothpick inserted in center comes out clean. Let stand for 10 minutes; serve hot or warm.

Serves 12.

160 CALORIES PER SERVING: 3 G PROTEIN, 5 G FAT, 27 G CARBOHYDRATE; 161 MG SODIUM; 18 MG CHOLESTEROL.

Rice Pudding With Apricots

These molded rice puddings, the creation of French chef Michel Guérard, are a snap to make.

½ cup long-grain white rice
2¼ cups skim milk
¼ cup sugar
2 oz. dried apricots, cut in ¼" dice (about ⅓ cup)

1 tsp. vanilla extract
1 tsp. vegetable oil
1 15-oz. can apricots in light syrup
fresh mint leaves for garnish (optional)

Combine rice, milk and sugar in a heavy-bottomed saucepan and bring to a boil. Reduce heat, cover partially and simmer 30 minutes, stirring from time to time with a wooden spoon, until the rice is tender and the mixture has a creamy consistency. Transfer to a large bowl, stir in dried apricots and vanilla and cool.

Brush 4 ramekins lightly with oil and divide rice evenly among them. Smooth the tops, cover with plastic and refrigerate for at least 3 hours or overnight.

Pour off the syrup from canned apricots, reserv-ing ½ cup. Combine apricots with reserved syrup in a saucepan and simmer over medium heat for 10 minutes, or until the apricots fall apart. Remove from heat and puree in a food processor or blender. Transfer to a bowl and refrigerate.

To serve, dip each ramekin in hot water for about 30 seconds, run a knife around the edge of each pudding and invert it onto a dessert plate. Surround with the apricot puree. Garnish with fresh mint, if desired.

Serves 4.

290 CALORIES PER SERVING: 7 G PROTEIN, 2 G FAT, 64 G CARBOHYDRATE; 77 MG SODIUM; 2 MG CHOLESTEROL.

Fresh Fruit & Ricotta Parfaits

Light and nearly effortless to make, these amaretto-flavored
parfaits make a fine conclusion to an Italian dinner or a heavy meal.

1 cup part-skim ricotta cheese
⅓ cup sugar
2 Tbsp. amaretto liqueur
1¼ tsp. vanilla extract
1 tsp. unflavored gelatin

½ cup nonfat yogurt
2 large ripe peaches, peeled, pitted, cut into
   ½" cubes and tossed with ½ tsp. lemon juice
1 cup fresh strawberries, halved
¾ cup fresh blueberries

Combine ricotta, sugar, 1 Tbsp. amaretto and vanilla in a blender and blend until very smooth, about 1 minute. Refrigerate until chilled, for at least 1 hour or up to 24 hours.

Mix remaining 1 Tbsp. amaretto with 1 Tbsp. water and sprinkle gelatin over. Let stand for 5 minutes to soften. Heat the mixture over medium-low heat, stirring until the gelatin dissolves. Place the gelatin mixture in a large mixing bowl and slowly whisk in yogurt. Set the bowl in a larger bowl of ice water and stir until the mixture thickens to the consistency of egg whites and begins to jell, about 4 minutes. Im-

mediately beat the mixture with an electric mixer on high speed for 4 to 5 minutes until it is light and about tripled in volume. Immediately whisk in chilled ricotta mixture by hand.

Toss together peaches, strawberries and blueberries. Spoon a layer of ricotta cream into a parfait glass. Top with a layer of fruit, then another layer of ricotta, ending with a layer of fruit. Repeat with remaining glasses. Serve immediately or refrigerate for up to 2 hours.

Serves 6.

159 CALORIES PER SERVING: 7 G PROTEIN, 3 G FAT, 24 G CARBOHYDRATE; 68 MG SODIUM; 13 MG CHOLESTEROL.

Fruit Cup With Marsala Sauce

Nothing looks more handsome than a bowl of jewel-bright fruits: glistening red berries,
burnished plums, blueberries with their dusky bloom. This combination is exceptionally tasty,
particularly when the plums have an edge of tartness. Sweeter fruits can be substituted; chunks of
nectarines, cherries and gooseberries go together delightfully, as do cantaloupe, blackberries and kiwis.

1 cup raspberries
1 cup prune plums, halved and pitted
1 cup blueberries

Marsala Sauce *(recipe follows)*
6 sprigs mint or pineapple sage

Mix fruit gently and arrange in six small bowls. Top each with a dollop of sauce, garnish with herb leaves

and serve at once.

Serves 6.

97 CALORIES PER FRUIT-CUP SERVING: 3 G PROTEIN, 1 G FAT, 21 G CARBOHYDRATE; 28 MG SODIUM; 2 MG CHOLESTEROL.

Marsala Sauce

1 cup raspberries

1 cup low-fat yogurt

1 Tbsp. sweet Marsala (Italian wine)

2 Tbsp. sugar or to taste

Blend raspberries in a food processor or blender. Pour into a bowl. Stir in yogurt and Marsala. Add sugar. Cover tightly and chill.

Makes 1¼ cups.

15 CALORIES PER TABLESPOON: 1 G PROTEIN, 0 G FAT, 3 G CARBOHYDRATE; 9 MG SODIUM; 1 MG CHOLESTEROL.

Fruit Compote With Almond Jelly

*A refreshing end to any heavy meal, this fruit salad can even
be made with canned mandarin oranges and pineapple in the winter.*

2 envelopes unflavored gelatin (5 tsp.)

½ cup sweetened condensed milk

¼ cup sugar

1 Tbsp. almond extract

1 small cantaloupe, seeded and cut into balls or diamonds

1 pt. strawberries, rinsed, hulled and halved

1 20-oz. can litchis in syrup

½ cup unsweetened pineapple juice (optional)

3 Tbsp. minced candied ginger

1 Tbsp. shredded coconut

Place an 8- or 9-inch square or round cake pan in the freezer to chill. In a small saucepan, sprinkle gelatin over ½ cup water. Let stand for 1 minute or longer to soften. Heat over low heat for 1 to 2 minutes, stirring, until the gelatin has dissolved. Place 2½ cups water, condensed milk, sugar and almond extract in a mixing bowl and stir to dissolve the sugar. Add the dissolved gelatin and mix again. Pour into the chilled pan, then cover and refrigerate until firm, at least 4 hours or overnight.

About 1 hour before serving, combine fruit, pineapple juice (if using) and candied ginger in a large serving bowl. Toss lightly, cover and chill. Shortly before serving, cut the jelly into 1-inch diamonds and add to the fruit bowl. Carefully fold them into the fruit and sprinkle coconut over top.

Serves 6.

247 CALORIES PER SERVING: 6 G PROTEIN, 3 G FAT, 53 G CARBOHYDRATE; 46 MG SODIUM; 9 MG CHOLESTEROL.

Poached Pears in Raspberry Sauce

Delicious and surprisingly easy to make, this should be served in fancy bowls for an elegant finale.

2 cups dry red wine
1½ cups frozen apple-juice concentrate
2 sticks cinnamon
1 slice gingerroot
¼ tsp. ground nutmeg

6 firm pears, peeled, cored from the bottom, leaving the stem intact
1½ cups fresh raspberries, or frozen, without sugar syrup
2 Tbsp. arrowroot
fresh mint for garnish (optional)

Bring wine, 3 cups water and 1 cup apple-juice concentrate to a boil. Add cinnamon, ginger and nutmeg. Reduce heat to a simmer.

Drop in pears and poach until tender, about 20 to 35 minutes, depending on their ripeness. The pears are done when a knife can be slipped into the fruit without resistance. (Test from the core end so no marks will show.) If the pears are overcooked, they will fall apart.

Remove pears from liquid and set onto a serving platter or individual plates. Discard the cinnamon sticks, ginger and all but 3 cups of the poaching liquid. Add remaining ½ cup apple-juice concentrate to the poaching liquid and boil about 15 minutes until it is reduced to half its original volume (to just under 2 cups).

Reduce heat to a simmer and add raspberries, reserving a few for the garnish. In a small bowl, stir together ¼ cup water and arrowroot. Remove poaching liquid from the burner and slowly add the arrowroot mixture, stirring constantly. Return to low heat and stir until the sauce thickens and looks clear. Strain. Pour the sauce around the pears. Insert a mint leaf near the stem and place a few fresh raspberries in the sauce. Serve warm or chilled.

Serves 6.

239 CALORIES PER SERVING: 1 G PROTEIN, 1 G FAT, 47 G CARBOHYDRATE; 63 MG SODIUM; 0 MG CHOLESTEROL.

Bananas Poached in Apple Juice

Serve this sweet compote immediately after making it.

2 cups apple juice
3 Tbsp. raisins or currants
1 Tbsp. vanilla extract
1 3" cinnamon stick

3-4 firm, ripe bananas, peeled and sliced
nutmeg, preferably freshly grated
4-6 Tbsp. nonfat yogurt

Combine apple juice, raisins or currants, vanilla and cinnamon in a saucepan and bring to a simmer. Cook for 5 minutes. Add bananas, cover and simmer for 8 to 10 minutes, or just until bananas are tender. Remove cinnamon stick, sprinkle nutmeg over top and serve immediately with yogurt.

Serves 4.

175 CALORIES PER SERVING: 2 G PROTEIN, 1 G FAT, 42 G CARBOHYDRATE; 21 MG SODIUM; 1 MG CHOLESTEROL.

Late Summer Compote

Bill Neal's judicious blend of late summer and autumn fruits is a perfect end to a heavy meal.

½ cup sugar
1 cinnamon stick or 6 whole allspice berries
3 strips lemon zest
1 large green apple, peeled, cored and sliced
2 firm, ripe pears, peeled, pitted and sliced

3 ripe peaches, blanched, peeled, pitted and sliced
¼ cup blackberries or seeds from 1 large pomegranate

Bring 3 cups water, sugar, cinnamon or allspice and lemon zest to a boil in a medium-sized nonaluminum saucepan. Cook for 5 minutes, reduce heat to low, drop in apples and simmer for 10 minutes. Add pears and after 5 minutes, add peaches. Poach for 2 minutes and let cool in the liquid. Refrigerate.

Serve cold, removing cinnamon stick and adding blackberries or pomegranate seeds at the last minute. Serves 4.

191 CALORIES PER SERVING: 1 G PROTEIN, 1 G FAT, 50 G CARBOHYDRATE; 1 MG SODIUM; 0 MG CHOLESTEROL.

Poached Dried Fruit

This anise-scented dessert is a light finish to any meal.
Dried cherries may be ordered by mail through American Spoon Foods,
P.O. Box 566, 1668 Clarion Avenue, Petoskey, MI 49770-0566; (800) 222-5886.

1½ cups Chardonnay or Gewürztraminer or other white wine
1-4 Tbsp. honey
2 tsp. anise seed

zest of 1 lemon, cut in ½" strips
½ lb. dried apricots
½ lb. dried pears
¼ lb. dried cherries or raisins (¾ cup)

In a large pot, combine wine, 2 cups cold water, 1 Tbsp. honey, anise and lemon zest and bring to a simmer over low heat. Add apricots and pears. If necessary, add more water to cover the fruit. Simmer, covered, for 5 minutes. Add cherries or raisins, cover and simmer for another 5 to 10 minutes, until the fruit is tender. Remove zest, taste and add more honey, if desired. *(The fruit can be made up to 2 days ahead and refrigerated.)* Serve hot, warm or cool with some of the liquid.

Serves 8.

149 CALORIES PER SERVING: 2 G PROTEIN, 0 G FAT, 39 G CARBOHYDRATE; 32 MG SODIUM; 0 MG CHOLESTEROL.

Poached Dried Fruit

Salad of Exotic Fruits

This bountiful fruit salad can be served in a hollowed-out pineapple half.

1 pineapple, peeled, eyes removed, cored
   and cut into bite-sized pieces
1 ripe mango, peeled and cut into bite-sized
   pieces
1 grapefruit, peeled and separated into sections
1 large orange, peeled and separated into
   sections

½ ripe cantaloupe, peeled, seeded and cut
   into bite-sized pieces
2 apples, cored and cut into bite-sized pieces
½ cup dark rum
2 Tbsp. dark brown sugar
pinch cinnamon
pinch nutmeg

Place fruit in a bowl. Stir in dark rum, brown sugar, cinnamon and nutmeg. Mix well. Chill in the refrigerator for at least 2 hours or overnight. Serve chilled. Serves 6 to 8.

165 CALORIES FOR EACH OF 6 SERVINGS: 1 G PROTEIN, 1 G FAT, 31 G CARBOHYDRATE; 6 MG SODIUM; 0 MG CHOLESTEROL.

Frozen Berry Yogurt

It is worth hoarding berries all season in the freezer just to make this frozen yogurt. Though it may be made with only one kind of berry, a combination will deliver a richer, more complex flavor.

4 cups fresh or frozen and thawed berries
   (raspberries, blackberries and/or blueberries)
1 banana
½ cup brown sugar

½ cup frozen orange-juice concentrate
1 tsp. vanilla extract
2 cups low-fat yogurt

In a food processor or blender, puree berries until smooth. Pass through a sieve to remove seeds. (There should be about 2 cups.) Puree banana in the food processor; add berry puree, brown sugar, orange juice and vanilla, then blend. Add yogurt and blend briefly. Freeze in an ice-cream freezer, following manufacturer's instructions, or see page 241 for alternate tray-freezing method. *(The yogurt may be stored in a tightly covered container in the freezer for up to 4 days. If the yogurt has frozen solid, allow to soften in the refrigerator for 30 minutes before serving.)* Serves 8 to 10.

155 CALORIES FOR EACH OF 8 SERVINGS: 4 G PROTEIN, 1 G FAT, 33 G CARBOHYDRATE; 44 MG SODIUM; 4 MG CHOLESTEROL.

Rum-Raisin Frozen Yogurt

*This frozen yogurt mellows when the raisins have a
chance to drink up the rum overnight. Dark rum is essential.*

⅓ cup dark rum
1 cup dark seedless raisins
⅓ cup evaporated skim milk
1 envelope unflavored gelatin

½ cup brown sugar
½ cup light corn syrup
½ tsp. vanilla extract
1 quart low-fat yogurt

Combine rum and raisins in a small bowl and allow to stand for several hours or overnight. Combine milk and gelatin in a small saucepan and allow gelatin to soften, about 1 minute. Stir in sugar and cook, stirring, over medium-low heat until sugar and gelatin are just dissolved. Remove from heat and add corn syrup and vanilla. Let cool and stir in yogurt and rum-raisin mixture. Transfer to an ice-cream freezer and freeze according to manufacturer's directions or see page 241 for alternate tray-freezing method. Pack in a container and store in the freezer for at least 2 to 3 hours before serving. Allow yogurt to soften in the refrigerator for ½ hour before serving in chilled dishes.

Serves 6 to 8.

361 CALORIES FOR EACH OF 6 SERVINGS: 11 G PROTEIN, 2 G FAT, 69 G CARBOHYDRATE; 151 MG SODIUM; 10 MG CHOLESTEROL.

🍂

Ginger Sorbet

*This simple ice has a vivid, lively flavor and makes a spirited palate cleanser between
courses as well as an invigorating dessert. Use more or less ginger to vary the effect.
Strain for smoother texture, less fire. It's also delicious with fresh blueberries on the side.*

2 cups sugar
2 Tbsp. peeled, minced gingerroot

2 tsp. finely grated lemon zest
⅓ cup fresh lemon juice

In a heavy-bottomed saucepan, combine sugar, ginger, lemon zest and 4 cups water. Bring to a boil, stirring often. Boil, uncovered, over medium heat for 10 minutes. Cool. Stir in lemon juice. Freeze the mixture in an ice-cream maker, following manufacturer's directions or see page 241 for alternative tray-freezing method. Break into chunks and whirl in a food processor until smooth. Transfer to a chilled airtight container and return to the freezer for 30 minutes to 1 hour, or until firm. *(The sorbet can be made ahead and stored in the freezer for up to 4 days. Thirty minutes before serving, transfer it to the refrigerator to soften slightly.)*

Makes 5 cups.

149 CALORIES PER ½ CUP: 0 G PROTEIN, 0 G FAT, 40 G CARBOHYDRATE; 1 MG SODIUM; 0 MG CHOLESTEROL.

Peach Sherbet

*Though it doesn't have any fat, this sherbet tastes rich and
intensely peachy. It is simple to make and will keep for weeks in the freezer.*

2 lbs. ripe peaches
5 Tbsp. fresh lemon juice
¼ tsp. almond extract

⅓ cup mild-flavored honey
mint leaves for garnish

Bring a large pot of water to a boil and blanch peaches for 20 seconds. Drain, refresh with cold water and remove the skins. Pit and place in a blender or food processor, along with lemon juice and almond extract. Blend to a puree for about 1 minute and set aside in the refrigerator.

Combine 1 cup water and honey in a large saucepan at least twice their volume (the honey will bubble up dramatically), and bring to a boil. Reduce heat and simmer 10 minutes, stirring occasionally. Remove from heat and allow to cool.

Blend together the honey syrup and the peach puree. Transfer to an ice-cream maker and freeze according to manufacturer's instructions or see page 241 for alternative tray-freezing method.

Transfer sherbet to individual serving dishes or an attractive bowl and cover with plastic, then tightly with foil (if foil is in direct contact with the fruit, the aluminum will react with the acid in the fruit). Work quickly to cover and return to the freezer before the mixture melts to a liquid, or ice crystals will form when it freezes. About half an hour before serving, place the sherbet in the refrigerator to soften. Unmold and serve in individual bowls, garnished with mint leaves.

Serves 6.

125 CALORIES PER SERVING: 1 G PROTEIN, 0 G FAT, 33 G CARBOHYDRATE; 1 MG SODIUM; 0 MG CHOLESTEROL.

Plum-Raspberry Ice

This prettily colored ice has a pleasant tartness and is a breeze to make.

2 plums, peeled and chopped
⅓ cup dry white wine
1 Tbsp. honey

¼ cup frozen apple-grape-raspberry
concentrate, thawed
2 tsp. fresh lemon juice

Place all ingredients plus ¼ cup water in a blender or food processor and puree until smooth. Freeze in an ice cream maker following manufacturer's instructions or see page 241 for alternative tray-freezing method.

Serves 4.

61 CALORIES PER SERVING: 13 G PROTEIN, 0 G FAT, 0 G CARBOHYDRATE; 15 MG SODIUM; 0 MG CHOLESTEROL.

Peach Sherbet

BEVERAGES

❧

'Ti Punch

This is the classic aperitif of the French Antilles. Old men sit in cafés on city squares, sipping their 'ti punch and watching the world go by.

1 jigger white rum (1½ oz. or 3 Tbsp.)
1 tsp. fresh lime juice

1½ tsp. brown sugar or to taste

Place ice cubes in a small wine glass. Add rum and lime. Add brown sugar to taste and stir to mix well.

Serves 1.

123 CALORIES PER SERVING: 0 G PROTEIN, 0 G FAT, 7 G CARBOHYDRATE, 14 G ALCOHOL; 2 MG SODIUM; 0 MG CHOLESTEROL.

Cranberry-Grapefruit Cooler

An eye-opener whose proportions may be varied according to taste.
By squeezing the grapefruit yourself, you get the fiber as well as the vitamin C.

juice of 3 large grapefruit, pink or white, with pulp (about 3 cups)

2¼ cups cranberry-juice cocktail
6 slices melon (optional)

In a pitcher, combine grapefruit and cranberry juice. *(The drink can be made ahead and held in the refrigerator overnight.)* Pour into tall glasses half-filled with ice cubes. Garnish with melon slices, if using. Serves 6.

103 CALORIES PER SERVING: 1 G PROTEIN, 0 G FAT, 25 G CARBOHYDRATE; 5 MG SODIUM; 0 MG CHOLESTEROL.

Sparkling Limeade

Rick Bayless's limeade nicely complements Mexican dishes—
even some of the most refined ones, and it makes a very special nonalcoholic
choice at any dinner party. The sparkling water must be added at the last minute.

½-⅔ cup sugar
1⅓ cups fresh lime juice (8-10 limes)

1 qt. sparkling water

Add ½ cup sugar to the lime juice and stir until the sugar is dissolved. Add sparkling water, stir and taste for sweetness; add more sugar if desired. Pour over ice and serve immediately. Makes about 5 cups.

90 CALORIES PER CUP: 0 G PROTEIN, 0 G FAT, 25 G CARBOHYDRATE; 1 MG SODIUM; 0 MG CHOLESTEROL.

Frothy Hot Chocolate

*Whipping this otherwise old-fashioned hot chocolate creates the illusion of creaminess.
If you have a cappuccino maker, use the steam nozzle to heat and
froth the milk. Note: To vary this recipe, substitute 1 Tbsp. sambuca (anise liqueur)
for the coffee liqueur, omit the vanilla and cinnamon and add ¼ tsp. instant coffee granules.
Or 1 Tbsp. brandy may be substituted for the liqueur (omit the cinnamon).*

¾ cup skim milk
1 Tbsp. sugar
1 Tbsp. coffee liqueur, such as Kahlúa or
 Tía Maria (optional)

2½ tsp. unsweetened cocoa powder
¼ tsp. vanilla extract
¼ tsp. cinnamon

In a mug, blend 1 Tbsp. milk, sugar, coffee liqueur (if using), cocoa, vanilla and cinnamon into a smooth paste. Heat remaining milk until steaming. Remove from heat and whisk vigorously or pour into a blender and whip until frothy. Pour into cocoa mixture in the mug and stir until blended.

Serves 1.

131 CALORIES PER SERVING: 7 G PROTEIN, 1 G FAT, 24 G CARBOHYDRATE; 96 MG SODIUM; 3 MG CHOLESTEROL.

BASICS

RX FOR RECIPES

Reducing Fat in Conventional Recipes

Before using a recipe, ask yourself:
- Are the meat portions appropriate? (4 oz. uncooked meat per person or 3 oz. cooked is often more than enough.)
- Can I reduce the fat called for? (If a recipe calls for 2 Tbsp. oil, 1 Tbsp. or less is often sufficient. Use a heavy, nonstick frying pan for sautéing.)
- Can I use vegetable oil instead of butter, shortening or margarine? (Oil can be used successfully in many recipes, particularly in sautés. Substitutions in baked goods, however, are trickier.)
- If oil is drizzled over, as in pizzas and Middle Eastern dishes, would the dish taste just as good without it? (Generally it does. If not, try brushing on a film of oil.)
- Will the dish work without fatty meats? (Eggplant and wild mushrooms make good meaty substitutes. Small amounts of lean beef or Canadian bacon provide lots of flavor.)
- Is cheese necessary? Can it be reduced or replaced? (Pizzas, for instance, can be topped with vegetable combinations instead of cheese. Alternatively, using smaller amounts of grated cheese on top will make the flavor seem more pronounced.)
- Is cream the only possibility for thickening and enriching? (Try grated potatoes, evaporated skim milk or buttermilk in soups and low-fat yogurt in vegetable purees.)

Other tips for fat reduction:
- Trim the fat from meat before cooking. If the meat will be marinated or braised, remove the skin be-fore cooking. If the meat will be roasted, the skin can be removed after cooking; the meat will not absorb the fat. For fish, remove the skin after cooking.
- Substitute skim, evaporated skim or low-fat milk for whole milk and cream.
- Reduce oil in salad dressings by replacing some of it with defatted chicken stock or fruit juice. For example, if a salad dressing calls for ¼ cup oil and 1 Tbsp. vinegar, use 2 Tbsp. oil, 2 Tbsp. defatted chicken stock and 1 Tbsp. vinegar.
- Thicken sauces and soups with flour, cornstarch or arrowroot dissolved in a little liquid instead of the traditional butter-flour roux.
- Whenever possible, reduce egg yolks. For example, if the recipe calls for 3 whole eggs, try it with 1 egg plus 2 egg whites.
- Small amounts of butter or browned butter give a buttery flavor without contributing a lot of fat.

STOCKING UP

Particularly in the health-conscious kitchen, where it is used in place of or in addition to oil to sauté vegetables and make sauces and salad dressing, and of course, soups, a good stock is nothing short of indispensable.

The following stocks can be stored in 1-pt. containers in the freezer, where they will keep for up to 6 months. For smaller portions, freeze stock in ice-cube trays covered with foil and pop out cubes as needed.

To remove fat from stocks:
- If the stock will be used immediately, skim off the fat on the surface with a spoon and draw a paper

towel over the surface to remove any remaining traces.

- For best results, refrigerate the stock and spoon off the solidified fat.

A Note About Our Numbers

Nutritional analyses for Beef Stock, Chicken Stock, Fish Stock, Fish Fumet (page 57), Chinese Chicken Stock (page 136), Rich Chicken Stock (page 188) and Vegetable Stock (page 240) are not provided because no precise data is available. After the stocks have been strained and skimmed of fat, they contain fewer than 10 calories per ¼ cup, small amounts of protein and traces of fat, carbohydrate, sodium and cholesterol. The analyses of recipes that contain these stocks are approximated accordingly.

Beef Stock

Veal bones make a particularly rich, gelatinous stock. If you don't have them, substitute an equal amount of beef bones. The step of roasting the bones, which imparts fuller flavor, may be omitted if time is short.

3 lbs. assorted beef bones (shin, shank, short ribs or marrowbones)
4 lbs. veal bones
2 large onions, left whole
6 whole cloves
5 carrots, left whole
2 stalks celery, left whole
1 leek, white part only, rinsed thoroughly
1 large head garlic, unpeeled
5 sprigs fresh parsley
3 sprigs fresh thyme or ½ tsp. dried
1 bay leaf

Preheat oven to 375 degrees F. Place bones in a large roasting pan and roast for 40 minutes, or until golden. Stud onions with 3 cloves each. Place bones in a large stock pot with 5 qts. cold water. Bring to a boil, skim foam and reduce heat to low. Add remaining ingredients and simmer for 5 hours, uncovered. Strain through a fine sieve. Skim fat, if using immediately, or refrigerate overnight and remove solidified fat. *(The stock can be refrigerated for up to 2 days or frozen for up to 6 months.)*
Makes about 3 qts.

Chicken Stock

7-8 lbs. chicken pieces (backs, necks and wings)
2 carrots, unpeeled
1 large onion, studded with 3 whole cloves
1 head garlic, unpeeled (optional)
5 sprigs fresh parsley
3 sprigs fresh thyme or ½ tsp. dried
1 bay leaf

Place chicken in a large stock pot with 4 qts. cold water. Bring to a boil, skim foam and reduce heat to low. Add remaining ingredients and simmer, uncovered, for 3 hours. Strain stock through a fine sieve. Skim fat, if using immediately, or refrigerate overnight and remove solidified fat. *(The stock can be refrigerated for up to 2 days or frozen for up to 6 months.)*
Makes about 2 qts.

Fish Stock

3 lbs. white fish heads and bones
2 cups dry white wine
2 onions, chopped
2 leeks, white parts only, rinsed thoroughly and chopped
2 stalks celery, chopped
2 cloves garlic, crushed
6 sprigs fresh parsley
3 sprigs fresh thyme or ½ tsp. dried
1 bay leaf

Rinse fish bones in cold water. Place in a stock pot with remaining ingredients and enough cold water to cover, about 3½ qts. Bring just to a boil, immediately reduce heat to low and simmer, uncovered, for 30 to 35 minutes. Skim foam. Strain stock through a fine sieve. *(The stock can be refrigerated for 2 days or frozen for up to 6 months.)*

Makes about 3½ qts.

Vegetable Stock

4 carrots, chopped
2 medium-sized onions, chopped
2 leeks (white parts only), rinsed thoroughly
   and chopped
2 stalks celery, left whole
8 mushrooms, cleaned, trimmed and sliced
1 tomato, quartered
5 sprigs fresh parsley
3 sprigs fresh thyme or ½ tsp. dried
1 bay leaf

Place all ingredients in a large stock pot with 4 qts. cold water. Bring to a boil over medium heat and cook, uncovered, for 30 minutes, skimming foam. Strain through a fine sieve. *(The stock can be refrigerated for up to 2 days or frozen for up to 6 months.)*

Makes about 4 qts.

EGG-WHITE KNOW-HOW

Due to incidences of salmonella poisoning traced to raw or undercooked eggs, eggs should be handled and cooked with particular care. Researchers believe that salmonella may be introduced in the chicken through an infection in the ovaries before the shell of the egg is formed. Whites are slightly less likely than yolks to harbor bacteria, but no chances should be taken with them.

To guard against salmonella:

- Refrigerate raw and cooked eggs; keep work areas, utensils and storage containers scrupulously clean; and discard leaking or cracked eggs.
- Cook all eggs—including whites—to at least 160 degrees F, the temperature at which microorganisms are likely to be destroyed. To ensure that temperature in meringues, which are traditionally only lightly baked, the egg whites must be warmed over hot water, bringing their temperature to about 100 degrees F.

  A 239-to-242-degree sugar syrup is then beaten into the whites in a quick, steady stream. The syrup-heated meringue can be used in place of raw meringue on lemon pie and browned briefly in the oven or folded into mousses and other unbaked, chilled desserts.
- To bring egg whites to room temperature safely, set the bowl of whites in a larger bowl of very warm water and stir gently for a few minutes.

To separate and whip egg whites:

- Chilled eggs are easier to separate, but egg whites whip best at room temperature or warmer.
- Be careful to prevent any yolk from invading the white, since egg yolks contain fat, which keeps whites from foaming.
- While separating eggs, place the white and the yolk in individual dishes; transfer each white to a bowl with the rest of the whites. This method prevents a bit of yolk from ruining a whole batch of whites.
- To remove any yolk from whites, use a spoon, not an egg shell, which may contain bacteria.
- To whip egg whites, use grease-free, nonplastic, nonaluminum bowls and utensils. To remove invisible grease, rinse them with a little lemon juice or vinegar and hot water.
- Egg whites should be beaten until foamy and opaque before adding salt, lemon juice or cream of tartar, which keeps the whites smooth and

stable but slow the foaming process.

- Once the stabilizers have been added, beat the whites just until soft peaks form, then immediately incorporate the sugar or sugar syrup.

CHIFFON BASICS

- Prepare baking pans and preheat the oven so the cake can be baked as soon as the batter is ready; standing batter begins to deflate, resulting in a heavy cake.
- Measure accurately. For dry ingredients, use measuring containers that hold exactly the amount needed so that you can level the top off with a knife. If a recipe calls for sifted flour, sift it directly into the measuring cup, then level the top.
- Beat egg whites with care; they leaven the cake. *(To separate and whip egg whites, see page 240.)* Before adding the sugar, beat them until foamy. Then add sugar gradually and beat the whites until "stiff but not dry." They should be glossy and just hold their shape. Continue to beat them, just until the peaks are stiff and no longer droop. (If you beat them too much, they will become dry and separate into clumps, though they can usually be saved by whipping in another egg white.)
- Lightly fold the flour-oil batter into the beaten egg whites; stirring deflates the fragile structure.
- To bake chiffon cupcakes, grease and flour the tins or use paper liners and reduce the baking time to 15 to 17 minutes for 2½-inch diameter cups.
- If the cake sinks after baking, the egg whites were overwhipped. If the cake is rubbery or tough, they were underwhipped. Dry lumps mean that the dry ingredients were improperly sifted or improperly combined with the wet ingredients.
- Low-fat chiffon cakes are not ideal candidates for long-term freezer storage; they can, however, be frozen for up to a week if double-wrapped in plastic and foil.

TRAY-FREEZING YOGURT, SHERBET OR SORBET

Even if you don't own an ice-cream machine, you can still make your own frozen yogurt, sherbet or sorbet. Pour frozen-yogurt, sherbet or sorbet mixture into a shallow metal pan. Cover and freeze until almost solid, about 6 hours. Break mixture into chunks, place in a food processor and blend until smooth. Transfer to a chilled, tightly covered container and return to freezer for 30 minutes to 1 hour, or until firm.

YOGURT CHEESE

One of the most useful low-fat dairy items for the cook to have on hand is yogurt cheese. Made by draining the whey out of yogurt, it can make a soft "cheese" with the texture of soft cream cheese. It can be used for a savory appetizer or as a substitute for whipped or sour cream in desserts.

Do not use yogurts containing additives like modified food starch, vegetable gums or gelatin; these thickeners inhibit the release of the whey. Once the whey has been released, you will end up with about ⅓ of the original volume of yogurt. Therefore, if a recipe calls for 1 cup yogurt cheese, use 3 cups yogurt to make the cheese.

To make yogurt cheese:

Line a colander with a large cotton towel or double thickness of cheesecloth, and place the colander in the sink. Pour in low-fat yogurt. After 15 minutes, transfer colander to a bowl. Cover with plastic wrap and refrigerate for 24 hours or overnight. Gathering the edges of the towel together, gently squeeze out any remaining liquid. Transfer cheese to a separate container. Refrigerate until ready to use. Keeps 1 week.

42 CALORIES PER OUNCE: 3 G PROTEIN, 1 G FAT, 3 G CARBO-HYDRATE; 27 MG SODIUM; 4 MG CHOLESTEROL.

VEGETABLE TACTICS

Roasting vegetables gives them a mellow, smoky intensity that makes oil or butter unnecessary.

To Roast Peppers:

Place peppers directly over the flame of a gas burner or a charcoal fire. When one side is lightly charred, turn and continue charring until they are blistered and blackened all over, about 8 to 10 minutes.

Alternatively, broil them about 4 inches from the heat for 10 to 15 minutes until they are blistered and blackened all over. Place in a paper bag and set aside for about 15 minutes. Slip off the skin, rinse, cut off stalk, slit open peppers and remove seeds.

To Roast or Boil Tomatoes:

To roast, lay whole, unpeeled tomatoes on a foil-lined baking sheet, as close to a preheated broiler as possible, and let them roast, turning once, until soft and blackened, about 12 to 15 minutes, depending on size. Cool, peel away the skin and cut out the core.

To boil, place them in water to cover, bring to a boil and simmer over medium heat until tender, about 5 to 10 minutes, depending on size and ripeness. Remove with a slotted spoon, cool, slip off the skin, and cut out the core.

TOASTING NUTS, BREAD CRUMBS OR SEEDS

• Peanuts, pine nuts or sesame seeds:
Heat a heavy-bottomed, dry skillet over medium-high heat. Add nuts or seeds and cook, stirring constantly or shaking the pan, for 2 to 3 minutes, or until lightly browned and fragrant. Let cool.
• Bread crumbs, walnuts, pecans, almonds or hazelnuts:
Spread crumbs or nuts on a pie plate or baking sheet. Toast in a 350-degree-F oven for 5 to 10 minutes, stirring occasionally, or until they are lightly browned and fragrant. (Rub hazelnuts in a clean towel to remove any loose bits of hull.) Let cool.

SOURCES

Joyce Chen Unlimited
423 Great Road
Acton, MA 01720
(508) 263-6922
A wide range of Oriental ingredients and cookware.

Dean & DeLuca, Inc.
560 Broadway
New York, NY 10012
(800) 221-7714
A large selection of international ingredients for Italian, Mexican, Oriental and Indian cooking; cocoas (Bensdorp, Drosti); mustards (Creole, Provençal); herbs and spices; oils and vinegars; pastas, rice and other grains; flours; cookware.

De Wildt Imports, Inc.
RD #3, Fox Gap Road
Bangor, PA 18013
(800) 338-3433
Indonesian, Thai, Vietnamese, Indian and Oriental foods, including rice paper, sticky rice, Oriental noodles, mirin, soybean sauce, tamarind concentrate; Oriental cookware.

G.B. Ratto International Grocers
821 Washington Street
Oakland, CA 94607
(800) 325-3483
A wide variety of ethnic foods: mustards, spices (herbes de Provence, garam masala, tamarind concentrate); chilies, including ancho; pastas (orecchiette, pappardelle); vinegars, including sherry and balsamic; rices, including Arborio; flours, including masa harina.

Williams-Sonoma
100 North Point Street
San Francisco, CA 94133
(415) 421-4242
A large selection of cookware; fine cocoas, including Pernigotti and Dark Jersey.

METRIC GUIDELINES

These guidelines were developed to simplify the conversion from Imperial measures to metric. The numbers have been rounded for convenience. When cooking from a recipe, work in the same system throughout the recipe; do not use a combination of the two.*

Metric Symbols

Celsius: C	gram: g
liter: L	centimeter: cm
milliliter: mL	millimeter: mm
kilogram: kg	

Oven Temperature Conversions

IMPERIAL	METRIC
250 F	120 C
275 F	140 C
300 F	150 C
325 F	160 C
350 F	180 C
375 F	190 C
400 F	200 C
425 F	220 C
450 F	230 C
475 F	240 C
500 F	260 C

Length

IMPERIAL	METRIC
¼ inch	5 mm
⅓ inch	8 mm
½ inch	1 cm
¾ inch	2 cm
1 inch	2.5 cm
2 inches	5 cm
4 inches	10 cm

Developed by the Canadian Home Economics Association and the American Home Economics Committee.

Volume

IMPERIAL	METRIC
¼ tsp.	1 mL
½ tsp.	2 mL
¾ tsp.	4 mL
1 tsp.	5 mL
2 tsp.	10 mL
1 Tbsp.	15 mL
2 Tbsp.	25 mL
¼ cup	50 mL
⅓ cup	75 mL
½ cup	125 mL
⅔ cup	150 mL
¾ cup	175 mL
1 cup	250 mL
4 cups	1 L
5 cups	1.25 L

Mass (Weight)

IMPERIAL	METRIC
1 oz.	25 g
2 oz.	50 g
¼ lb.	125 g
½ lb. (8 oz.)	250 g
1 lb.	500 g
2 lb.	1 kg
3 lb.	1.5 kg
5 lb.	2.2 kg
8 lb.	3.5 kg
10 lb.	4.5 kg
11 lb.	5 kg

Some Common Can/Package Sizes

VOLUME		MASS	
4 oz.	114 mL	4 oz.	113 g
10 oz.	284 mL	5 oz.	142 g
14 oz.	398 mL	6 oz.	170 g
19 oz.	540 mL	7¾ oz.	220 g
28 oz.	796 mL	15 oz.	425 g

RECIPE & PHOTOGRAPHY CREDITS

Recipes previously published in Eating Well *magazine:*

Nancy Baggett: Frozen Lemon Mousse With Blackberry Sauce, p. 193; Old-Fashioned Raisin-Spice Cake With Sea-Foam Frosting, p. 202; Strawberry-Raspberry Meringue Icebox Torte, p. 205; Cranberry Dacquoise, p. 210; Summer Fruit Tart With Yogurt Custard, p. 212; Lime Chiffon Angel Pie, p. 213; High-Summer Pudding, p. 215; Brown Sugar-Pecan Meringue Cookies, p. 216; Chocolate Meringue Drop Cookies, p. 217; Meringue Hearts With Brandied Sour Cherries, p. 221; Fresh Fruit & Ricotta Parfaits, p. 225.

Rick Bayless: Wheat-Flour Tortillas, p. 44; Northern-Style Shredded Chicken With Tomatoes, p. 124; Cold Chicken & Avocado With *Chile Chipotle*, p. 126; Shrimp With Lime Dressing & Crunchy Vegetables, p. 154; Northern-Style Shredded Beef With Tomatoes, p. 163; Quick-Cooked Tomato-Chili Sauce, p. 186; Quick-Cooked Tomatillo-Chili Sauce, p. 187; Sparkling Limeade, p. 236. From *Authentic Mexican: Regional Cooking from the Heart of Mexico,* © 1987 by Rick Bayless with Deann Groen Bayless. Illustrations © 1987 by John Sanford. Reprinted with permission of William Morrow and Company, Inc. Publishers, New York.

Bruce Beck: Broiled Salmon With Papaya-Mango Relish, p. 139; Poached Cod With "Melted" Tomatoes, p. 142; Grilled Orange Roughy Margarita, p. 145; Braised Tuna Milanese-Style, p. 147; Stir-Fried Monkfish & Asparagus, p. 148; Oven-Steamed Flounder With Cantonese Flavors, p. 150; Catfish en Papillote With Lime & Chives, p. 151; Baked Bluefish au Poivre, p. 153.

Terry Joyce Blonder: Chinese Dumpling Rolls, p. 25; Mushroom Lasagna, p. 95; Apple-Cider Chicken, p. 115; Red Sauce, p. 185; Poached Pears in Raspberry Sauce, p. 227. From *For Goodness' Sake: An Eating Well Guide to Creative Low-Fat Cooking.* © 1990 by Terry Joyce Blonder, Camden House Publishing.

Jean Carper: Greens With Garlic & Walnuts, p. 69; Spinach With Strawberries & Honey Dressing, p. 83; Dr. Duke's Anticancer Slaw, p. 85; Stir-Fried Scallops With Walnuts & Snow Peas, p. 150; Chinese Pepper Steak, p. 161. From *Food Pharmacy Guide to Good Eating,* © 1988 by Jean Carper. Used by permission of Bantam Books, a division of Bantam Doubleday Dell Publishing Group, Inc.

James Chatto: *Hortopitta* (Pie of Assorted Greens), p. 43; Artichokes in Egg-Lemon Sauce, p. 77; Chicken & Pasta, p. 123.

Naomi Duguid and Jeffrey Alford: Chicken & Cellophane-Noodle Soup, p. 53; Sticky Rice (*Xoi*), p. 103; Vietnamese Chicken Salad, p. 125; Vietnamese Shrimp Rolls, p. 155; *Nuoc Cham*, p. 155; Barbecued Beef & Lemon Grass, p. 166; Peanut Sauce, p. 168.

Darra Goldstein: Beef Soup With Herbs, p. 61.

Jessica B. Harris: Salad of Exotic Fruits, p. 230. From *Iron Pots and Wooden Spoons,* © 1989 by Jessica B. Harris. Reprinted with permission of Atheneum, MacMillan Publishing Company. 'Ti Punch, p. 235. From *Sky Juice and Flying Fish,* © 1991 by Jessica B. Harris. Reprinted with permission of Simon & Schuster, Inc.

Jeanne Jones: Cranberry Chutney, p. 179. From *Diet for a Happy Heart,* © 1988 by Jeanne Jones. Published by 101 Productions. Reprinted by permission of The Cole Group.

Barbara Kafka: Sweet Garlic Puree, p. 187; Barbara Kafka's Sweet Garlic "Mayonnaise," p. 188; Rich Chicken Stock, p. 188.

Diana Kennedy: Serbian Vegetable Caviar, p. 21. From *Nothing Fancy,* © 1984 by Diana Kennedy, North Point Press.

Ann Lovejoy: Bruschetta With Tomatoes & Capers, p. 23; Fresh Pea Soup, p. 47; Potato-Vegetable Stock, p. 50; Roasted Bell Peppers, p. 70; Warm Dandelion Greens, p. 73; Garlic-Tip Dressing, p. 80; Italian Potato Salad, p. 109; New Potatoes & Peas, p. 111; Crusty Herbed Chicken, p. 120; Broiled Lamb Chops or Medallions, p. 175; Rhubarb Chutney Sauce, p. 180; Lemon Meringue Kisses, p. 218; Biscotti, p. 219; Fruit Cup With Marsala Sauce, p. 225; Ginger Sorbet, p. 231; Vegetable Stock, p. 240.

Deborah Madison: Blanched Winter Vegetables With Thyme, p. 65; Broccoli With Roasted Peppers, Olives & Feta Cheese, p. 66; Winter Greens & Potatoes, p. 68; Escarole With Garlic & Chili, p. 69; Red Cabbage Braised in Red Wine, p. 70; Parsnips With Brown Butter & Bread Crumbs, p. 73; Cauliflower With Paprika & Garlic Sauce, p. 74. From *The Savory Way,* © 1990 by Deborah Madison. Used by permission of Bantam Books, a division of Bantam Doubleday Dell Publishing Group, Inc.

Tamara Murphy (*Campagne,* Seattle, WA): Rabbit Marinated in Cider & Peppercorns, p. 133; Rack of Lamb à la Provençal, p. 177.

Joan Nathan: Rumanian Zucchini-Potato Latkes, p. 41; Herkimer Chicken Soup, p. 53; Matzo Balls With Ginger & Nutmeg, p. 54. From *The Jewish Holiday Kitchen: New and Expanded Edition,* © 1988 by Joan Nathan. Reprinted by permission of Schocken Books, a division of Random House, Inc.

Bill Neal: Red Slaw, p. 83; Vegetarian Jambalaya, p. 101; Shrimp & Grits, Crook's Corner Style, p. 158.

Late Summer Compote, p. 229. From *Biscuits, Spoonbread, and Sweet Potato Pie,* © 1990 by Bill Neal. Reprinted by permission of Alfred A. Knopf, Inc.

Dean Ornish: Pizza Provençal, p. 45; Pasta Primavera With Dijon Vinaigrette, p. 94; Italian Dressing, p. 94; Dijon Vinaigrette, p. 95; Bananas Poached in Apple Juice, p. 227. From *Dr. Dean Ornish's Program For Reversing Heart Disease,* © 1990 by Dean Ornish, MD. Reprinted by permission of Random House, Inc.

Fred Plotkin: Marinated Mushrooms & Peppers, p. 76; Salad of Mixed Greens, p. 80; Poached Dried Fruit, p. 229.

Spaghetti With Shrimp, p. 89; Orecchiette with Vegetable Sauce, p. 93; Pappardelle With Squab, p. 96. Adapted from *The Authentic Pasta Book,* © 1985 by Fred Plotkin. Reprinted by permission of Simon & Schuster, Inc.

Susan Purdy: Pineapple Chiffon Cake, p. 196; Cocoa Chiffon Cake, p. 199; Spiced Apple Chiffon Cake, p. 204; Frozen Framboise Chiffon Cake, p. 208.

Richard Sax: Smoked Salmon & Potato Cakes With Dill Cream, p. 31; Vegetable Hash Baked in a Skillet, p. 32; Potato & Smoked Fish Frittata, p. 34; Toasted Cornmeal-Apple Muffin Wedges, p. 35; Maple-Walnut Yogurt Swirl, p. 37; Cranberry-Grapefruit Cooler, p. 236.

Chris Schlesinger: Plum-Nectarine Chutney, p. 180; Tomato & Peanut Salsa, p. 181; Avocado & Corn Salsa, p. 182; Cucumber-Pineapple Sambal, p. 185.

Regina Schrambling: Roasted Potatoes With Rosemary & Garlic, p. 110; Quick-Roasted Chicken With Chili Essence, p. 114; Roasted Salmon With Mustard Crust, p. 137; Roasted Veal Chops With Gremolata, p. 170; Pineapple & Jalapeño Salsa, p. 182; Tomato-Herb Concassée, p. 186; Roasted Shallot Sauce, p. 190.

Ellen Schrecker, John Schrecker and Chiang Jung-feng: Dr. Hammerschmidt's Blood-Thinning *Mapo Doufu,* p. 62. From *Mrs. Chiang's Szechuan Cookbook,* © 1976 by Chiang Jung-feng and John Schrecker and Ellen Schrecker, Trustees. Reprinted by permission of HarperCollins Publishers.

Martha Rose Shulman: Belgian Endive With Smoked Salmon & Goat Cheese, p. 16; Smoked Fish Canapés, p. 16; Phyllo Triangles With Spinach Filling, p. 19; Crostini With Mushroom Topping, p. 20; Smoky Eggplant Puree, p. 21; Mushroom Caps With Wild Rice, p. 24; Mussels on the Half Shell, p. 27; Puree of Vegetable Soup, p. 48; Marinated Vegetables Vinaigrette, p. 84; Refried Black Beans, p. 104; Thin Salmon Scallops With Herb Dressing, p. 140; Rice Pudding With Apricots, p. 224; Peach Sherbet, p. 233.

Spinach & Red Pepper *Torta Rustica,* p. 40; Provençal Fish Soup, p. 56; Fish Fumet, p. 57; Moroccan Ramadan Soup, p. 58; Slow-Baked Tomatoes, p. 68; Orange & Olive Salad With Cumin, p. 87; Spaghetti With Eggplant & Tomato Sauce, p. 90; Potato Gratin, p. 111; Baked Chicken With 40 Cloves of Garlic, p. 117; Mushroom Ragoût Gravy, p. 191. From *Mediterranean Light,* © 1989 by Martha Rose Shulman. Illustration © 1989 by Anthony Russo. Used by permission of Bantam Books, a division of Bantam Doubleday Dell Publishing Group, Inc.

Nina Simonds: Pumpernickel Toast With Salmon, p. 15; Chicken in Miso Soup With Noodles, p. 51; Chicken Soup With Mushrooms, p. 54; Glazed Onions, p. 76; Sweet Potatoes Anna, p. 79; Rainbow Salad With Spicy Chili Dressing, p. 86; Chinese Rice Salad With Vegetables, p. 87; Pan-Fried Egg Noodles With Chicken & Broccoli, p. 98; *Pad Thai* (Thai Fried Rice Noodles), p. 99; Cold Soba Noodles, p. 100; Wild Rice Pilaf, p. 102;

Lacquered Cornish Game Hens, p. 113; Grilled Salmon Steaks With Black-Bean Sauce, p. 135; Grilled Swordfish With Spicy Hot-&-Sour Sauce, p. 143; Eight-Treasure Seafood Noodle Pot, p. 156; Steak & Vegetable Kebabs, p. 162; Saucy Chinese Noodles, p.169; Stir-Fried Korean Noodles, p. 171; Spicy Pear Chutney, p. 181; Almond Tuiles, p. 218; Pumpkin Caramel Custard, p. 222; Fruit Compote With Almond Jelly, p. 226.

Ruth Spear: Shrimp & Snow Pea Hors d'Oeuvres, p. 18; Currant-Mustard Dip, p. 18; "Zero-Fat" Herb Dressing, p. 81; Japanese Spinach Salad With Sesame Seeds, p. 81; Bulgur Pilaf With Currants & Pine Nuts, p. 106; Barley-Scallion-Pine Nut Casserole, p. 106; Turkey Scallopini Marsala, p. 129; Teriyaki-Grilled Swordfish, p. 145. From *Low Fat & Loving It,* © 1991 by Ruth Spear. Reprinted by permission of Warner Books, Inc.

Lucia Watson *(Lucia's,* Minneapolis, MN): Hearty Grain Bread, p. 39.

Recipes contributed by Eating Well *readers*

Kay Briggs (Duncanville, TX): Grilled Mustard Chicken, p. 120.

Jean Cobt (Winthrop, MA): Chocolate Cake, p. 201.

Louise Curtis (Cape Girardeau, MO): Oatmeal & Whole-Wheat Bread, p. 30.

Rick Emmer (San Francisco, CA): Barley-Root Chowder, p. 50; Seafood Risotto, p. 102.

Sara Fielder (Brownsville, OR): Frozen Berry Yogurt, p. 230.

Cathryn Frere (Morgantown, WV): Green Beans Indian-Style, p. 74; Fennel & Lemon Green Bean Salad, p. 85; Tandoori Leg of Lamb With Fresh Mango Chutney, p. 176.

Tamara Frey (Tecate, CA): Ranch Granola, p. 30.

Mr. and Mrs. Howard Freyensee (San Diego, CA): The Best Corn Bread, p. 38.

Marlene Gabel (Skokie, IL): Zesty Dill Potato Salad, p. 110; Sweet & Sour Turkey Meatballs, p. 130.

Darcy Gorris (San Luis Obispo, CA): Marbled Melon Soup, p. 63.

Margery Ann Hart (Rochester, MN): Portuguese Sausage Soup, p. 55.

Laura Johnson (Gahanna, OH): Turkey Chili, p.132.

Joan Kendall (Hamden, CT): Plum-Raspberry Ice, p. 233.

Maria Kourebanas (Essex Junction, VT): Athenian Orzo, p. 107.

Elizabeth Lowe (Burlington, VT): Sesame Asparagus, p. 79.

Kathleen Matney (Scottsdale, AZ): Peppers Stuffed With Turkey, p. 131.

Mark Messner (Arcade, NY): Spicy Rice, p. 103.

Doris Mishkin (Bethesda, MD): Brioche Bread, p. 38.

Arlen Nimchuk (Winnipeg, Manitoba): Curried Beef Ambrosia, p. 170.

Mrs. M. Polkinghorn (Mohawk, MN): Mexican Soup, p. 55.

Glenn Weber (New York, NY): Glenn's Easy Pollo Cubano, p. 115.

Desiree Witkowski (Long Beach, CA): Pueblo Pumpkin Stew, p. 105; Garam Masala, p. 105.

Photographers

Fred Bird: cover; courtesy of *Canadian Living,* 1985.

Ed Carey: p. 178.

John Dugdale: p. 173.

Brian Hagiwara: p. 192, p. 214.

Steven Mark Needham: p. 42, p. 49, p. 60, p. 122, p. 128, p. 134-135, p.138, p. 141, p. 144.

Alan Richardson: p. 10-11; p. 33, p. 36, p. 59, p. 88, p. 91, p. 92, p. 97, p.116, p. 183, p. 184, p. 197, p. 198, p. 209, p. 220, p. 228, p. 232.

Maria Robledo: p. 17, p. 157.

Teri Sandison: p. 127.

Ellen Silverman: p. 152, p. 206, p. 234.

Jerry Simpson: p. 14, p. 22, p. 46-47, p. 52, p. 72, p. 78, p. 82, p. 108, p. 112-113, p. 121, p. 149, p. 160, p. 167, p. 174, p. 189, p. 222; back cover (center & right).

Mark Thomas: p. 28; back cover (left).

Lisa Charles Watson: p. 64-65, p. 67, p. 71, p. 75.

INDEX

(Page numbers in italics indicate color photographs.)